AF579211

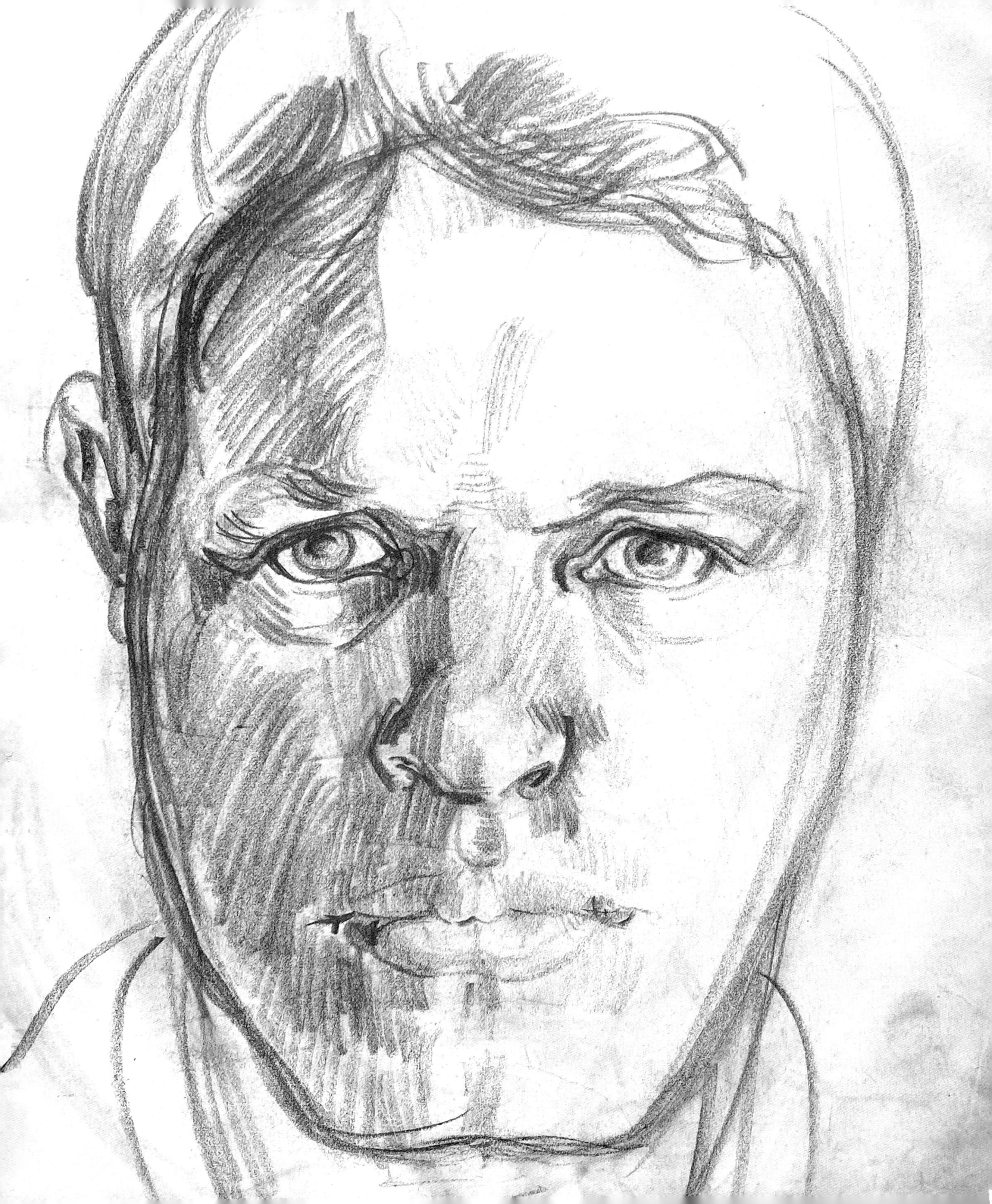

J. A. Jerichau
Great Times Are Upon Us

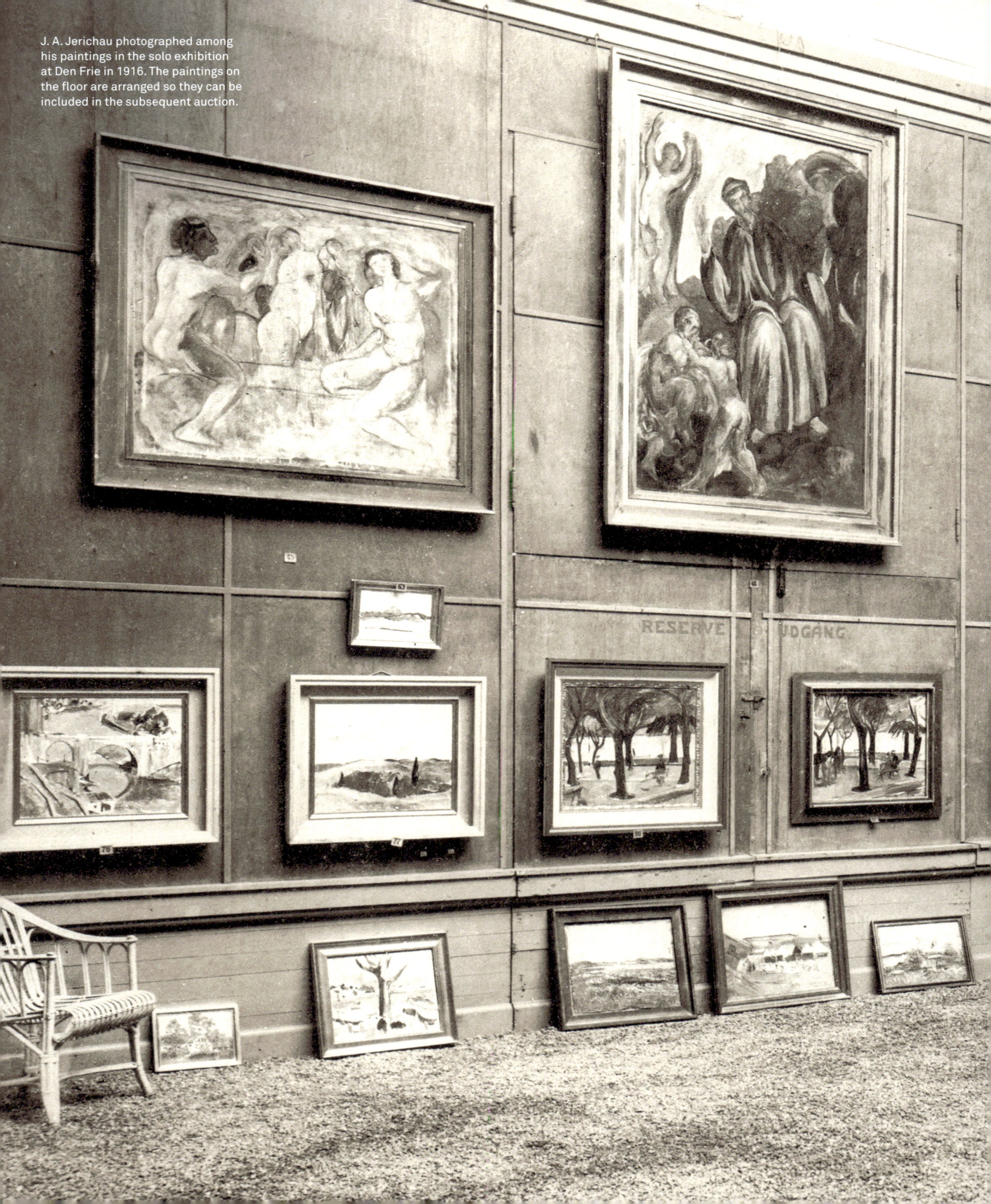

J. A. Jerichau photographed among his paintings in the solo exhibition at Den Frie in 1916. The paintings on the floor are arranged so they can be included in the subsequent auction.

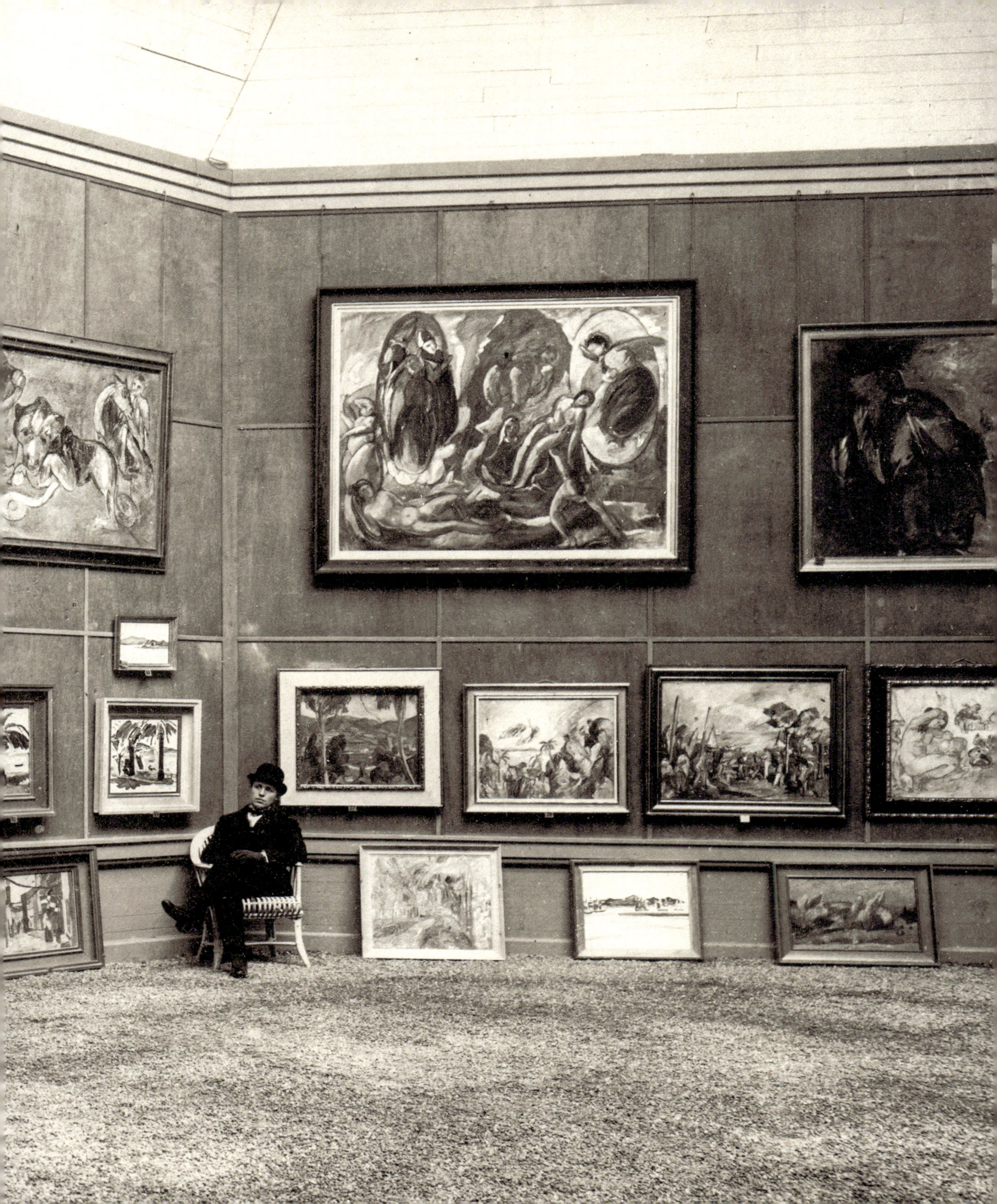

Foreword

The painter Jens Adolf Jerichau (1890-1916) is hardly a central figure in the history of Danish art. For that his practice was too short and the exhibitions of his work too few. But despite his status as a marginalized painter, Jerichau has been key to several luminaries of Danish art. In the 1960s, Asger Jorn noted his connection to Jerichau through "the very method of painting". In the late 1970s, Per Kirkeby singled out Jerichau as an un-Danish painter, who was synonymous with the "grand style" of painting that Kirkeby himself aspired to, which is "one big movement that organizes the picture from the inside". Jorn's and Kirkeby's appreciation of Jerichau indicates a discrepancy between the canon that they themselves are part of and the reception of art. That is, between the narrative of art and art's impact as a generator of new art. Jerichau's significance to us lies in the latter: his pictures begat new, vital pictures. What could be more important than that?

The Louisiana's exhibition is the first major presentation of Jerichau's work at a Danish museum ever. Some may be surprised that it is housed here. While the Louisiana has always oriented itself to international art movements, its birth and identity are closely tied to Danish modernism. Louisiana founder Knud W. Jensen collected Danish art before he found Beuys and Warhol. And as veteran Louisiana-goers will remember, a Jerichau painting used to hang prominently in the Villa facing the Sculpture Park. For those of us who work with exhibitions here, mounting a Jerichau show is a perfect fit.

The exhibition, the biggest ever of the artist's work, has three overarching goals: First, to present as comprehensive a view of Jerichau as possible. Many of the artist's works remain in private collections, inaccessible to art professionals and art lovers alike. Showing Jerichau on such a lavish scale is bound to stimulate further interest and research into this singular artist beyond what is showcased in this exhibition and publication. Second, to add to the story of the artist. We have made an exhaustive effort to locate previously unknown works, and we are proud that this exhibition includes four paintings by Jerichau that have never been shown to the public before. We are here for the art. It is art we look to to make us wiser. And new works mean new ideas. Finally, we make a point of viewing Jerichau and his art from a contemporary perspective, so that his work is conveyed not only through an understanding of his life and times but also through today's changed sensibilities, which have a huge impact on the perception of his work. We are taking a special look at Jerichau's obviously androgynous representations of men and women. Complemented by his correspondence, they more than suggest that Jerichau's art was preoccupied with challenging convention, especially regarding gender and sexuality.

It would be a stretch to call this a retrospective. Jerichau committed suicide at the tender age of 25, and there is not a long career to look back on. What we do have are six to seven years of work testifying to an artistic talent that developed at a meteoric pace. Art history is brimming with cases of rapid artistic maturation followed by an early exit. In Jerichau's own day, the early deaths of August Macke (1887-1914) and Egon Schiele (1890-1918) bracket his. Nonetheless, in art history their works are treated not as juvenilia or promises of what might have been but as fully realized bodies of work. Without otherwise likening Jerichau to those two giants, we believe he deserves equal treatment. He, too, left behind a large body of work despite his short life.

The Jerichau exhibition continues an unofficial series of exhibitions of painters from early modernism, who for one reason or another have been overlooked or downplayed by art history. We have previously showcased the work of Marsden Hartley, Gabriele Münter, Paula Modersohn-Becker and Hilma af Klint. Through these exhibitions, the Louisiana aims to contribute to a worldwide retelling of the history of art, carving out a space for more artists and their works, and enriching us all.

Acknowledgments
This exhibition is made possible by the gracious cooperation of the many private and institutional lenders. We have been met with tremendous support for the project from all sides – and patience, since the global pandemic entailed repeated changes of plan. A sincere thanks to the lenders for their generosity and adaptability. Jerichau's works are scattered across Denmark, but with particular clusters, which was key to the project's success. We have been particularly reliant on support from the Museum Jorn, which is also home to the Jerichau archive; the Canica Art Collection in Norway; and, not least, the National Gallery of Art and the Royal Collection of Graphic Art in Copenhagen, which provided invaluable aid to this exhibition and lent us everything we asked for. We are indebted to all three for their support. Our knowledge about Jerichau comes in large part thanks to Troels Andersen, who from the early 1960s was collecting material, interviewing people who knew the artist and finding artworks in cellars and attics. This exhibition would have been impossible without the dedicated efforts of this powerhouse, whom

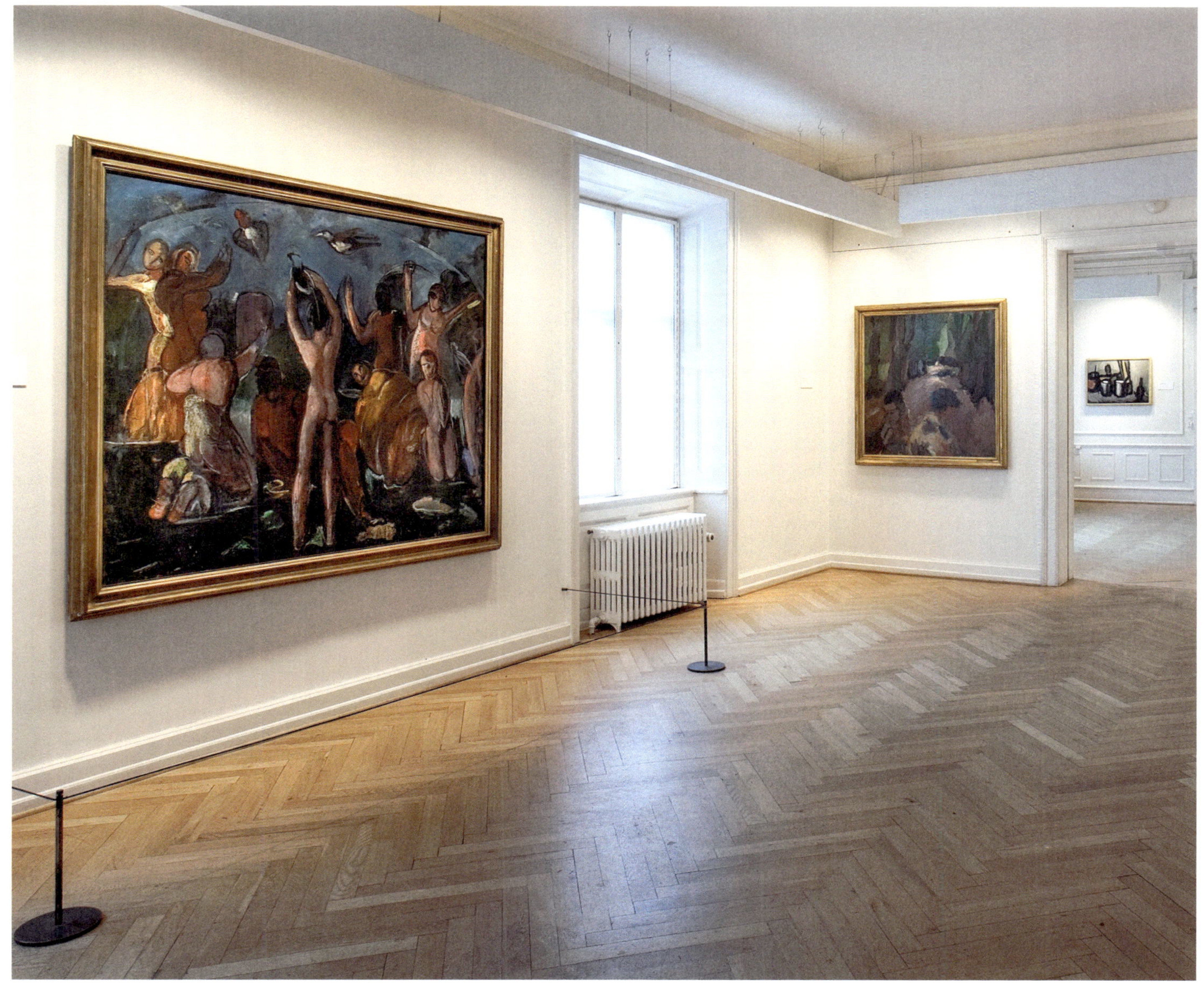

J. A. Jerichau's painting *The Sacrificial Feast. Man Seeking Omens. Opus III* from 1915 is part of the Louisiana's collection and formerly had its regular place in the Louisiana's Villa. It was most recently hung up in 2010, which is when this photograph was taken.

sadly we must thank posthumously for his near-archaeological efforts into the artist and his work. The Louisiana's exhibition was sparked in particular by Mikael Wivel's comprehensive 2019 monograph, *Penslen og pistolen – maleren Jens Adolf Jerichau* (The Paintbrush and the Pistol: The Artist Jens Adolf Jerichau). Wivel agreed to act as co-curator of this exhibition and made all his material and knowledge available to us – from contacts to private lenders to transcriptions of Jerichau's letters. Thank you for your invaluable contribution.

Thanks as well to the writers of this catalogue for their fine perspectives on Jerichau's life and work. Finally, we are profoundly grateful to our funders who made it all possible: Lektor Peer Rander Amundsens Legat and the Beckett Foundation.

Poul Erik Tøjner
Director

Mathias Ussing Seeberg
Curator

1906-1912
Hørsholm, Copenhagen, Roskilde, Funen, Hesselø

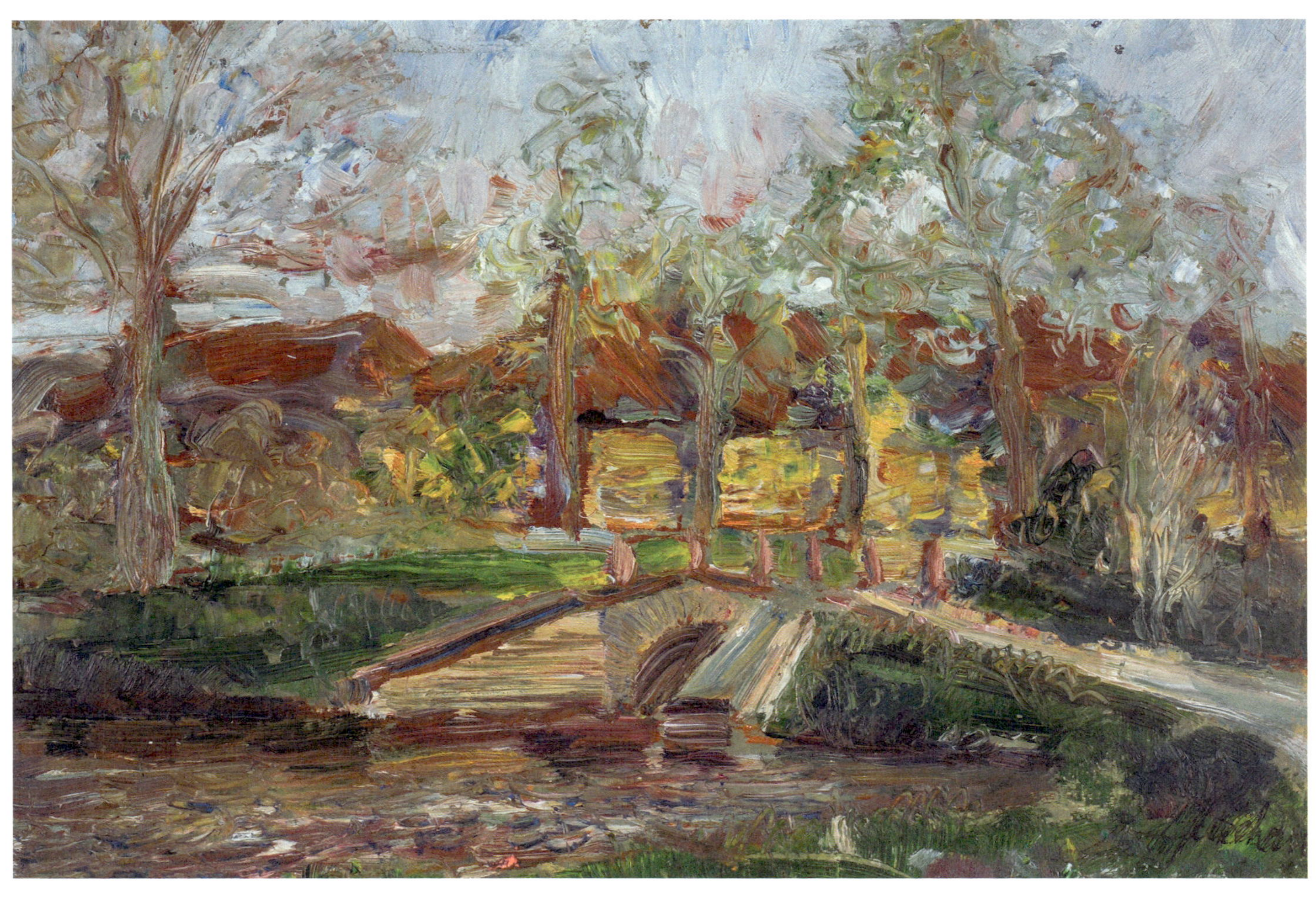

1 *The Bridge to the Church*, 1906

3 *Landscape*, 1910

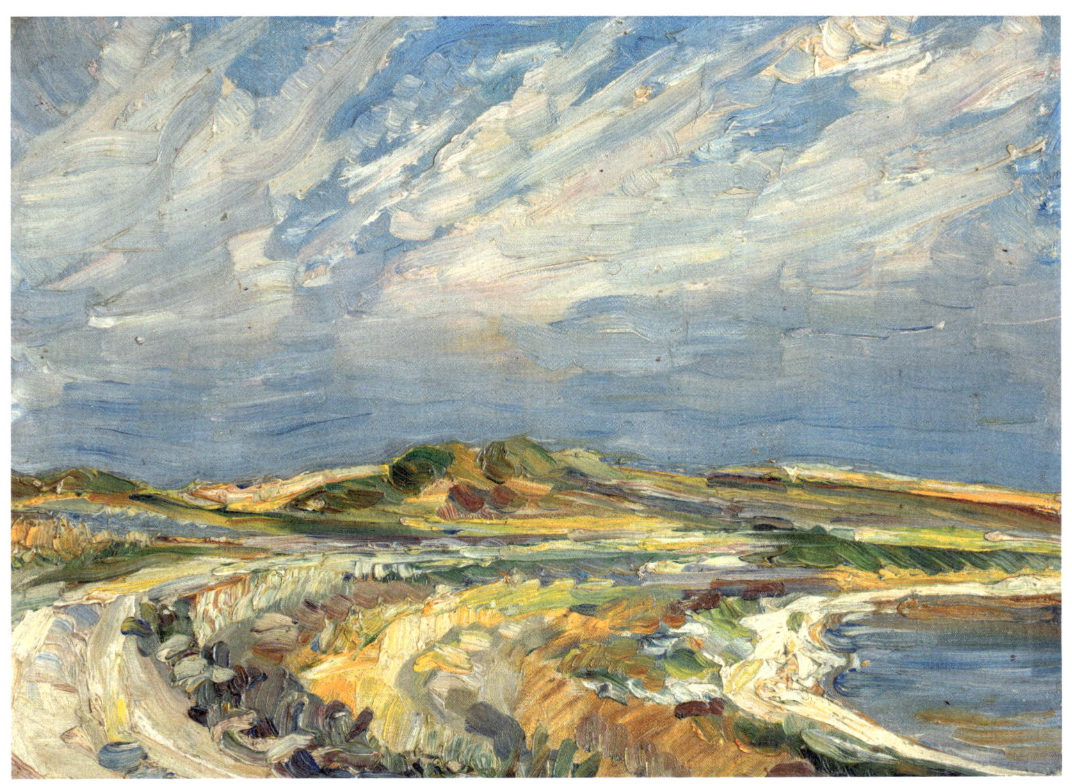

5 *Landscape*, 1910

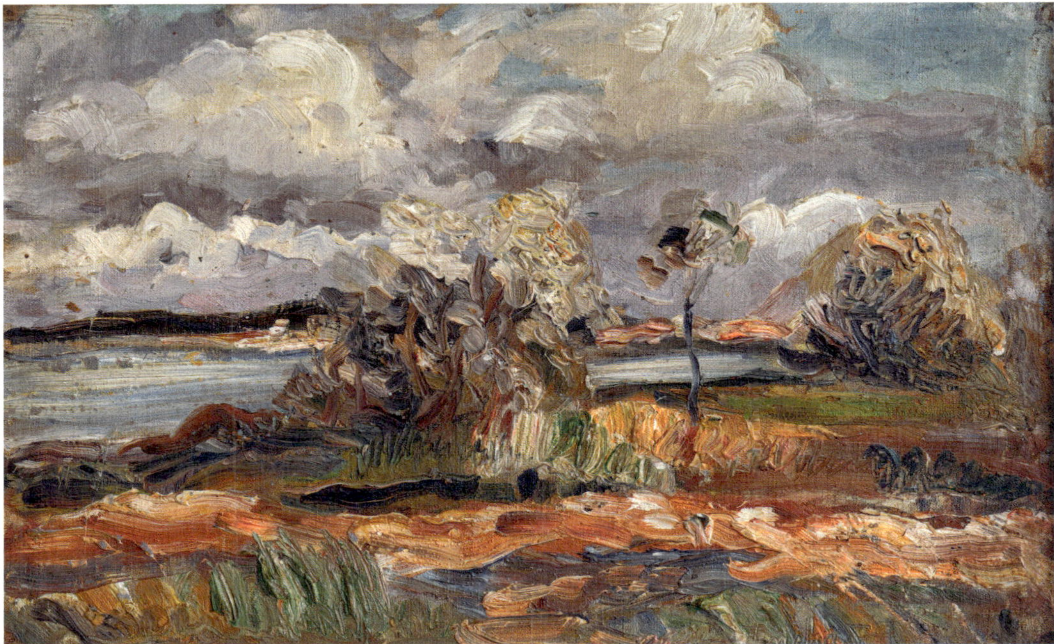

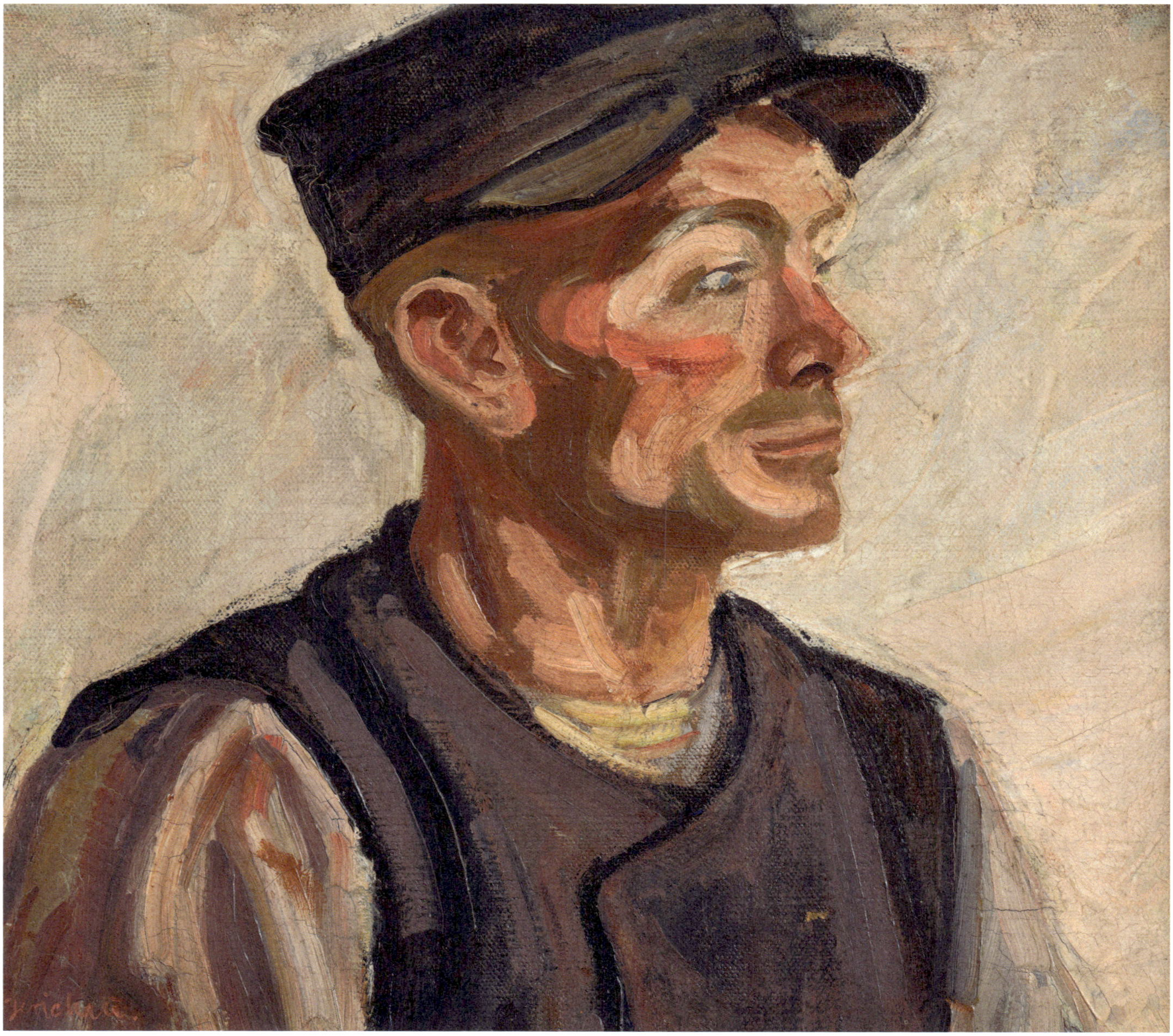

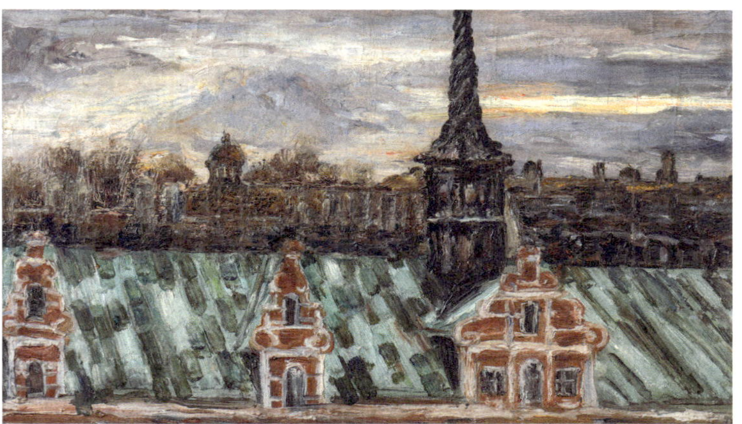

4 *A Farmer from Zealand*, 1910

2 *View of the Stock Exchange*, 1909

8 *Tomato Plant*, 1911

9 *Poppies in Bloom*, 1912

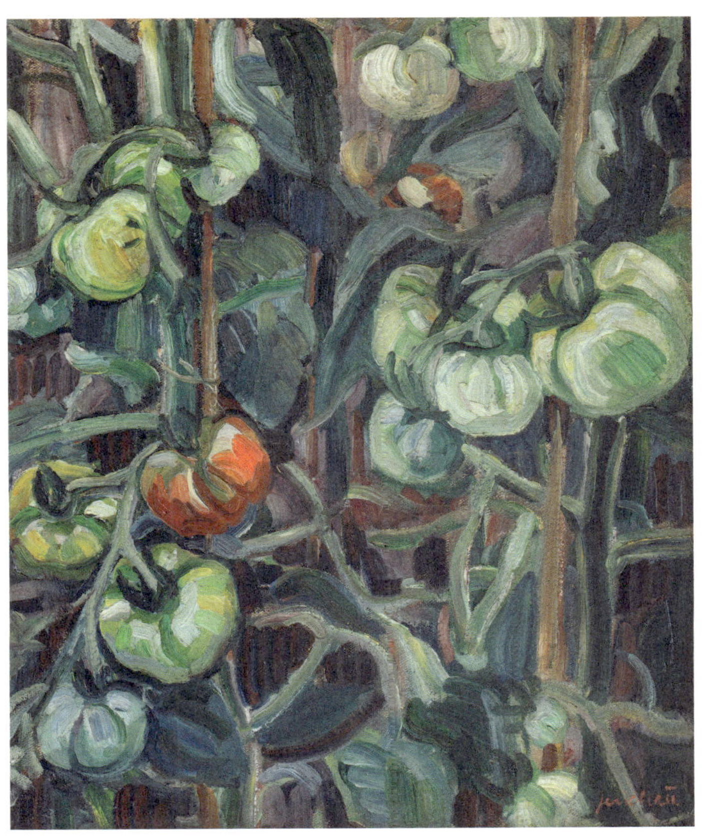

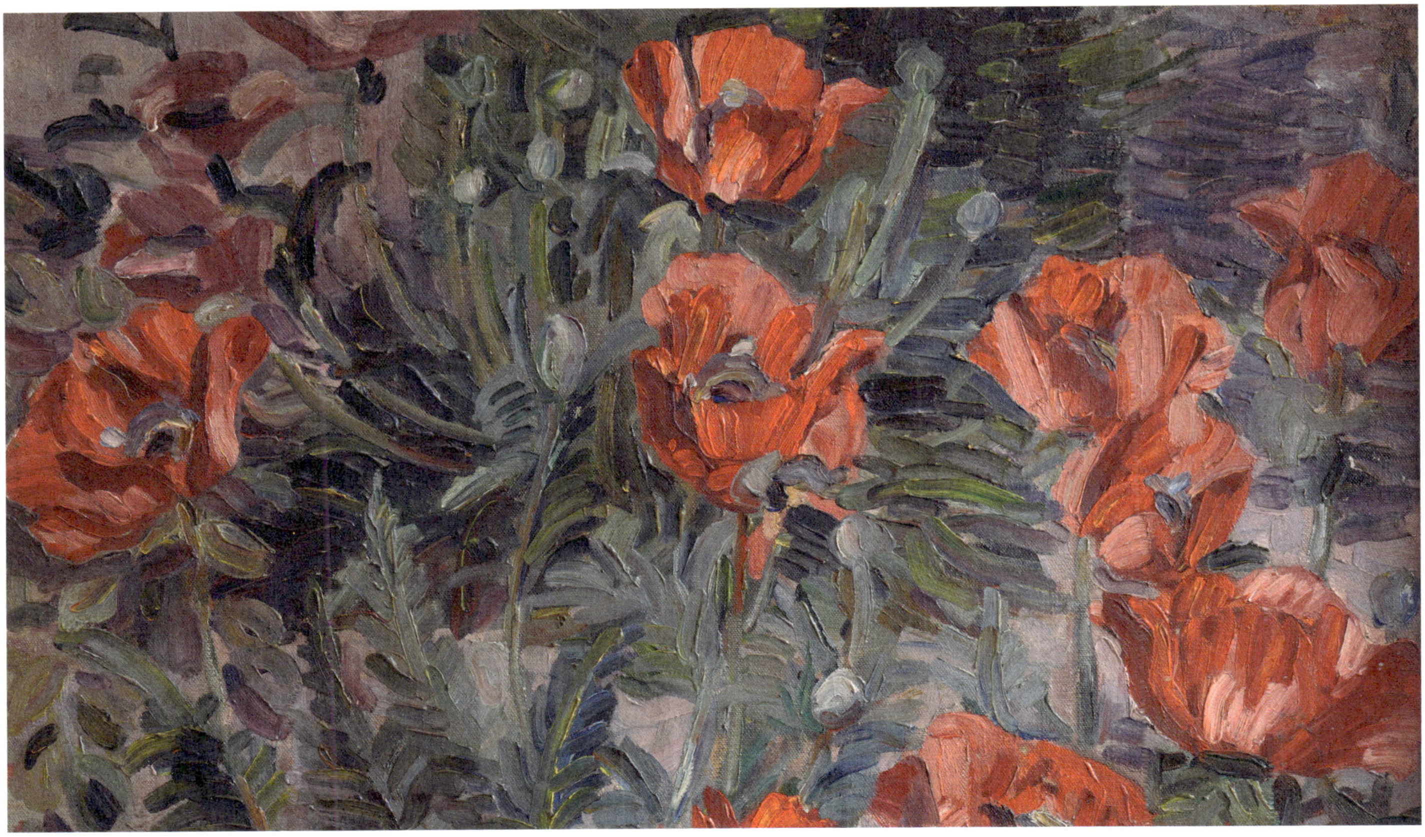

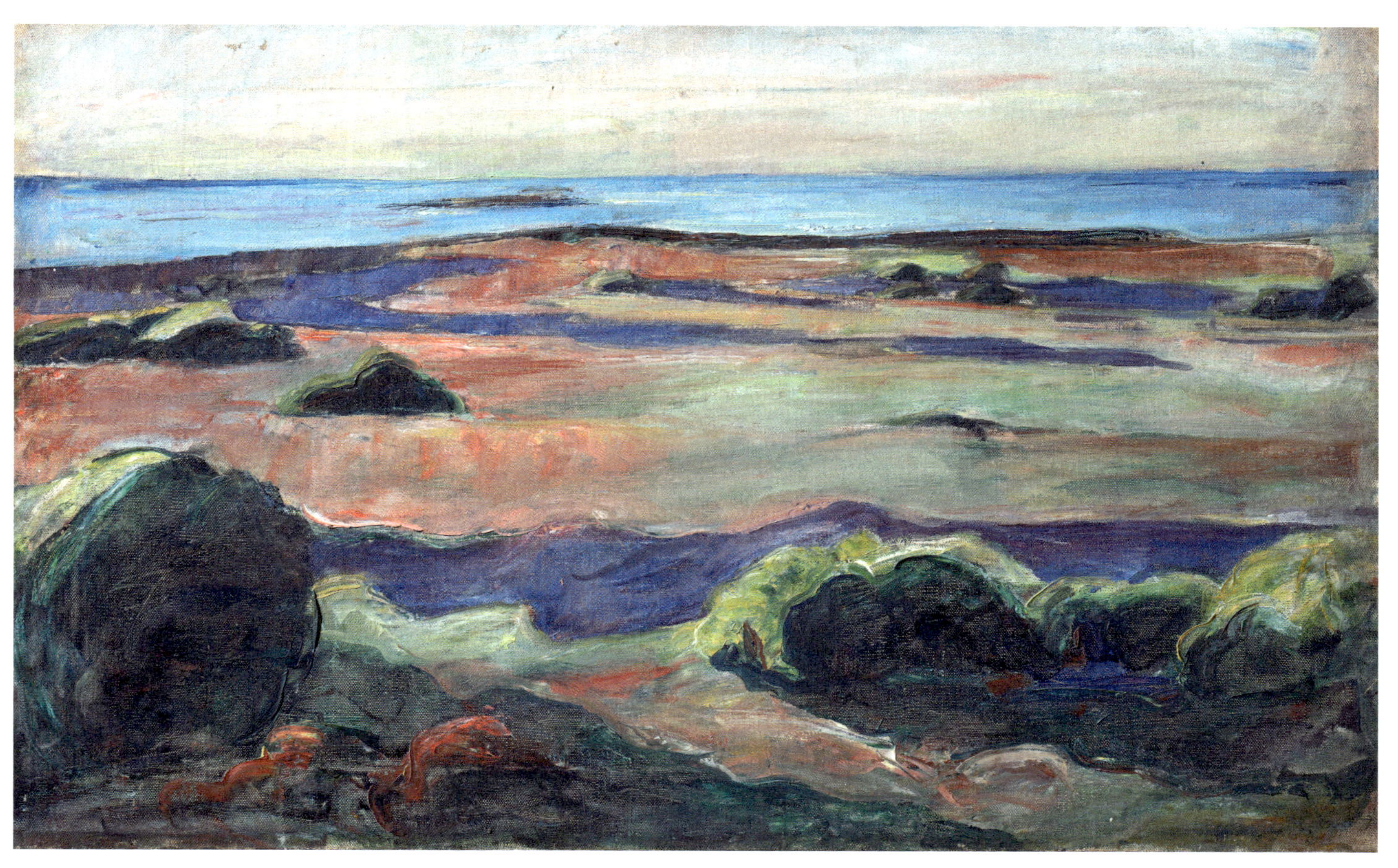

7 *Hesselø*, 1911

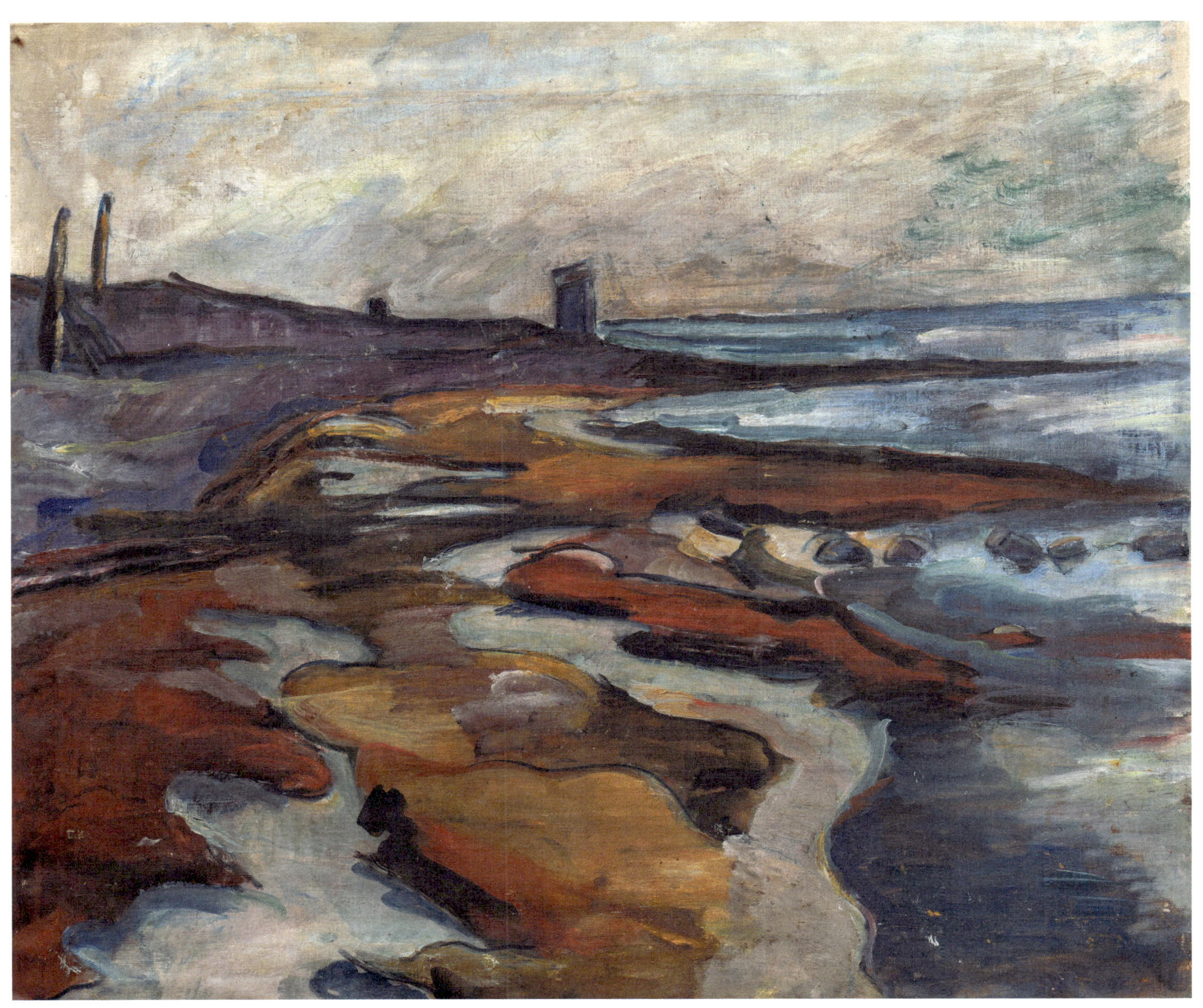

6 *Landscape*, 1911

Great Times Are Upon Us: On the Existential Struggle in Jerichau's Art

Mathias Ussing Seeberg

Among the papers left behind by the Danish painter Jens Adolf Jerichau (1890-1916), a 1916 fragment reads, "I am hardly quite normal."[1] The year before he had written to his sister Lisbeth from Bandol in southern France, "This is not vanity, but I do not think I am like other people – and I know I *never* want what others want."[2] Feelings of this nature haunted his short life and left a mark on his art. Jerichau was caught between the life his family thought he should lead, the life society expected of him and the life he really wanted for himself.

From an early age, he felt a strong call to be an artist, which did not come out of thin air. At age 19, he wrote in his journal about a feeling he had experienced during a walk in his hometown of Hørsholm, "Memories of the greatness of my lineage washed over me. I felt that I myself was born to be somebody, the greatest perhaps of our line."[3] The lineage is that of his paternal grandparents, the sculptor J.A. Jerichau (the Elder, 1816-1883) and the painter Elisabeth Jerichau-Baumann (1819-1881), who both had major careers as artists. Jerichau's father, Holger Jerichau (1861-1900), was a painter as well, but never reached the same heights as his parents. His death at age 39 in 1900, when Jens Adolf was just 10 years old, marks a symbolic, final break with the heritage of the Danish Golden Age, as represented by Holger Jerichau, and the arrival of a new, more experimental style that his son very early on knew he wanted to pursue. A new century and a brand new art.

The earliest work in this exhibition, from 1906, is an expressionist depiction of the bridge between the Cavalier Houses in Hørsholm, where he grew up, and the local church. Jerichau had yet to feel the call of art, the rush of his ancestors, but he was already a better and freer painter than his father ever was or dared to be. Other early works by Jerichau are in a similar vein, conventional in subject matter – landscapes, portraits, still lifes – but with a clear orientation away from the petit bourgeois. *Poppies in Bloom* (1912) is as straightforward as the title implies, painted in wild colours and impasto. This simple yet beautiful painting tells us something fundamental about Jerichau. The sensitivity of his paintings lies not only in the pathos of a particular subject, though there is a lot of that in his work, but in the pulsating brushwork itself. That is one effect of these small, unostentatious paintings on us when we study Jerichau. We see his talent in a purer form. The landscapes he painted during his last stay in southern France, in 1915, evoke the best of German Expressionism, in particular Emil Nolde's (1867-1956) paintings of the South Seas.[4]

More than anything, Jerichau's world was populated by big figure compositions, in which he articulated a new artistic expression by looking back in time. He liked to paint according to Renaissance principles of composition and toured Europe, studying the masters: Tintoretto, Velázquez, Rubens, Raphael, Michelangelo. He read Plato and Dante and cultivated heroic figures, great men of singular ability or with a singular calling. Jerichau called them prophets, and he might even have believed that he was or could become one of them. However, his interest in this subject matter was not reactionary. Jerichau knew and studied the latest experimental European art as well – the artists' collective Der Blaue Reiter, Pablo Picasso (1881-1973) and Henri Matisse (1869-1954), to name a few. In well-worn subjects from art history – Adam and Eve, the Three Magi, Dante, bacchants and so on – Jerichau saw an opportunity to reinvent painting *through* tradition. In Jerichau's hands, these subjects held up a mirror to the contemporary world and his own life, offering an opportunity to juxtapose the present with a glorious past.

Loving Both Black and White at Once

Jerichau struggled with life; a cliché, perhaps, but true. He suffered from a mental illness (we do not know which), as several

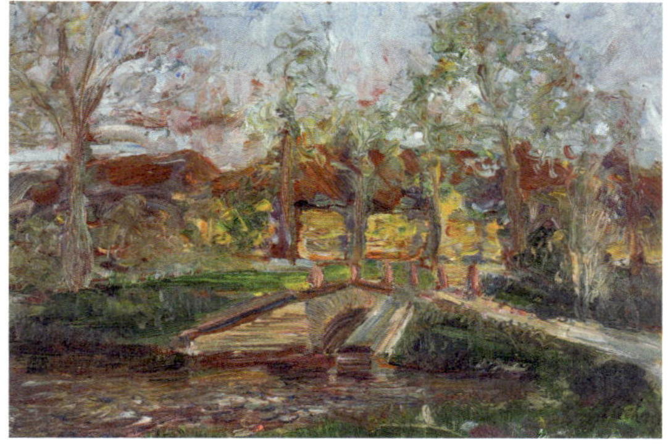

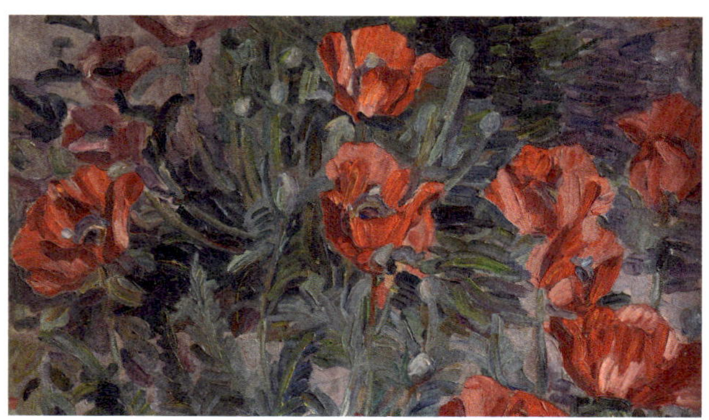

members of his father's family had done before him.[5] His illness seems to have involved wild mood swings, from ecstatic (and charming) states to bouts of depression weighing him down from an early age with thoughts of suicide as an all but inevitable outcome. One year before his death, he wrote to his sister Lisbeth, "The misfortune is that what I need most of all is time, and always I feel the knife at my throat."[6] In addition to mental illness, Jerichau fought with his mother, who tried to control her son's career and love life. He faced a lot of resistance, especially about his last known relationship, to Sigrun Schalburg (1882-1969). Eight years his senior, Schalburg was a single mother with four children. They met in the fall of 1914 and stayed in Madrid together in 1915. In a letter that Jerichau sent to his mother in February of that year, we sense her disapproval of his relationship with Schalburg, "And you should also know that the woman I love, she is worthy, she is necessary to me - and that it is for the good. I cannot and will not love that which is nothing. You think it is strange to love black and white - at once - not separately; but, mother, I do, and I can."[7] Jerichau's relationship with Schalburg has been documented and described several times in the literature on the artist. Mikael Wivel sees Jerichau's breakup with Schalburg as a contributing factor to his suicide.[8] However, the above excerpt from Jerichau's letter to his mother, in which he defends his relationship with Schalburg, also indicates a significant but under-examined detail about Jerichau's life which is crucial to the legacy of his art: loving both black and white.

In 1931, Jerichau's mentor, Vilhelm Wanscher (1875-1961) - who taught him about Renaissance art, composition principles and techniques - wrote the first biography on the artist in the series *Vor tids kunst* (Art of Our Time). In the volume, published 15 years after the artist's death, Wanscher writes that Jerichau, "in the erotic, like Michelangelo, had a 'duality' in his nature, which can be perceived in his representation of figures."[9] Calling attention to Jerichau's erotic duality - which, perhaps, is what Jerichau meant by loving black and white - was unusual in 1931. Clearly, Wanscher raises the issue at this point in time because, with a delay of several years, he has arrived at the conclusion that it is key to understanding the artist, whom he was so fond of and who was so fond of him.[10]

Wanscher was crucial in unfurling Jerichau's talent for painting. But in terms of making Jerichau realize and express the dual nature that Wanscher saw in his work, the most important acquaintance in Jerichau's life was the writer Aage Barfoed (1879-1960).[11] Barfoed and Jerichau had a relationship from the time Jerichau was 18 and up to 1912. The relationship was intellectually stimulating for Jerichau but also, at least for a brief period, had a more intimate dimension, as witnessed by the fact that they bathed and shared a bed.[12] We know that Barfoed was gay, but we do not know if Jerichau was. Homosexuality is, however, a recurring theme in Jerichau's letters to his mother and sisters. In one letter, he writes that he is not homosexual, but that he has "been a previous life, it is at any rate quite natural to understand homos."[13] Such clues abound, not only in his letters. In one early drawing, Jerichau depicts himself from the back and nude with an obvious accentuation of his rear. For all intents and purposes, he is playing with, exploring and questioning his sexuality.[14]

This essay builds on Wanscher's informed reading of Jerichau's figures through "the duality of his nature,"[15] on the pioneering Jerichau scholar Troels Andersen's reading of Jerichau's life as torn "between the sexual forces and the death drive"[16] and Mikael Wivel's (albeit qualified) suggestion that Jerichau was bisexual.[17] Accordingly, my approach to Jerichau's paintings and imagery is based on speculations about his "nature". Jerichau's figure paintings reveal a general interest in themes and subjects that are part of a contemporaneous homoerotic canon, and that have not been significantly unpacked in the existing literature on the artist.[18] Furthermore, I identify painterly strategies that can be viewed in this light as well. Jerichau's works are characterized by overpainting, hiding images that can barely be discerned. He also liked to paint on the backs of his canvases. Playing with the hidden, an aspect of one's identity that cannot be shown, is a strategy that was expressed in many different ways particularly among queer artists in Jerichau's day. One was Marsden Hartley, whose work was the subject of an exhibition at the Louisiana Museum in 2019.[19] Codes were used in art and literature to insinuate what was going on behind closed doors and drawn curtains, while indulging the dream of letting oneself be known.[20] Today, such strategies would be described as inherently queer (in relation to the notion of normality) and non-normative. When Jerichau writes that he is not normal, he is not necessarily referring to his battle

Opposite page from the left:

Jens Adolf Jerichau: *The Bridge to the Church*, 1906 (1)

Jens Adolf Jerichau: *Poppies in Bloom*, 1912 (9)

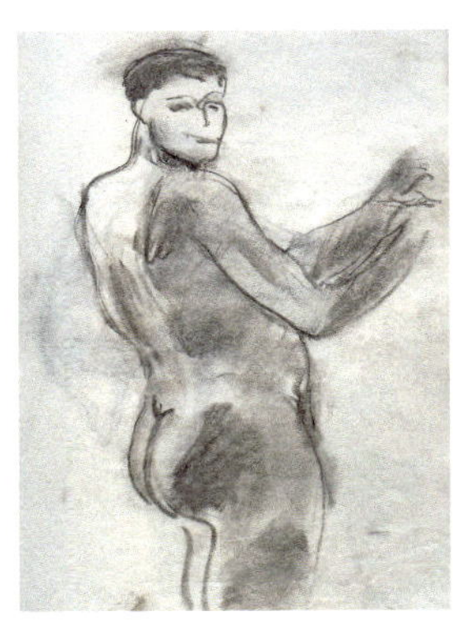

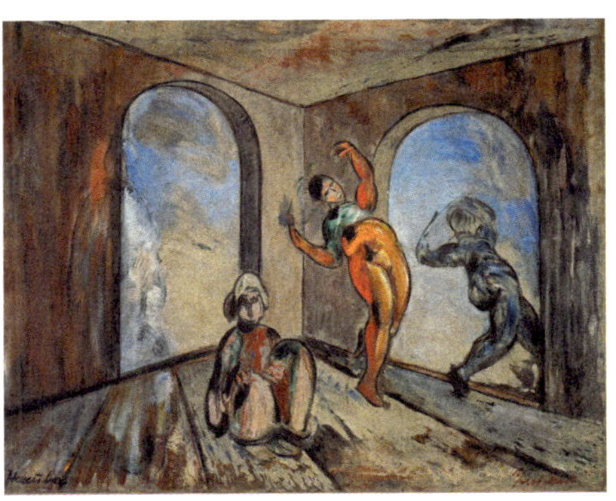

This page from the left:

Jens Adolf Jerichau: *Self-portrait, Standing Nude*. Sketchbook (138)

Jens Adolf Jerichau: *Hecuba*, 1916 (95)

with mental illness but generally remarking on his identity as an outsider. In this essay, I attempt to identify an interpretive material in Jerichau's work related to his own understanding of who he was that has previously only been superficially examined.

Hidden Images

On the backs of many of Jerichau's paintings are more images. Jerichau often painted a composition on one side of the canvas, then turned the canvas over and worked with the stains of paint that had bled through to the other side. Mikael Wivel singles out *Pietà* (1914, cat. no. 35, p. 37), at Ribe Art Museum, in which a figure on the front of the canvas matches the mirrored image on the back. As the modern Danish painter Asger Jorn saw it, this method of painting underscored the lesser importance to Jerichau of the iconography, demonstrating the great freedom with which he painted.[21] For Jerichau, the starting point for something new was often a gift from the existing – not unlike the Surrealists' "exquisite corpse" game of folded paper, where one artist continues another's unseen drawing. Only here, Jerichau works from his own marks on the canvas as a special category of spontaneous painting, repeating the figure as the basis for something new. In Jerichau's sketchbooks, there are numerous examples of drawings filled in on the reverse side of the page.[22] At the very least, this relationship between the front and the back can be regarded as orchestrated randomness.

There are compositions hidden under the surface of the paintings, as well. In his 1916 masterpiece *Hecuba* (cat. no. 95, p. 76), a figure has been painted over, but not so effectively that we fail to sense its presence. In 1962, in the journal *Signum*, Troels Andersen wrote, "For Jerichau, painting over a picture was not an indifferent process or a mere rejection. To him, it meant working on top of the content of ideas he had already put down on the canvas. In his mind, the picture, in an almost mystical way, contained the event or person it depicted."[23] I propose that we consider the backs of the paintings in a similar light. Like his German colleagues in the artists' collective Der Blaue Reiter, Jerichau was interested in Theosophy and mysticism, and may have felt that the pictures would be spiritually enriched and gain gravity by containing hidden compositions.[24]

The front of *A Bishop* (1912) shows the figure of a bishop with a bird in his hand, while the back shows a palimpsest-like self-portrait of the artist emerging like a ghost from a figure composition set at a 90 degree angle to it. The two compositions are clearly interrelated; one is not simply painted on top of the other. The simple explanation for Jerichau's use of the back of the canvas, proposed by Wivel and others, is that he was in a hurry, "and usable canvases were [...] often in short supply in his studio. For that reason, there are numerous examples of him flipping his canvases over and painting something new on the back. This was simply routine. He could not wait for the paint shop to open in the morning".[25] To my eye, the practice looks more methodical, though practical considerations like those described by Wivel obviously played a part. Jerichau's last self-portrait, painted in Paris, shows a worn out, tortured man. It is a profoundly sad picture, painted in a more conventional and uninspired style than his figure compositions from the same period. The self-portrait itself now lives in the shadows, since there is another picture on the front of the canvas. That picture, *The Graves of Fallen Warriors* (1916), of a tombstone in the shape of a cross, is the only work by Jerichau that directly refers to the raging First World War. The relationship between the two subjects intrigues me: one is a defeated man, the other is the grave of a defeated man. One image seems to lead to the other. Something similar is seen in *A Bishop*. Bishops are a motif in Jerichau's work, a holy or enlightened figure or prophet. Likewise, the bird in the bishop's hand recurs as an image of inspiration or connection to the higher powers. The images on the front and the back of the canvas are linked: on the front, the bishop with his bird; on the back, Jerichau and his iconic figures. Two pictures with related meanings, or Jerichau with and without a disguise.

Apart from the concrete relationship between the front and the back of the canvas, between a composition and what lies behind it, it is important to consider the act of "hiding" as the existential condition of a queer person, especially at that time in history. In his day and age, mental illness as well as "deviant" sexual and gender identities had to be hidden from public view. The mere fact that something is not shown, or shown as hidden and out of sight, can be regarded as a queer artistic device, playing with what is not known to everyone

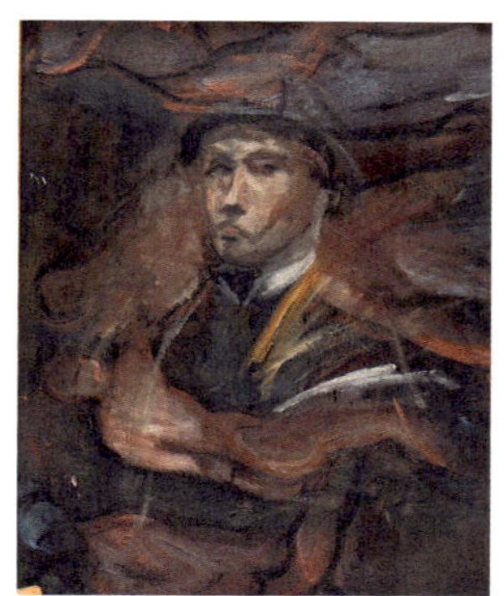

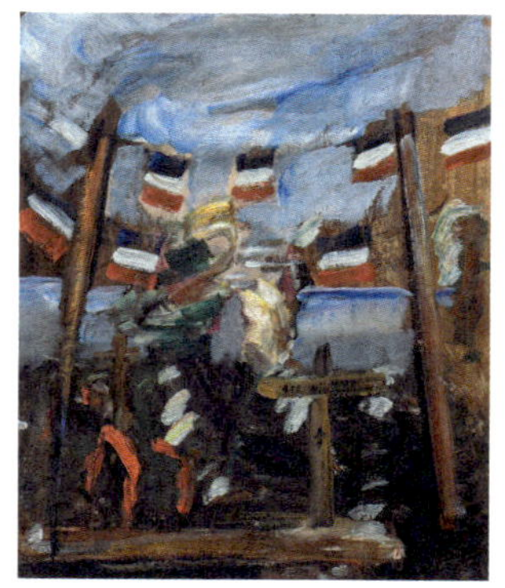

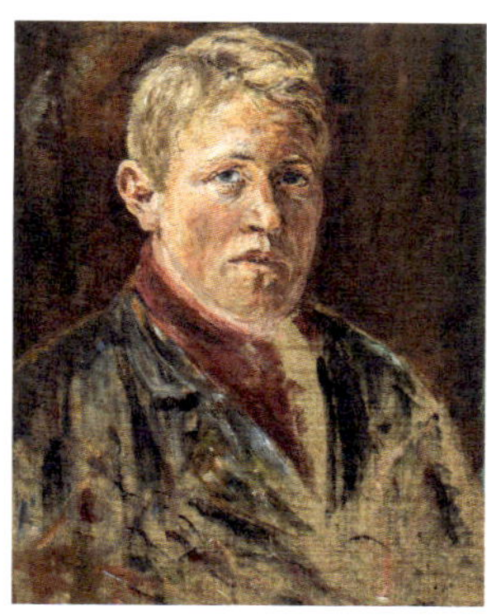

and everyone is not allowed to know. A contemporaneous English term for homosexual, "invert", (from "sexual inversion", the title of a study by Havelock Ellis), also implies the notion of being turned inside out.

Subject Matter

Jerichau alternated between innocuous, "small" subjects, like the ones he started out painting – in particular landscapes, as mentioned – and ostensibly more heroic pictures after or inspired by the Bible and classical imagery from art history, Dante's *Divine Comedy*, antiquity and more. However, even when he starts from a familiar iconography or sticks to historical events, his very handling of the material suggests that something else is going on. In the biblical pictures he painted in Copenhagen between 1913 and 1915 – *The Deposition* (1913), *Pietà* (1914) and *The Road to Calvary* (1913-1914, cat. no. 32, p. 36) – Jerichau seems merely to be using Bible stories as jumping-off points. His handling of the subject turns The Road to Calvary, from the Passion of Christ, into a strange, almost perverse ritual rendered particularly corporeal and sexual. Severing the ties between signification and source, Jerichau unleashes a whole other potential of interpretation in the picture, connecting entities like shame and sexuality with religious persecution and, indeed, the Passion of Christ.

Beyond the subject matter's partial correspondence to the Bible stories, there is an internal or invisible correspondence to Jerichau's own life. The artist himself is not immediately visible in the work, but knowing his life, the letters he wrote and received, his notes and sketchbooks, we can state with some certainty that he was personally invested in his choice of subject matter. Indeed, we can say this without first considering whether it even matters to the interpretation of the respective works, or whether it more accurately belongs to an anecdotal category. Jerichau's last painting, *The Ancestors Beckon* (1916, cat. no. 98, p. 89), can immediately be connected to Jerichau's notions about the distinguished line of artists from which he was descended, and his place therein. The young man in the painting, who is summoned by his ancestors in the clouds, can moreover be connected to Jerichau's suicidal ideation, which dominated his last days in Paris. On 24 July 1916, about three weeks before his death, Jerichau writes in his journal, "Only death I think about, glorious death which will fill me and swallow me up."[26] Jerichau's tragic life can very specifically be viewed in relation to what he painted. There are other correspondences, as well. Less specific than the above example, they are even more important for understanding and expressing a specific aspect of this essay's intention, which is to indicate Jerichau's interest in subject matter, which hints at his queer identity.

A small, easily overlooked portrait may hold the key to unlocking some of Jerichau's motifs and cast of characters. Jerichau painted *Socrates (Portrait of Vilhelm Wanscher)* (1912, cat. no. 23, p. 47) after making several sketches of a bust in the Royal Collection of Graphic Arts at the National Gallery of Denmark.[27] However, as the title also makes clear, this is actually a portrait of his mentor, Vilhelm Wanscher, or, more accurately, it is Jerichau's way of connecting the two persons in a single image. In other words, Jerichau is juxtaposing a person from his own life with one of the greatest thinkers of antiquity. This opens the possibility of regarding the other historical and biblical figures that Jerichau painted as stand-ins for himself and for people he knew, or at least as images of his own day and age. Dante, whom Jerichau painted several times, is not necessarily the historical figure that Jerichau had read and admired. In Jerichau's cosmology, Dante could also be someone who is "like Dante", in the same way that Christ could be "like Christ" – the latter very possibly himself. This switch is crucial to understanding Jerichau's work and gives credence to the theory that Jerichau was taking his own time and interests as his subject matter.

The Glorious Age of Greece

Antiquity is the source for a number of Jerichau's most important paintings, particularly ones he made during his years in Copenhagen, between fall 1912 and spring 1915, and the last ones he made before his suicide in Paris. In addition to the portrait of Socrates, there are *Philosophers* (1913, cat. no. 25, p. 48) and a painting that Wivel, based on a list of subjects in Jerichau's sketchbook, persuasively argues is an androgynous image of *Alcibiades* (1913, cat. no. 26, p. 47).[28] In a 1935 poem, Jerichaus close friend, the ceramicist Axel Salto, addresses Jerichau as Alcibiades. In addition to his beauty, young Alcibiades was known for his relationship with the much older Socrates.[29] Repeating Jerichau's device, Salto connects his

Opposite page from the left:

Front and back:
Jens Adolf Jerichau:
A Bishop, 1912 (21)

Front and back:
Jens Adolf Jerichau:
The Graves of Fallen Warriors, 1916 (90)

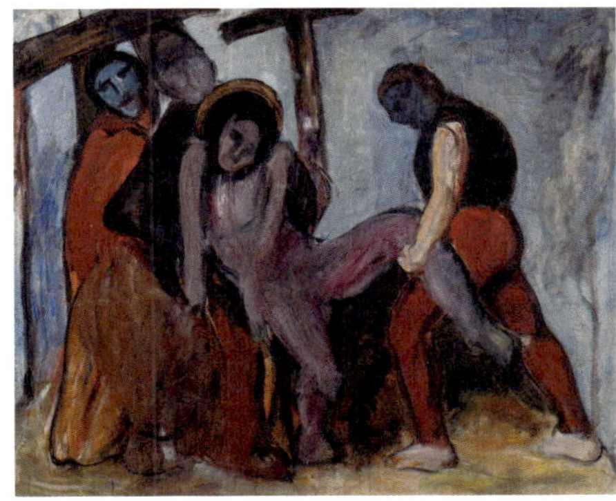

Jens Adolf Jerichau:
The Deposition, 1913 (31)

friend, 19 years dead, with an idol from antiquity. This makes Salto the second friend of Jerichau's (after Wanscher) who, in the 1930s, seems to be describing Jerichau's homosexual inclinations. In his description, Wanscher referred to the Renaissance and Michelangelo, while Salto turned to antiquity, which bolsters our understanding of what antiquity and its rebirth in the Renaissance could have meant to Jerichau as not only an artistic but a spiritual and sexual ideal.

This interest in antiquity and ancient times was hardly unique in Jerichau's day, but flourished in Denmark and abroad, and not only among artists who considered themselves outsiders. According to Timothy Hyman, Henri Matisse, in his iconic *Dance* (1909-1910), imagined "a community reborn in primal liberty; an icon of earthly joy, whose antecedents are in Gauguin's Tahiti and Cézanne's bathers, in the 'primitive' worlds evoked by African tribal sculpture, but also in Greek and Roman literature." The idea of the dance was bound up with a myth about a golden age, "a time before hierarchy, class, nation, gender, religion or race divided humankind."[30]

Alcibiades, whom Jerichau depicted as a figure of ambiguous gender, appears in a list he made in one of his journals under the headline "From the Glorious Times of Ancient Greece," which is also part of the title of three paintings he made in the last three years of his life: *The Golden Bird. From the Glorious Times of Ancient Greece. Opus I* (1913-1914), *The Arrival of Spring. From the Glorious Times of Ancient Greece. Opus II* (1915, cat. no. 48, p. 46) and *The Golden Bird. From the Glorious Times of Ancient Greece. Opus III* (1916, cat. no. 94, p. 79). Jerichau painted the last of these pictures in Paris shortly before his death. The subtitle, *From the Glorious Times of Ancient Greece*, recalls the last words Jerichau wrote in his journal before committing suicide, "Great times are upon us - glorious art awaits."[31]

"The Glorious Times of Ancient Greece" and "the great age of glorious art" appear to be different versions of the same idea. Writing "great times are upon us," it is as if Jerichau describes something like a season, destined to recur periodically. Jerichau evidently had a vision of the second coming of "his" Greece in his own time.[32] The golden bird paintings, especially the first two, seem to depict a link between artistic, spiritual and bodily liberation. The bird, a perennial motif for Jerichau, as described in connection with *A Bishop*, is an image of both freedom and inspiration, which Jerichau orchestrates in a seemingly promiscuous and liberated natural society.[33]

In Copenhagen, others besides Jerichau held up antiquity as an ideal. Jerichau may have seen the Danish painter Kristian Zahrtmann's (1843-1917) picture *Socrates and Alcibiades* (1911) when it was displayed in the art dealer Kleis's March exhibition of 1911.[34] Zahrtmann's interest in the subject stemmed from ideas about the erotic relationship between Socrates and Alcibiades. In general, antiquity was an important code for queer people at the time. Salto's description of Jerichau as Alcibiades appears to be a loving gesture, discreetly using the same device as Jerichau to place his friend in relationship to homoeroticism. Likely, it was Aage Barfoed who introduced Jerichau to the symbolic meanings of antiquity.

Antiquity as a Code

From 1909 to 1912, Jerichau had a relationship with the writer Aage Barfoed, as described in the beginning of this essay.[35] It was because of his relationship with Barfoed that Jerichau had to assure his mother that he did not like men, as seen in the draft of a letter he wrote,[36] "I am quite at ease going over there now [to Barfoed], simply because I am not a homo, if being so [...] means that one *prefers living with men* instead of women. I have never in a sexual regard been attracted to men. However, in a spiritual regard I have *most often* felt at home with men."[37] Because he is writing to his mother, who does not approve of the relationship, we cannot take Jerichau's words about whom he is attracted to at face value. We can merely note that he took pains to make sure that his mother would not worry. At any rate, Barfoed was enormously important to Jerichau. It is through Barfoed that Jerichau becomes acquainted with Oscar Wilde (1854-1900) and *De Profundis* (1897), a text Wilde wrote during his imprisonment in Reading Gaol for "gross indecency" because of his relationship with Lord Alfred Douglas (1870-1945). After a visit to Barfoed, Jerichau wrote in his journal about Wilde, "His defence of homosexuality I must get a hold of."[38]

Barfoed had studied literature at Oxford University, where Wilde was a student from 1874 to 1878. This was at a time when trendsetting homosexual personalities, among them Walter Pater (1839-1894), had helped to create a literary canon in the department at Oxford that covertly supported and

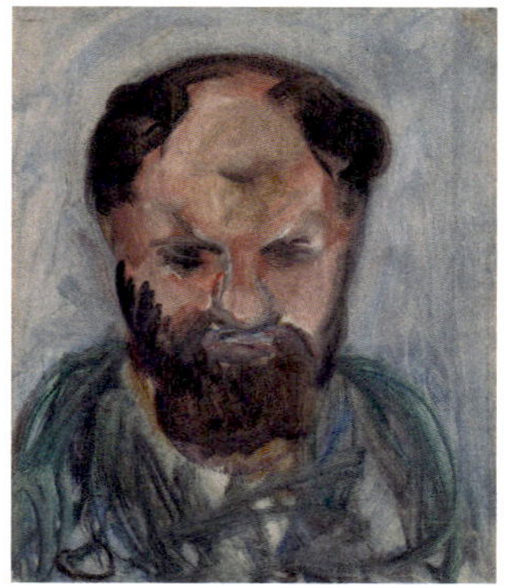

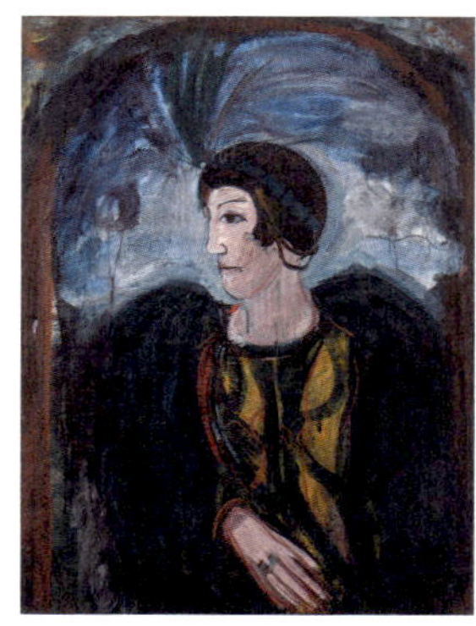

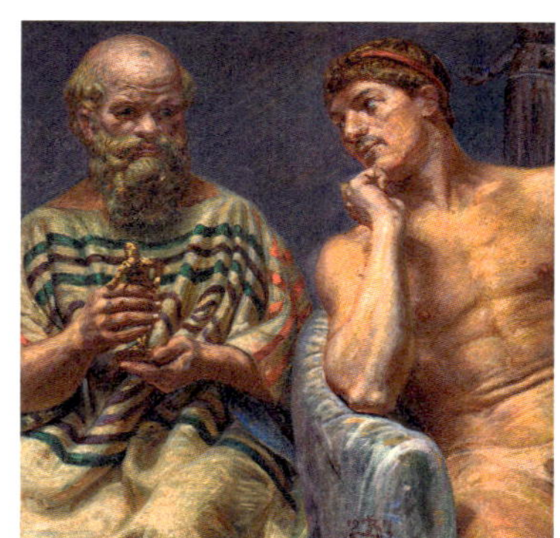

From the left:

Jens Adolf Jerichau:
Socrates (Portrait of Vilhelm Wanscher), 1912 (23)

Jens Adolf Jerichau:
Alcibiades, 1913 (26)

Kristian Zahrtmann:
Socrates and Alcibiades, 1911
Oil on canvas, 37 cm × 37cm
SMK, National Gallery of Art

justified homosexual love. Dante and Plato were read there. In turn, cultivating Greek philosophy, and using it to legitimize same-sex love, became a "homosexual code".[39] For instance, calling someone a "Platonist" was code for saying they were gay.[40] Through the Oxford canon, physical attraction between men was recoded into spiritual desire for the highest form of knowledge,[41] which is precisely how Jerichau puts it in the letter denying his homosexuality to his mother. He is not physically but spiritually attracted to men.[42] Through Barfoed, Jerichau connects sexual desire with intellectual appetite and artistic aspiration. He is able to justify homosexuality as spiritual refinement. In Barfoed, Jerichau encountered a "Platonist" capable of giving his, if not homosexual, then at least bisexual feelings a language, form and purpose that was not only meaningful but made attraction to men a symptom of a uniquely powerful artistic sensibility.

Dante

Antiquity was not the only source of subject matter that preoccupied Jerichau, but it was certainly one of the most important. Another subject that Jerichau returned to over and over again, from the time he first started making figure compositions, in 1912, and until his death in Paris in 1916, was Dante Alighieri (1265-1321). Andersen writes that a portrait of Dante hung in Jerichau's childhood home,[43] but it was probably also through Barfoed[44] (and Wilde) that Jerichau became so fascinated with the Italian poet. A series of sketchbook portraits shows Jerichau contemplating Dante and Socrates side by side.[45] Wilde studied Dante in depth during his imprisonment, and Dante was commonly used as an argument to justify same-sex love in the late 19th century. Stefano Evangelista points to Havelock Ellis's study *Sexual Inversion* (1897), in which "Ellis uses Dante's evidence to confirm his hypothesis that 'homosexuality is especially common among men of exceptional intellect'".[46]

The interest in Dante among an intellectual queer community was due in particular to Dante's descriptions of homosexual love and desire in *Inferno* (Cantos 15 and 16) and *Purgatorio* (Canto 26). Gary Cestaro, who has mapped queer-theoretical readings of Dante up to the present day, importantly points out that "queer readers can't help but queer Dante – sensing sympathy, or in defiance, or often with some conflicted mixture of the two," noting that Dante has been a subject for an endless array of queer artists – poets, painters, writers and filmmakers.[47] Jerichau was not the only one who saw a kindred spirit in Dante. Nonetheless, in Denmark there was also an interest in Dante as a subject for paintings that were not inherently queer. Edvard Weie's (1879-1943) paintings after Eugène Delacroix's (1798-1963) *Dante and Virgil in the Underworld* (1822) and Poul S. Christiansen's (1855-1933) *Dante and Beatrice in Paradise* (1895) portray different versions of the Italian poet.

Jerichau's pictures of Dante vary widely and often deal quite freely with the poet and his work. Dante is generally represented as an archetype, one of Jerichau's prophets, more than as the historical figure. One painting, however, looks to be lifted straight out of *The Divine Comedy*. Enigmatically titled *The Resurrection. Tribute to the Renaissance. Symbols. Opus IV* (1914-1915, cat. no. 44, p. 31), it depicts two greyish, ghostlike, androgynous figures and two other only partly visible, very muscular figures in an intense embrace, with Dante in the background wearing his characteristic red robe and cap, as if he were meeting these souls while passing through purgatory. Basically, it looks a lot like an illustration, which is rarely the case with Jerichau's pictures. Perhaps Jerichau wanted to create a work that specifically refers to Canto 26 of *Purgatorio*, where Dante explicitly describes homosexuality – or, more accurately, sodomy – with great engagement and compassion.[48] In Canto 26, Dante mentions shadow people who meet in kisses and hurry on.[49] At the centre of the painting, two very masculine, semi-transparent figures appear to be kissing and embracing very intensely. This image of homosexual love, in conjunction with the figure of Dante, makes it likely that there is a connection between the subject matter and the canto.

The title, *The Resurrection. Tribute to the Renaissance*, is curious, since Dante lived before the Renaissance. Jerichau's hero Oscar Wilde, however, described Dante as a precursor to great Italian Renaissance painting.[50] Writing to Wanscher, his friend and mentor, Jerichau linked this work to a Renaissance master, "I have laid out a canvas where the idea and composition are two stiff figures in profile [...] in relation to a very animated Michelangelesque figure that rushes into the pictorial space and experiences a wonderful effect."[51] The pairing of Dante and Michelangelo brings together two giants of

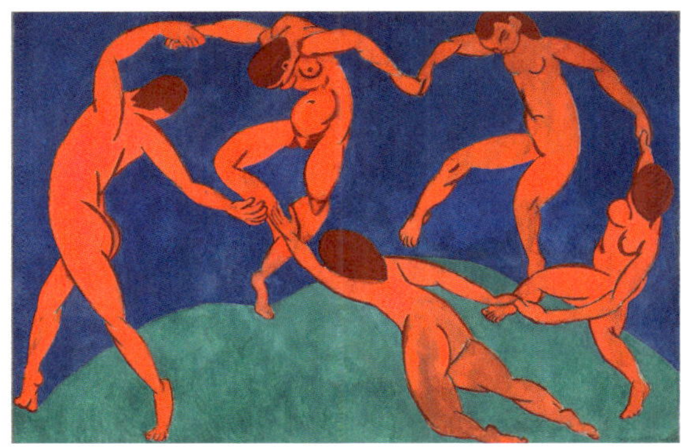

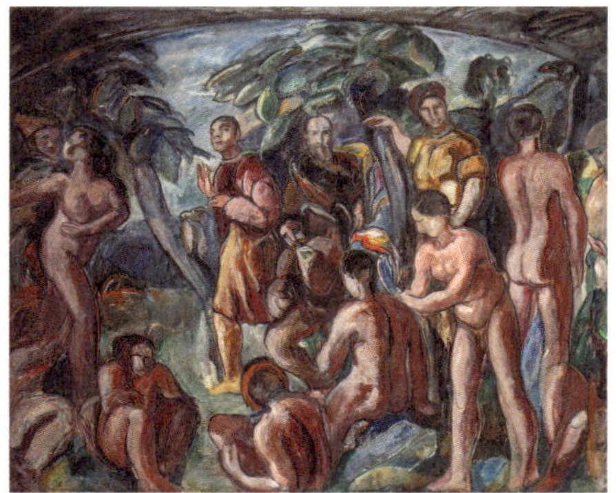

From the left:

Henri Matisse: *Dance*, 1909-1910
Oil on canvas, 260 × 391 cm
The State Hermitage Museum

Jens Adolf Jerichau:
The Golden Bird. From the Glorious Times of Ancient Greece. Opus I, 1913-1914 (34)

literature and art. However, Wanscher specifically tied Jerichau to Michelangelo through their "erotic duality". In his 1908 book *Raphael and Michelangelo*, which Jerichau surely read, Wanscher writes that Michelangelo was "undoubtedly" in love with both men and women, and refers to another book that looks at Michelangelo in the light of his erotic and romantic interest in men.[52] Combining Dante and Michelangelo may have been Jerichau's way of describing an affinity that went beyond the purely artistic.[53]

The Figures

Jerichau's figures do not all look alike. But there are general traits that reappear in most of his striking figure compositions. Above all, they are not anatomically correct. The faces he paints are often stylized and mask-like. That is distinctly the case in a series of three pictures, *The Sacrificial Feast. Man Seeking Omens. Opus I* (1914), *The Sacrificial Feast. Man Seeking Omens. Opus II* (1915, cat. no. 46, p. 42) and *The Sacrificial Feast. Man Seeking Omens. Opus III* (1915, cat. no. 47, p. 43). The latter painting, held in the Louisiana's Collection, links Jerichau's practice to that of a number of his international colleagues who cultivated primitivism, especially inspired by encounters with ethnographic collections in Berlin, Paris and elsewhere.[54] Jerichau used the primitivist strain as a way to separate the expression of his works from his own time, thereby connecting exactly his own time to a vision of something eternal, true and grand. Not unlike the aforementioned case of Matisse.

Jerichau not only removes his figures from his own day and age. Often, he also eliminates the characteristics that would allow us to unequivocally identify them as male or female. This is what Wanscher was pointing out. In Jerichau's handling of the figures, Wanscher recognized an attempt to express erotic duality. Many figures are completely genderless, while Jerichau's male figures are feminine, and his female figures masculine. In his analysis of *The Golden Bird. From the Glorious Times of Ancient Greece. Opus I* (1913-1914), Wivel writes that it is difficult to determine which figures are men and which are women, adding that it is not important anyway, because it is the "atmosphere of upheaval and liberation that marks their interaction".[55] I think Jerichau would agree with Wivel in this, although Wivel does not attach the same significance to this observation as I do in terms of Jerichau's work. I believe that Jerichau aspired to a liberation that a fixed gender and a normative understanding of identity would be unable to provide. In great times, for Jerichau, sexual, spiritual and artistic liberation go hand in hand.

Renaissance

Jerichau's last work, *The Ancestors Beckon*, has a counterpart, which is quite similar in composition and narrative but also crucially different. During his last days in Paris, Jerichau returned to a subject he had painted before, *The Magi and the Whore of Babylon* (first version, 1913-1914; final version, 1916). In the early version of the painting, a nude woman clings to a knight-like male figure, watched by the biblical Magi. In the late version, the nude woman stands with her back to us, while the three kings clearly distance themselves from her, the nearest of the Magi holding up his hand as if to stop her or turn her away. This is the polar opposite image of *The Ancestors Beckon*, where the ecclesiastical figures, another trio, beckon the nude man to them. As mentioned, *The Ancestors Beckon* has often been linked to Jerichau's suicide, though that is perhaps trivializing the work's grand theme in light of *The Magi and the Whore of Babylon*. The two paintings show conflicting feelings that are seen in any family and any society: rejection, on the one hand, and acceptance, on the other. Perhaps, the artist is trying to show us the ludicrousness of summoning one person and banishing the other. Does it matter that one is a man and the other a woman, or could they even be two sides of the same person? One that the family (or society) wants and one that they do not want, the hero and the whore. One who abides by a moral code and one who does not, which in the end is what determines entry to Heaven. In general, Jerichau's last images reveal an existential struggle. *The Golden Bird. From the Glorious Times of Ancient Greece. Opus III* (1916), for one, is markedly different from the two earlier versions described above. We now see a single androgynous figure at the centre of the picture. The figure stands alone, surrounded by the aforementioned images of liberation and inspiration, which the figure seems unable to approach, tantamount to a lack of ability to take part in the revelry, a hesitancy about taking the plunge. Whether this represents either fear of ultimate sexual liberation or a state of depression, in which it is

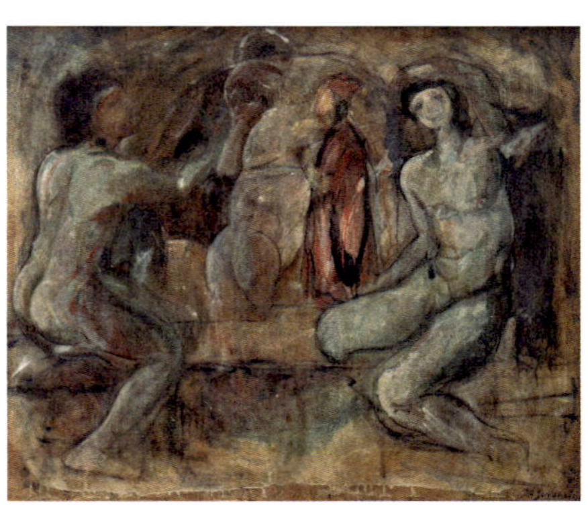

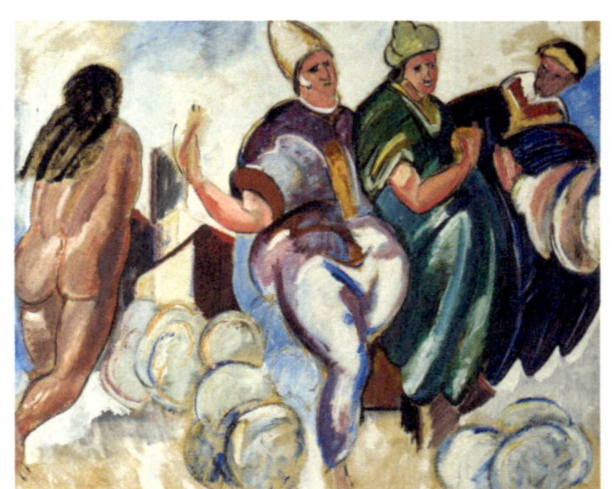

From the left:

Jens Adolf Jerichau:
The Resurrection. Tribute to the Renaissance. Symbols. Opus IV, 1914-1915 (44)

Jens Adolf Jerichau:
The Magi and the Whore of Babylon, 1913-1914 (33)

difficult to attain happiness in life – Jerichau struggled with both – may not be all that important. Both can be true at the same time. The painting is a profoundly moving image of what I would describe as an inability to approach what one craves and longs for.

I have already described Jerichau's struggle with his family, which went on his entire adult life. On 18 July 1915, Jerichau wrote to his sister Lisbeth from Bandol in southern France, "Why will Mother and my dear ones never take me as I am. [...] I will not become someone else because Mother pushes me away, but I must be allowed to live, and Mother ought rather be big and take me as I am. She should also know our family line, and I have often enough told her about my goals and ambitions – but in them she sees only danger, child-rearing is difficult. I say this also because I know they always wanted what was best for me, but never rightly understand how to take me. [...] I don't want to [be] too solemn, but I am so gnarly and complex that it is very hard for me to say straight out, This is how I am. I am still waiting *for something more* in myself. I am not the one I would like and wish to be – and *before* I am *that* – I am really nothing, or no one rather."[56] For Jerichau, destruction or non-existence are not necessarily bound up with suicide and death, although we know he often thought about ending his life. What Jerichau is suggesting in this and other letters is that a lack of acceptance from your loved ones is a form of existential eradication.

I would argue that we should be careful about interpreting the metaphorics of death in Jerichau's work, especially his late pictures – such as the masterful *Hecuba*, which shows a figure jumping out a window – as being directly linked to his suicide. The paintings strike me unequivocally as images of existential struggle, which is also why they are so moving. Leaping from a window can be a fever dream of leaving safe ground, breaking away from familiarity, and plunging into the unknown. When Jerichau auctioned off his works at Den Frie on 6 March 1916, he wrote this dedication in the catalogue, "In praise of the price of beauty, in praise of Hecuba." In many of his works, as described above, Jerichau depicts the highest artistic ideal as bound up with absolute existential liberation. That is the price of beauty.

In this article, I have tried to place the emphasis elsewhere compared to past readings of Jerichau by following a trail of clues left, but not pursued, by his three chief biographers. This essay supplements rather than replaces the existing readings of his work. Examining Jerichau's existential struggle, as revealed in letters and notes, not least regarding his mental illness and his sexuality, makes it clear that he saw himself as marginalized, someone who today would assume a queer position. Like many other men of his day, he was vividly engaged in justifying his attraction to men as evidence of a unique artistic exaltation, cultivating figures and subject matter that represented this. I have highlighted the works that confirm this reading. Obviously, in Jerichau's entire body of work, there are many examples that do not so transparently invite this analysis, nor is the point that Jerichau always employed such strategies, but simply that he sometimes did.

Jerichau told his family that he thought he had been homosexual in a past life. In general, Jerichau's notion of a renaissance, or rebirth, seems to involve spiritual and sexual liberation as much as purely artistic ideals. The two go hand in hand. Indeed, we could say that it is the combination of Wanscher and Barfoed that makes Jerichau. *The Book of Wisdom*, Jerichau's near-megalomaniacal journal, includes a kind of prose poem about a boy. The last line reads, "Everything shall come again, and victory is yours."[57] Jerichau saw his artistic realization in the liberation of his identity. The strange figures, the androgynous representations, the hidden images, the references to antiquity and the Renaissance were a way of alluding to but not directly tackling the issue and a refined reckoning and subversion of convention. Jerichau painted grand pictures after classical imagery and subject matter, but in his handling he transformed them into counterimages or distortions, artworks bucking bourgeois norms and morality. The last words Jerichau wrote in his diary, before committing suicide on 16 August, read "Great times are upon us – glorious art awaits."[58] On death's doorstep, Jerichau had a vision of an impending epochal age of art, but he did not himself have the means to stay and join the party. He could not take the plunge.

Mathias Ussing Seeberg is a curator at the Louisiana Museum of Modern Art. In addition to the Jerichau exhibition, he has curated *William Kentridge: Thick Time*, *Being There*, *Marsden Hartley: The Earth Is All I Know of Wonder* and *Arthur Jafa: MAGNUMB*.

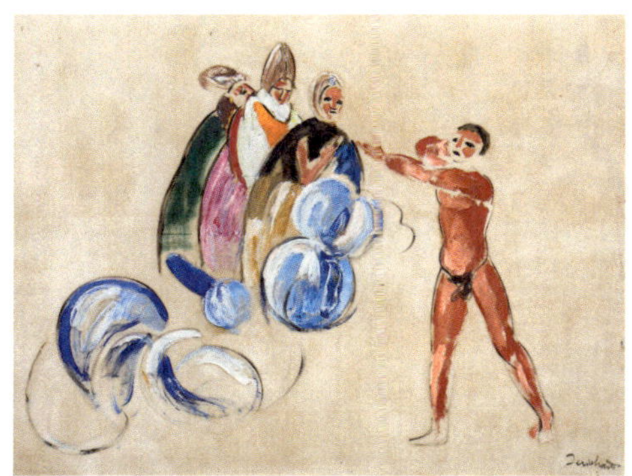

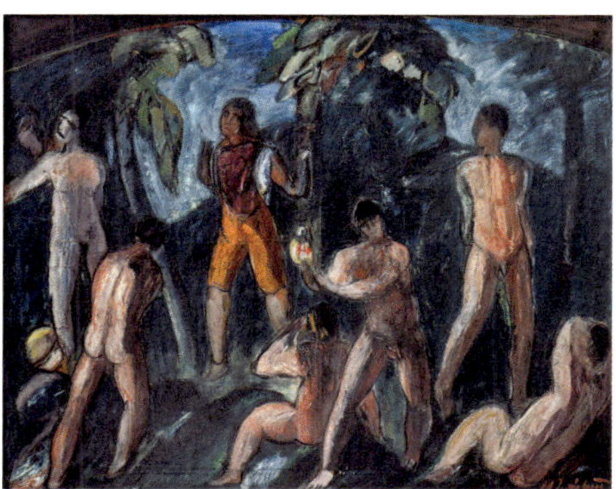

From the left:

Jens Adolf Jerichau:
The Ancestors Beckon, 1916 (98)

Jens Adolf Jerichau:
The Golden Bird. From the Glorious Times of Ancient Greece. Opus III, 1916 (94)

1912
Sanary, Bormes

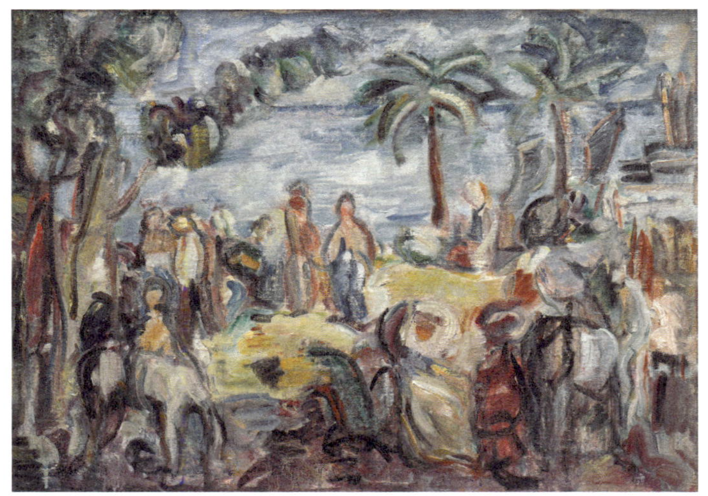

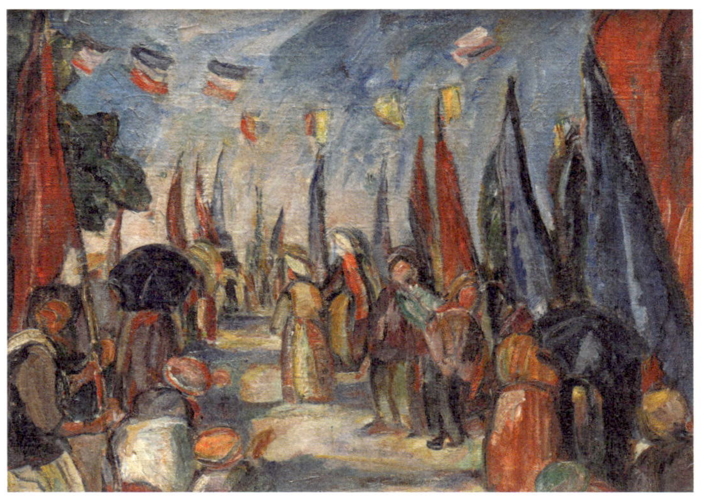

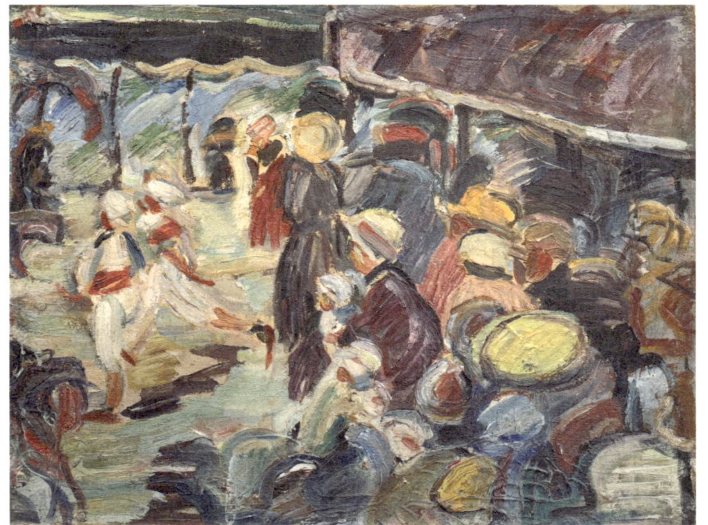

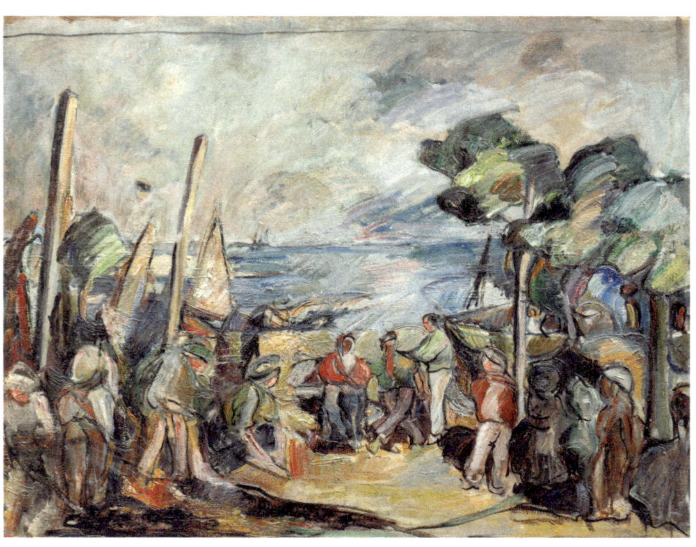

12 *Beachgoers*, 1912

14 *A Market Place*, 1912

15 *Traditional Festival, Southern France,* 1912

11 *From Provence*, 1912

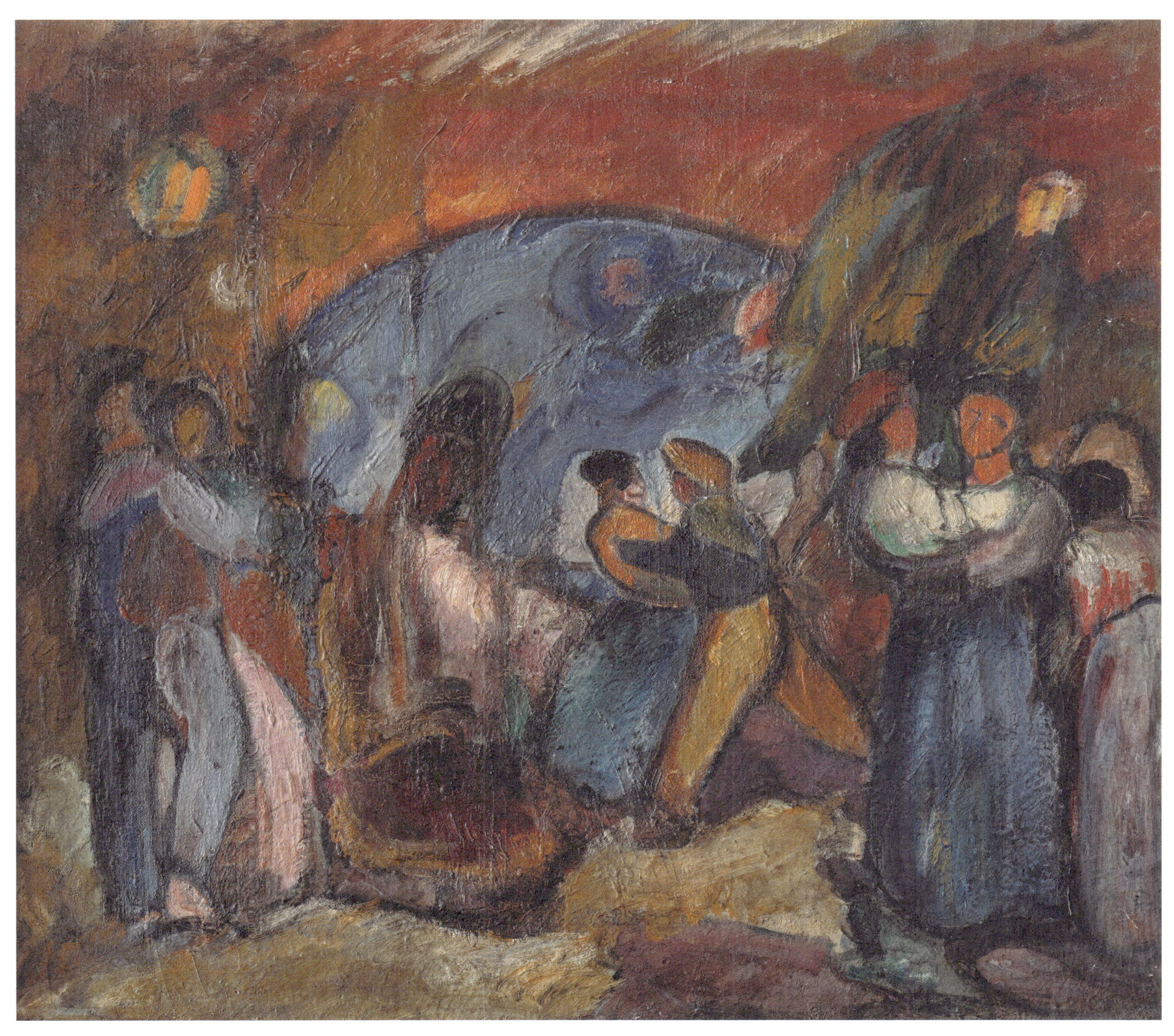

10 *Dance of the Sailors*, 1912

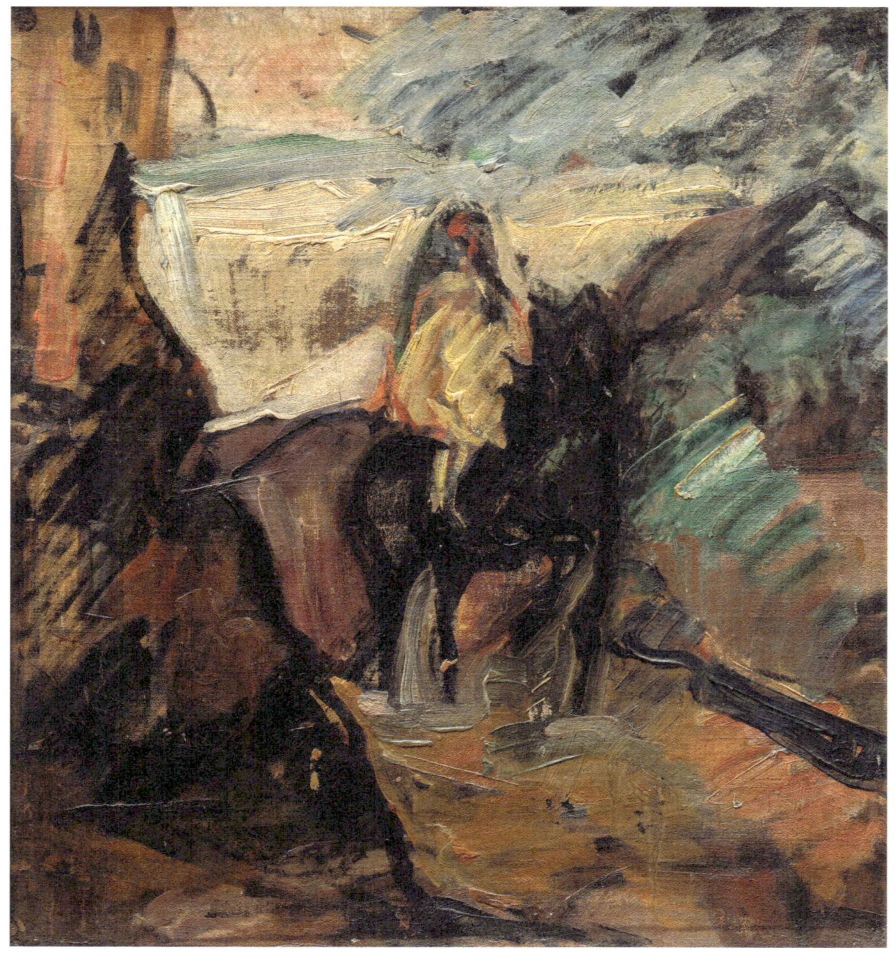

17 *Rider*, c. 1912

13 *Place Gambetta*, 1912

Opposite page:

16 *Susanna and the Elders (The Meeting in Heaven)*, 1912

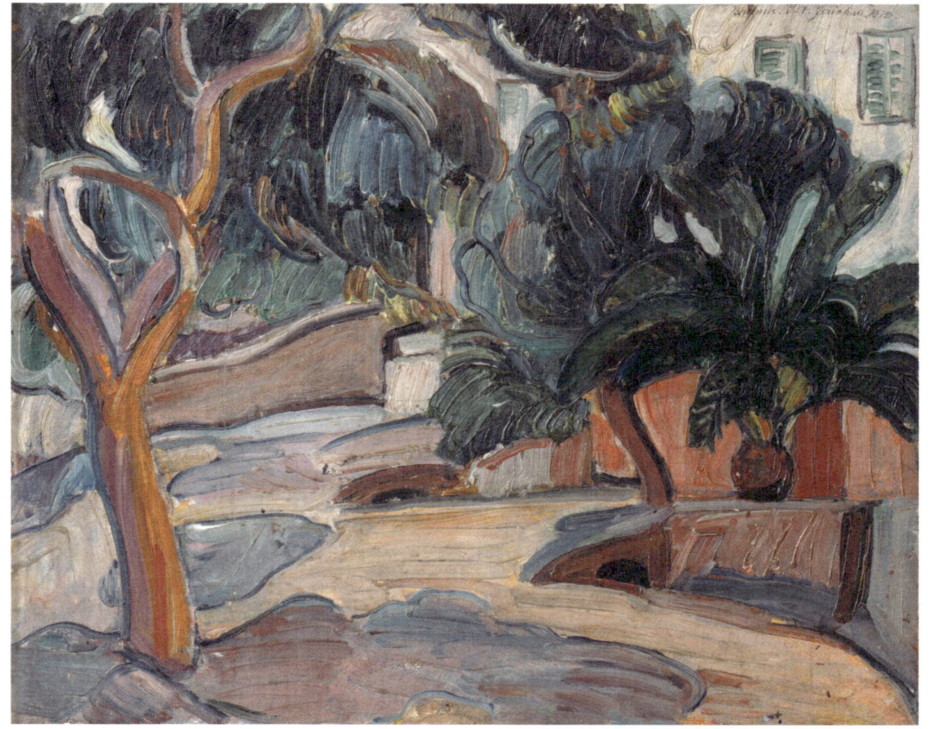

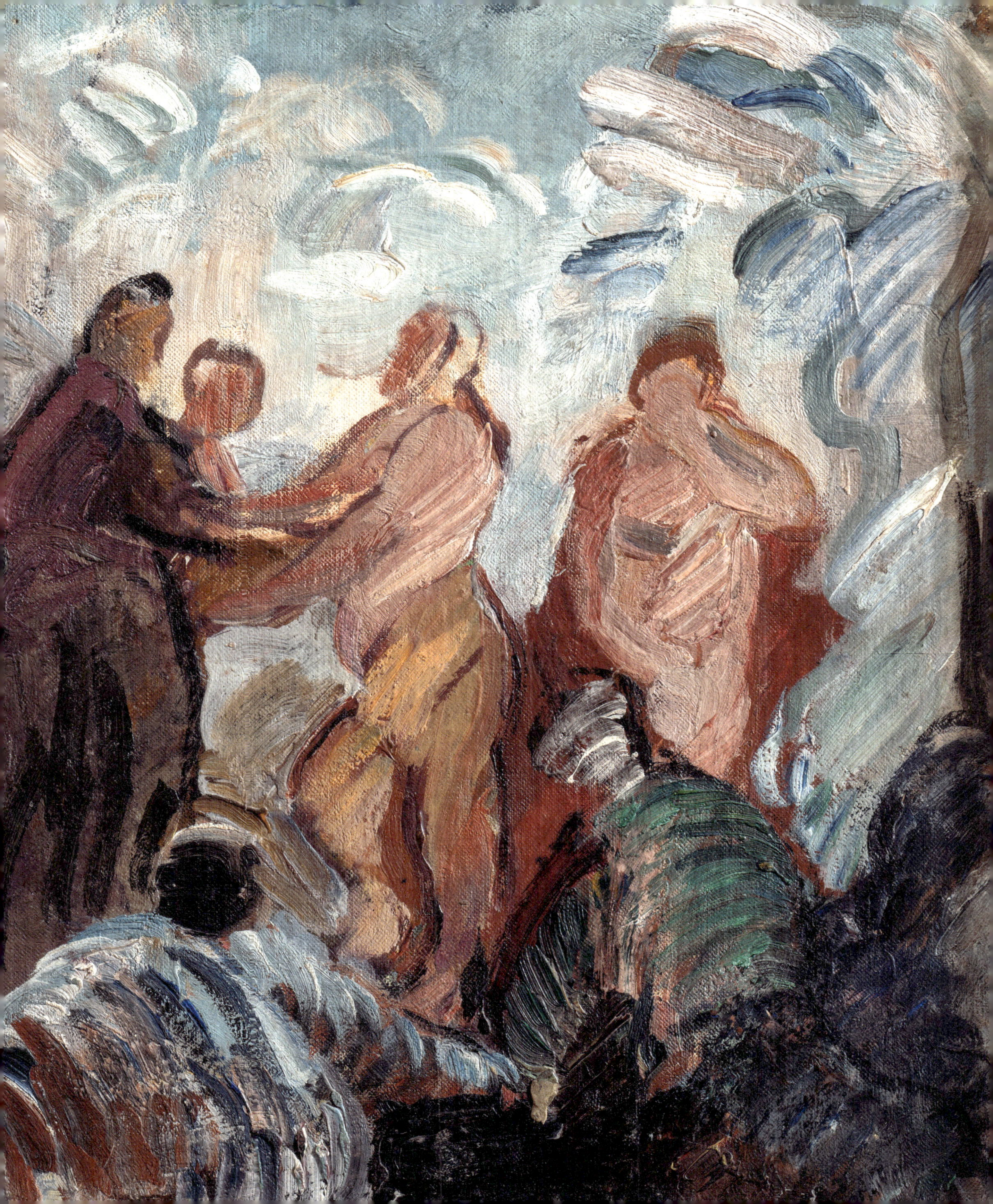

Trainer and Star – The Grand Style in Word and Deed

Mikael Wivel

The art historian Vilhelm Wanscher (1875-1961) was an inspiring speaker, and as a lecturer at the Royal Academy of Fine Arts in Copenhagen he was able to influence a whole generation of Danish artists with his lectures on the Italian Renaissance.[1] Among these there was no one who listened with greater attention to him than Jens Adolf Jerichau (1890-1916), and Wanscher in fact quickly saw the extent of the young man's talent. As his teacher and mentor he subjected Jerichau's compositions to the same close analysis that he applied to works by Raphael (1483-1520) and Michelangelo (1475-1564).

Wanscher was himself an excellent draughtsman and painter, but he was mainly active at the level of copying. His copies were almost all in natural size, precise in the detail and captivatingly well painted. When he was teaching and had to emphasize something essential, he also preferred to draw it on the blackboard in chalk. Of course he had black-and-white photographs at hand, but it was undoubtedly the drawings that did the trick for his listeners: when it comes to an understanding of Michelangelo's genius it is rather more inspiring to see *Night* come to life on the blackboard at the same time as one hears the sculpture expounded in words.

However, independent compositions were something Wanscher was unable to paint, and this was where Jerichau came in as a mediating figure. One thus gets a clear sense that this young desperado painted the pictures that his learned friend was himself predisposed to realize, but could only dream about when he dreamed himself away in the Renaissance.

In this distinctive symbiosis between teacher and pupil there is no doubt that with his words the older man inspired the younger to seek ever-bolder solutions to the problems. Jerichau was thus able with amazing speed to work his way out into areas where no other Danish painter had been before him. With unusually superior assurance he succeeded in balancing on the borderline between tradition and modernity and creating reconciliation upon reconciliation between these two opposing factors.

These reconciliations materialized in an impressive series of large figural compositions which Jerichau created between

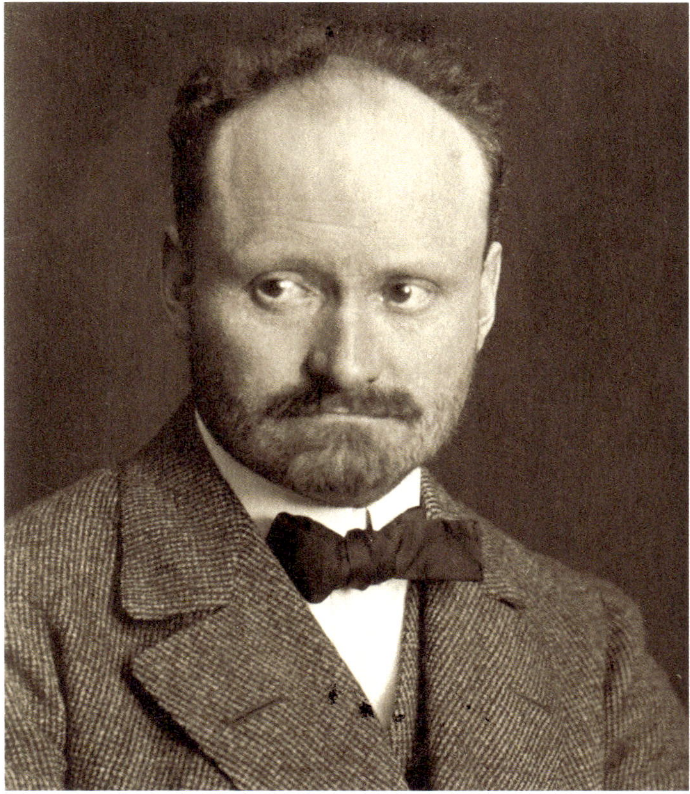

Vilhelm Wanscher, c. 1914

1912, when the spark of inspiration jumped the gap, and 1916, when he took his own life – four wondrous years during which he alternated constantly between firmly grounded solutions and more desperately formulated gambits.

The Grand Style

Taking his cue from the Italian Renaissance, Vilhelm Wanscher launched an overarching concept that he called 'the Grand Style'. This was at the beginning of the 20th century and in parallel with the series of ever more radical departures that characterized the modernist-oriented visual art of the time. One might therefore easily get the idea that Wanscher was a backward-looking figure who clung desperately to tradition and rejected the future. But this was certainly not the case.

Although there were also older artists who felt the force of Wanscher's theories about the Grand Style, it was first and foremost the young ones who listened to his words and came under his influence. This is one of the prime reasons why the Danish variant of international modernism had such a strong element of the authentic Romantic ideal.

For thanks to Wanscher the inspiration came not only from France, via artists like Paul Cézanne (1839-1906), Paul Gauguin (1848-1903), Vincent van Gogh (1853-1890), Henri Matisse (1869-1954) and Pablo Picasso (1881-1973) – but also and at least as much from Italy, by way of classic artists like Giotto (died in 1337), Masaccio (1401-1428), Raphael, Michelangelo and Tintoretto (1518-1594), the five artists who were the leading figures in Wanscher's canon.

It was thus not only a matter of purely stylistic changes in the formal idiom, but also of a more general shift in attitudes entailing that the modernist departures in Denmark did not simply mark a challenge to the established doctrines, but in addition a revitalization of certain values that had not been active in Danish art since the eighteenth century.

The painter who came more than anyone to personify this dual front was in fact Jens Adolf Jerichau. But there were of course also others than him. A number of his classmates from the Academy worked side by side with him and tried to keep up, although at a slower pace. This heroic process was brief and intense. It began around 1912, when Jerichau painted his first free figural composition but was definitively over by the beginning of the 1920s, when a more pragmatically determined consolidation phase made its impact. This was not only because Jerichau died in 1916, but also and especially because the mood in the years afterwards was different from the idealistic one that had created a basis for a modified understanding of Wanscher's ideas. The horrors of the World War had simply weakened their impact.

"The Grand Style is seriousness in art," wrote Wanscher in 1921, when he at last chose to give an account of his theories in a collected version – and he continued: "The seriousness is in the nobility of the soul, the full inner purity of thought; the situation in which the smaller becomes large with the right emphasis; which opens the eyes to the totality of things, and also in the end to their interrelations."[2] The formulation is as vague as it is high-flown. But Wanscher naturally clarified it with the aid of selected works painted by the artists who in his view possessed this "nobility of soul." In his eyes it was crucial to be able to create "the spiritual connections among people" and in a composition give an account of "the visual propagation of motion from person to person as if in a current" and to convey "the gradual transitions from one gesture to another."[3]

As will be evident, this involved an oddly indefinable kind of visual musicality. That is, something rather intangible, which Wanscher was nevertheless able to teach with such empathy that those who listened to him with an open mind were in no doubt that the solution of the enigma lay just ahead.

Socrates

It was Jerichau himself who in 1910 persuaded Wanscher to take him on as a private pupil and teach him to draw. But it was his aunt, Astrid Birch, who the same year and by agreement with her anxious sister, Jerichau's mother, ensured that Wanscher also took on the task as spiritual guide and mentor. He went along with the idea, and in a letter to Astrid Birch he writes among other things: "I shall do my best to keep your nephew constantly at work and perhaps also protect your sister a little in the future from over-hasty decisions from his side, if I can maintain the trust he seems to give me now. I think at all events that he has been given an impression that I will not accede to his whims, and that he must therefore watch out to a certain extent; but it cannot help either that I try to be a kind of strict guide; I must also, for my own sake, take just as much of his freshness into our service as is compatible with our studies."[4]

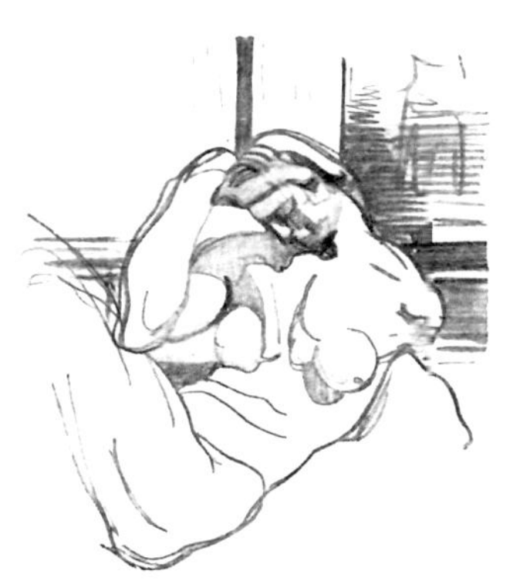

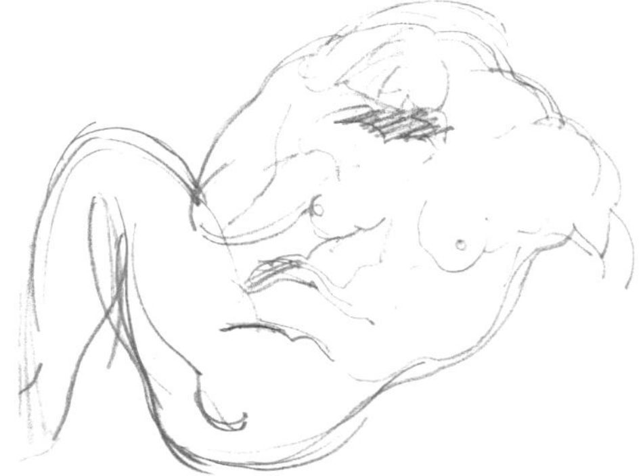

From the left:

Vilhelm Wanscher:
Sketch after the sculpture *Night* in the Medici Chapels in San Lorenzo, Florence, by Michelangelo, year unknown
Illustration in Vilhelm Wanscher: *Grækernes Syn på Kunst*, Copenhagen, 1914

Jens Adolf Jerichau:
Sketch after plaster cast of the sculpture *Night* by Michelangelo, 1914. Pencil on paper, 25.5 × 20 cm
SMK, National Gallery of Art

As an element in these studies Jerichau was sent at intervals into the The National Gallery of Art in Copenhagen to confront the originals. There it was not so much about the unfortunately rather few paintings from the Renaissance that are in the Collection of Paintings, as the many plaster casts of Greek, Roman and Italian sculptures to be found in the Cast Collection.

This incredibly rich collection was at that time housed in the actual museum on Sølvgade, and in Jerichau's sketchbooks we can follow his movements through it. One supreme outline follows another, and they alternate in lively succession between works from Greek antiquity and works by Donatello and Michelangelo – including *Night*, which Jerichau captures with his pencil in the same expressively registrative way as his teacher (p. 25). As the sketch demonstrates, he worked with a definite nerve in the line which also came to affect the figure painting that gradually became his actual goal. One of the finest examples is the 'portrait' he painted in 1913 and called *The Babylonian Astrologer* (cat. 39, p. 41).

His starting point was one of the figures in Raphael's fresco in the Vatican's *The School of Athens* – that is, the Babylonian astrologer Zoroaster. But Jerichau let himself be carried away by the inspiration, and suggested his own astrologer's presence with such immediacy that one would think this was actually a living model. The nerve lies in the constant precision of the line which makes it seem that the astrologer materializes while one stands looking at him. Jerichau's dynamic development in these younger years is evidence that Wanscher's influence lay both at the technical and the theoretical level. First he taught Jerichau to draw his way in around a subject, and then he taught him to paint up against the true 'big names' of western art.

Jerichau was fortunate enough also to have one-on-one lessons at home with Wanscher, where they undoubtedly also discussed much more than 'the Grand Style'. As early as 1914 Wanscher wrote about their dialogues: "I have followed his development; we have studied the classics together, especially Raphael, the mighty figural composer and colour artist – and we have held many a dispute about Cézanne and van Gogh."[5] It is implicit in the quotation that Wanscher could not to the same extent as his pupil see the relevance of these two modern masters. He undoubtedly thought that they could only distract his susceptible pupil from his true concern – that is, 'the Style.' Along the way Wanscher must have shown Jerichau the copies in water-colours he had himself made on his travels to Italy. They are water-colours painted on the spot, in among other places the Stanze and the Sistine Chapel in the Vatican. The ceiling is high and the pictures are far off. They are expressive in the brush-strokes but precise in their proportions – and then they are in colour, which was of great importance in the situation, since colour reproductions were a rare sight at the time.

Jerichau must have studied the copies intensely, and at one point in 1913 he also chose to copy one of them – or perhaps he was actually set it as an exercise? For this was not a random choice from the heap, but the most significant picture in the whole dizzying process on which his mentor focused – Raphael's already-mentioned fresco in the Stanza della Segnatura, *The School of Athens* – a large and complex figural composition, where crowds of beautifully draped figures, with Plato and Aristotle in the middle, are gathered for a discussion under light-filled vaults in a monumental architecture that is the very embodiment of the High Renaissance. Wanscher's copy seems to have been lost, but it must have been good, for Jerichau's copy is amazingly precise if one compares it to Raphael's fresco. All the figures stand or sit where they should, and although their drapes are only suggested with quick strokes, the colour is hit off with great assurance, just as the living rhythm that binds the figures together from edge to edge is kept intact.

Jerichau himself puts it as follows: "Raphael's School of Athens – I have analysed each finger and each toe and each corner of a mantle in my thoughts. Raphael in every part." In the same process he also mentions both Michelangelo and Tintoretto and then rounds it all off with the following underlined dictum: "Read and know Wanscher."[6]

The copy marks the beginning of the great analytical project to which Jerichau was prompted by Wanscher and in which he was confirmed on study trips to Berlin, Dresden, Vienna and Paris. It was a kind of disciplining of his wild talent but also, and in its inner lines, the establishment of a kind of 'picture-readiness' he could draw on when he stood working with his own compositions.

From Jerichau's posthumous sketchbooks it is clear that on his 'raids' in the Cast Collection he was just as interested in the works from antiquity as in Michelangelo's sculptures. Thus there is not only a wealth of lightning-fast sketches of various nude male figures depicting Greek gods, heroes and athletes, but also

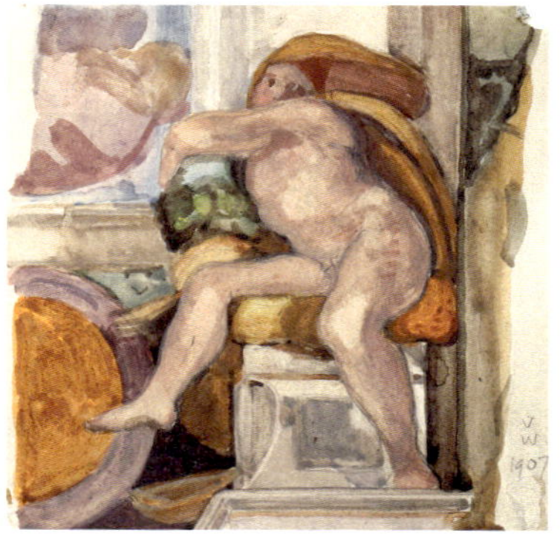

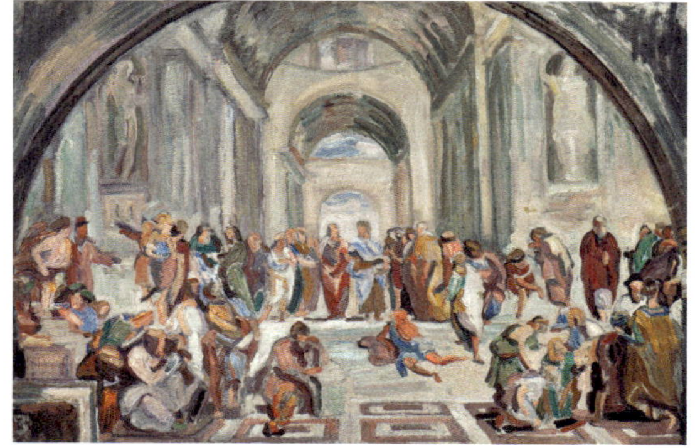

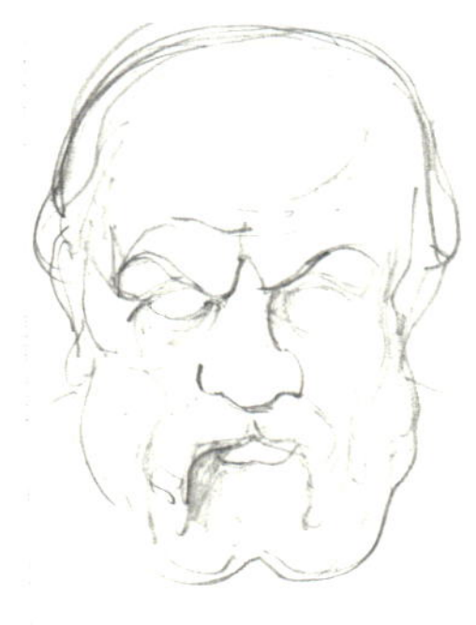

studies of portrait heads of the great Greek philosophers, in this case not least those of Plato and Socrates.

It must have been during the close study of one of the portrait busts of Socrates that the Greek philosopher's facial resemblance to Wanscher struck him. At all events he drew the head from several different angles and subsequently used one of the sketches as the model for a small and quickly painted 'portrait' of his mentor. It is a kind of coloured animation of the drawing, not a regular portrait, but it must certainly have amused Jerichau that in this way he could represent his own inspiring teacher as a modern reincarnation of the great Greek thinker.

With Rubens at His Side

The collections at the Danish National Gallery of Art include very few works from the Italian Renaissance, none of them painted by any of the five leading figures in Wanscher's canon. On the other hand the Flemish painters of the Baroque are richly represented. When Wanscher had to lecture on the Grand Style, illustrating what he said with original works, he therefore did so in front of Rubens' pictures and especially in front of the latter's dramatic figure composition *The Judgement of Solomon*.[7]

Rubens (1577-1640) took in the Grand Style at second hand. As a young man he had studied in Italy, and later on his own initiative went to work on the greatest Italian masters – not least Titian (d. 1576), whose mythological figure compositions he copied again and again. Although Rubens was not quite a match for the great Italians, he came close. He composed his pictures with a supreme breadth of view and realized them with a living use of line, brilliant colour and a distinctly sensual feel for the volume and vitality of the human body. The picture of *The Judgement of Solomon* is a splendid example of his mastery in all respects. It is dynamically composed with the aid of a number of crossing lines that intensify the drama inherent in the actual narrative. Everything is in balance, but everything is also in motion. Solomon's throne is in an ochre-coloured amber, but framed by blue-black drapes that seem to come flooding in from above and find their termination in the muscular headsman's azure loincloth. The blue colour thus encloses the scene tightly and in the last second around the man who stands ready with questioning eyes and his arm raised for the chop. It is the snapshot of a moment, but it is also a drama that Rubens has frozen forever. The observer stands with bated breath!

We do not know what Wanscher said to his audience when he stood in front of the picture. But there can be no doubt that it amused him to see how much Rubens was in control. The composition was the absolutely best example within the borders of the country of a great painter's total mastery of 'the Style'. Wanscher also chose to copy it himself so he could have Rubens at hand back home, and the copy was so good that it could itself be copied – for example by Jerichau. For it certainly does not appear that Jerichau painted his own copy in front of the original in the museum. The details are too few and the intensity too great. This is clearly an exercise in hitting the subject off and doing so without hesitation.

The drama must have gripped Jerichau during the process. This is revealed among other ways in a small, intense detail far out on the right, where he has suddenly gone in close and given the bad mother a pair of wild eyes and an open mouth,

This page:

Top, from the left:
Peter Paul Rubens, ascribed:
The Judgement of Solomon, 1914
Oil on canvas, 234 × 303 cm
SMK, National Gallery of Art

Vilhelm Wanscher: Copy after Rubens'
The Judgement of Solomon, year unknown
Oil on canvas, 116 × 154 cm
Private collection

Bottom, from the left:
Jens Adolf Jerichau: *The Judgement of Solomon*, 1912 (22). Copy after painting by Rubens at The National Gallery of Art, Copenhagen. Detail to the right

Opposite page from the left:

Vilhelm Wanscher: Sketch of Michelangelo's *Ignudo* in the Sistine Chapel ceiling in the Vatican, 1907

Jens Adolf Jerichau: *The School of Athens. Copy after Raphael*, 1913 (24)

Jens Adolf Jerichau: Sketch of plaster cast of an antique portrait of Socrates, 1913
Pencil on paper. Sketchbook, 25.5 × 20 cm
SMK, National Gallery of Art

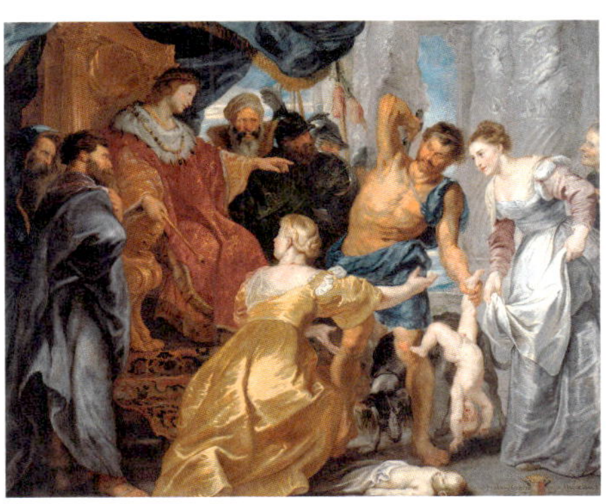

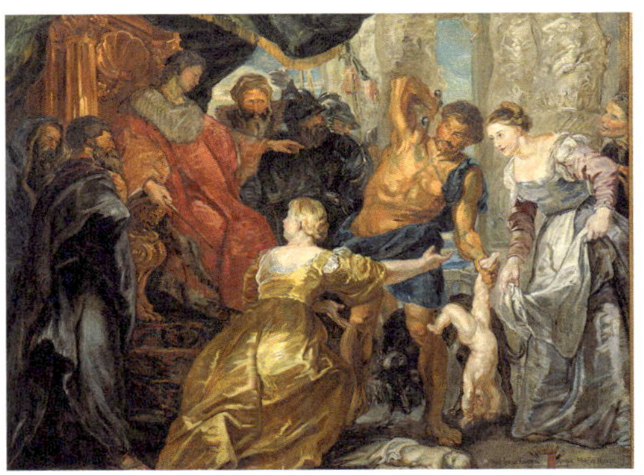

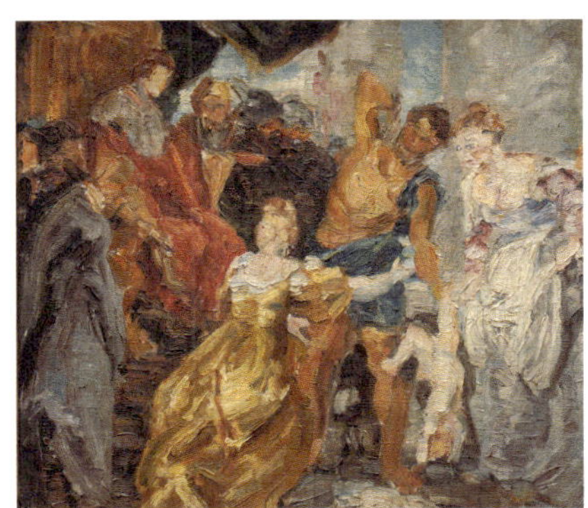

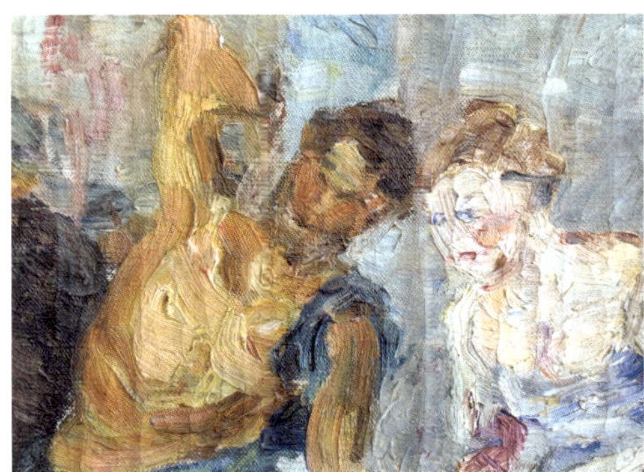

painted in with three lightning-fast flicks of blue and red alternately, as if he wanted to emphasize that these are also human beings – not only the Grand Style.

The Sacrificial Feast

Jerichau was wild at heart and on his way out in the galaxies to the great masters. Wanscher's theories about the Italian Renaissance were a kind of access ticket to a level that lay beyond the normal in contemporary art. For although the Style was burdened down by tradition, it could also set its painter free and permit him to take a liberal view of the modernist dogma that prevailed in the environment and reduced any picture's legitimate elements to an interplay of line, colour and form.

As Jerichau saw it, the subject of a picture need not be mute or passive. As a painter one was not forced to stick to so-called 'neutral' genres such as portraits, landscapes and still life paintings to be 'modern'. One could also choose to paint without a safety net and instead develop figuratively, tell stories, and give one's pictures content of an existential character.

This was at any rate what he attempted from 1912 until his death four years later, at an ever-accelerating pace and in ever-larger formats. These were exclusively figural compositions that alternated between monumental statements and pieces with a more ecstatic effect. Jerichau painted them in his studio in Tordenskjoldsgade in the middle of Copenhagen, but apparently drawing his subjects from remote regions and earlier times and always with the great masters out on the sidelines – as sparring partners. But only apparently. For although he mimed Raphael, he never did so without taking his starting point in his own time and his own situation. He did not lose himself in the Greek past, on the contrary he painted his way straight into his own Danish time. Existence itself was the issue. These were not dream images but symbolic images.

Jerichau started in earnest with a composition he called *The Golden Bird* and whose subject was in his own words taken from "From the Glorious Times of Ancient Greece." The scene shows a flock of young people gathered around an elderly philosopher. But if one looks closer, it is clear that it is not only about life in ancient Greece, but also life here and now, since Jerichau was clearly convinced that the mountain of the Muses, Parnassus, had been moved to Copenhagen for the event – with Vilhelm Wanscher in the role of the philosopher and Jerichau and his friends as his enraptured audience (cat. 94, p. 79). Jerichau continued his investigations with a composition he called *The Sacrificial Feast*, and whose subject was in his own words taken from "the people of the first age." We are now all the way back in prehistory, where a gathering of mainly nude people has come together in connection with a sacrificial ritual where they take omens from the flight of birds.

Jerichau painted three closely related yet different versions of this unsettling subject. They were done as a series in the course of the autumn and winter of 1914-1915, and there is no doubt that they deal metaphorically with the outbreak of World War I. In order to understand and depict this fatal shift in European history, Jerichau thought he had to go right back to the earliest times to arrive in a roundabout way at his own. Wanscher was on the sidelines in this rapid development. He says himself that he regarded the three versions of *The Sacrificial Feast* as the principal works in "the period of the dark pictures." The period of the bright pictures was the alternative one that developed in parallel, and whose most important statements were Jerichau's two interpretations of the meeting on Parnassus. He painted the last of these immediately before he left Denmark in 1915 to travel south to Italy, France and Spain.

Wanscher loved the bright pictures from the beautiful period of Greece, but was nevertheless more fascinated by the dark ones from the earliest times. In his far too short monograph about Jerichau from 1931 he fortunately writes intensely and extensively about what he can remember about the genesis of the first of the three versions of *The Sacrificial Feast* – the flash of memory is so illuminating that it deserves to be quoted in full:

"I saw the picture for the first time in the winter of 1915 when I visited Jerichau one evening in his studio on Tordenskjoldsgade [...], which he had furnished quite fantastically. Candles were burning here and there and the picture was placed up high. When I had looked at it long in great captivation, we began to discuss the interaction of the motional motifs and the colours; and I noted that a colour must be missing on the top right: "Yes. that is right enough; I have painted it out." Then he turned his back to the picture and repeated for himself how the deep red colour goes into the depths behind the nude standing figure in the middle and turns up towards the outside figure on the left, while another backward-leaning figure in the middle gathers the red in bright orange, and suddenly he went

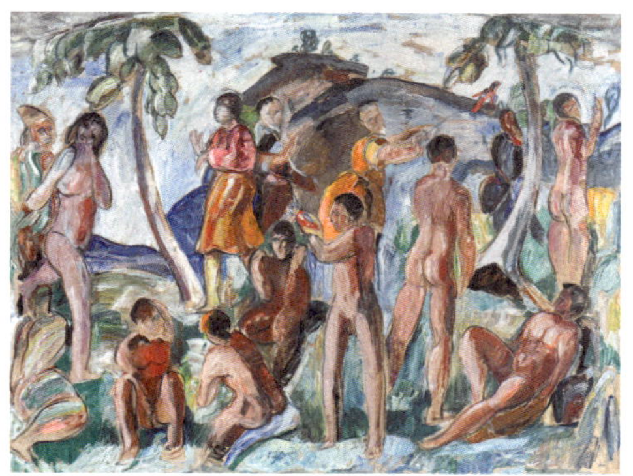

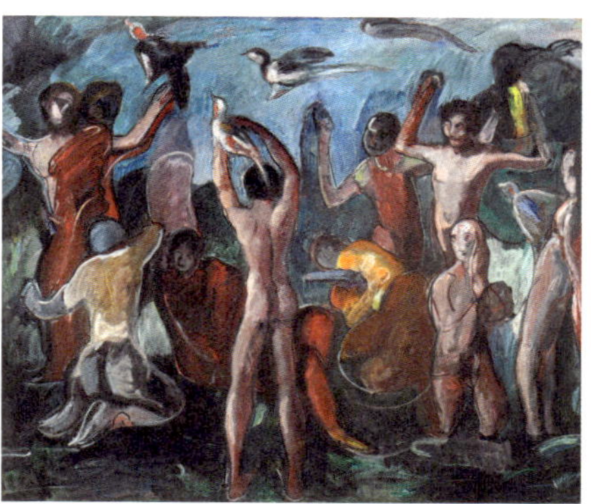

From the left:

Jens Adolf Jerichau: *The Arrival of Spring. From the Glorious Times of Ancient Greece. Opus II*, 1915 (48)

Jens Adolf Jerichau: *The Sacrificial Feast. Man Seeking Omens. Opus I*, 1914 (41)

over to his paint table at the other end of the studio, took the lemon cadmium on his palette knife and put two wide bright strokes in the right-hand corner above, by the raised arm of one of the nude figures. The totality was once more taut. That was what had been missing."[8]

The moment was completely magical. The two lemon-yellow strokes that Jerichau put in were not just to be a full stop after a long period of intense work, but also a supreme gesture that testified that he was now in earnest at the same wavelength as his great exemplars. Wanscher concluded: "How happy he was that evening, as a man who had consummated the great work for which his whole soul longed; he felt rightly that he understood what the very greatest artists in the Renaissance had wanted."

Finale

When it comes to Jerichau's starting point for *The Sacrificial Feast*, Wanscher suggests an artistic affinity with pictures by Tintoretto and Raphael, but Troels Andersen points to an "odd congruence" between the composition and a small but significant detail in one of El Greco's masterpieces – that is, *The Burial of the Count of Orgaz*.[9] The latter is the most interesting parallel because at the beginning of the 20th century El Greco (1541-1614) had cult status in the avant-garde – so much so that he was regarded as a regular Expressionist, ahead of his time. Jerichau entirely agreed, not least after having seen a number of his pictures on his travels to Dresden and Paris in 1911 and 1912.

He probably also discussed him with Wanscher, which was perhaps the reason why the latter at one point decided to paint a copy of the male portrait by El Greco that can be seen in the Danish National Gallery. It is from the early years of the Greek, but since it was the only original work by him in this country, it was also the only one he could try his strength with if, like Wanscher, he wanted to understand what it was the young painters saw in him.

However, Jerichau went more determinedly after El Greco. In 1915 he travelled to Spain, where he settled in Madrid for an extended period and visited both the Escorial and Toledo. He must have seen a multitude of El Greco's pictures during this stay; all the same not a single copy of any of them seems to be preserved. The only thing of that kind preserved is a small copy of a composition by Diego Velásquez (1599-1660) – that is, *Las Hilanderas* or *The Spinners* in the Museo del Prado. In a way

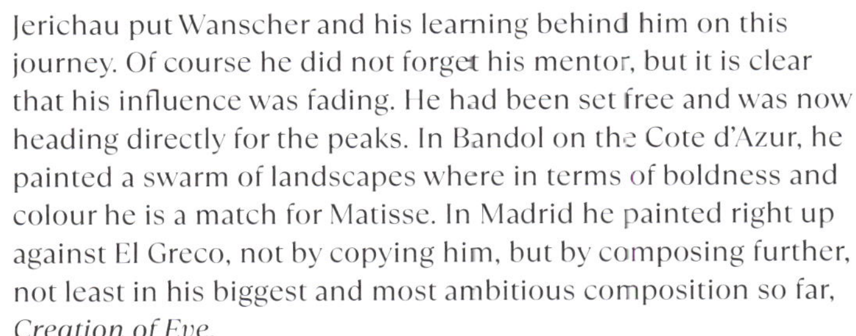

Jerichau put Wanscher and his learning behind him on this journey. Of course he did not forget his mentor, but it is clear that his influence was fading. He had been set free and was now heading directly for the peaks. In Bandol on the Cote d'Azur, he painted a swarm of landscapes where in terms of boldness and colour he is a match for Matisse. In Madrid he painted right up against El Greco, not by copying him, but by composing further, not least in his biggest and most ambitious composition so far, *Creation of Eve*.

Jerichau had moved up to an international level and then continued his ascent the next year when he went to Paris and engaged in dialogue with both Matisse and Picasso. Especially with the latter! Indeed, his pictures from there look very different from everything he had painted before. He has a quicker hand, is stronger in the colours and he stakes everything much more fiercely on the big lines.

The major work from the months in Paris is the composition he himself called *Hecuba* (cat. 95, p. 76). It depicts three figures, one seated, one dancing and one jumping who appears in a box-shaped scene which like a Zeppelin floats freely somewhere midway between Heaven and Earth. It looks as if the composition has been created in very few minutes, as if Jerichau has chosen to let go of it while the expectation of its completion is still only half realized. It seems to stand quivering on the borderline between life and death – just like Rubens' picture of *The Judgement of Solomon*. But perhaps it is in reality about Jerichau's imminent suicide?

He undoubtedly regarded it as his most important and most original composition from this last, hectic phase. For shortly before he took out the pistol and shot himself in the temple he chose to dedicate it to his mentor with the following words, which stand written with a broad brush on the back of the canvas: "To my friend Vilhelm Wanscher from your Jens Adolf Jerichau." Wanscher was thus with him to the end. With the picture of Hecuba Jerichau perhaps wanted to say that he had not forgotten the Grand Style, but had chosen to take it from the tradition in order to symbiotically enfold it in modernity.

Mikael Wivel is an art historian and doctor of philosophy. He is the author of a large number of books about Danish art and artists, among others the monograph *The Paintbrush and the Pistol: The Artist Jens Adolf Jerichau*, which was published in 2019. He has co-curated the Jerichau exhibition at the Louisiana.

From the left:

Vilhelm Wanscher:
Copy after El Greco's portrait of a man at SMK, National Gallery of Art, year unknown
Oil on canvas, 93 × 112 cm
Private Collection

Jens Adolf Jerichau:
The Spinners. Madrid (Copy after painting by Velázquez' Las Hilanderas), 1915 (77)

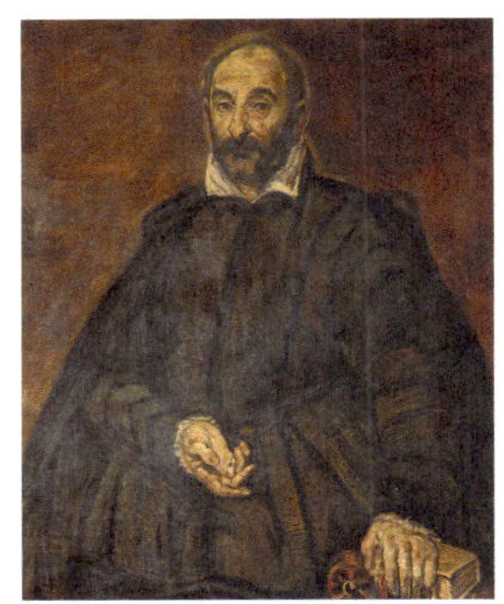

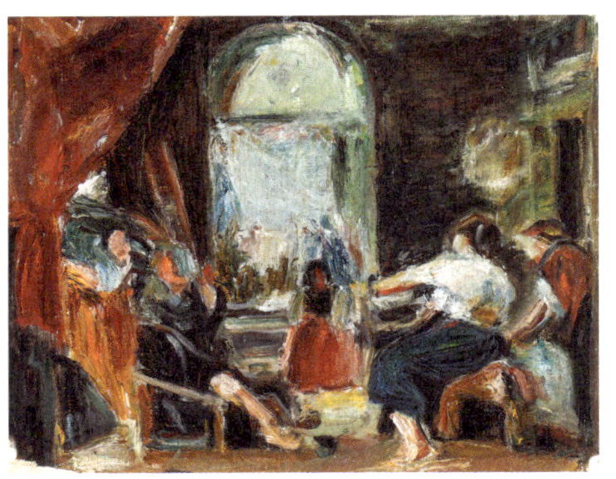

1912-1915
Copenhagen

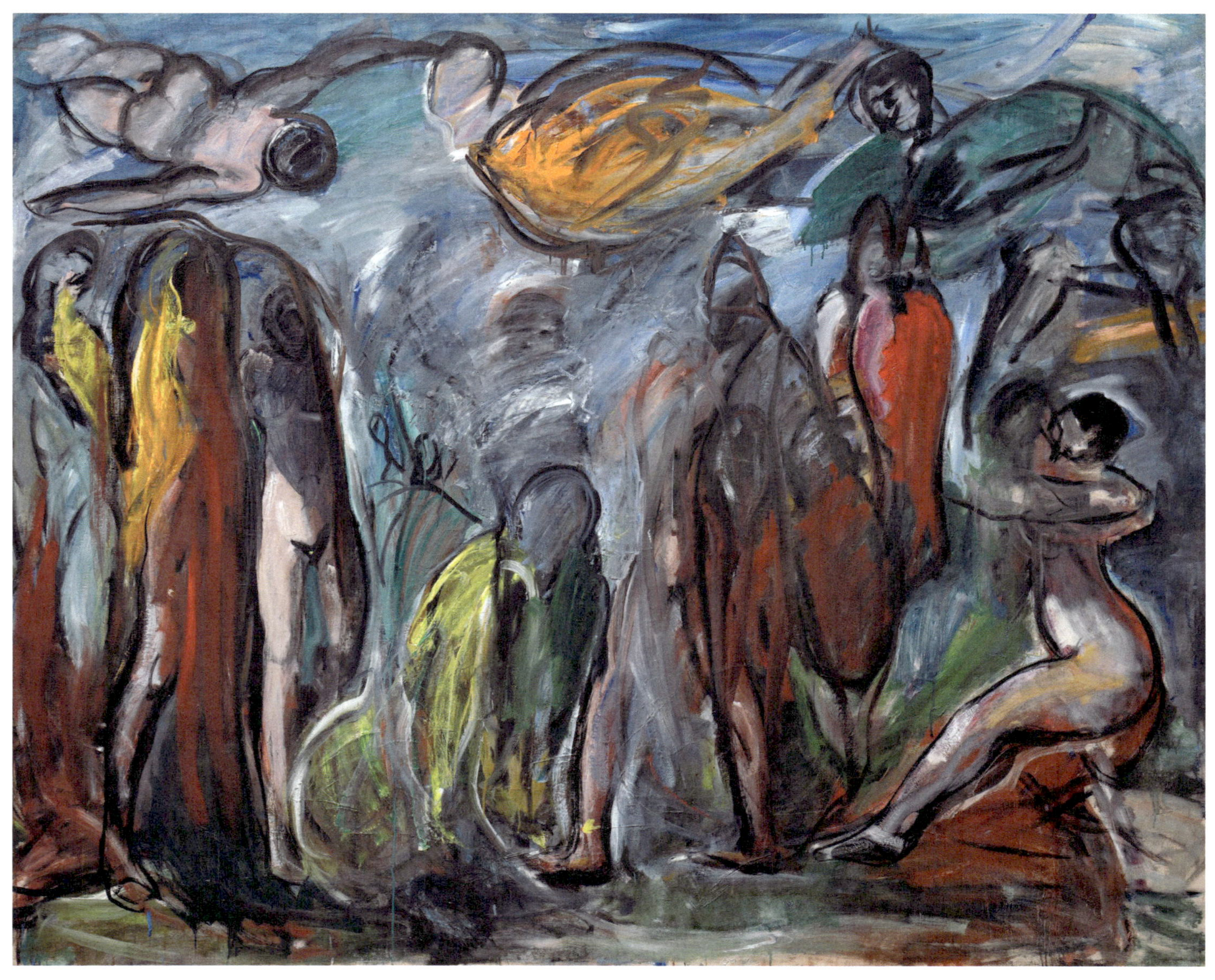

43 *Figure Composition (Dante Ascending – Dante Symbol)*, 1914-1915

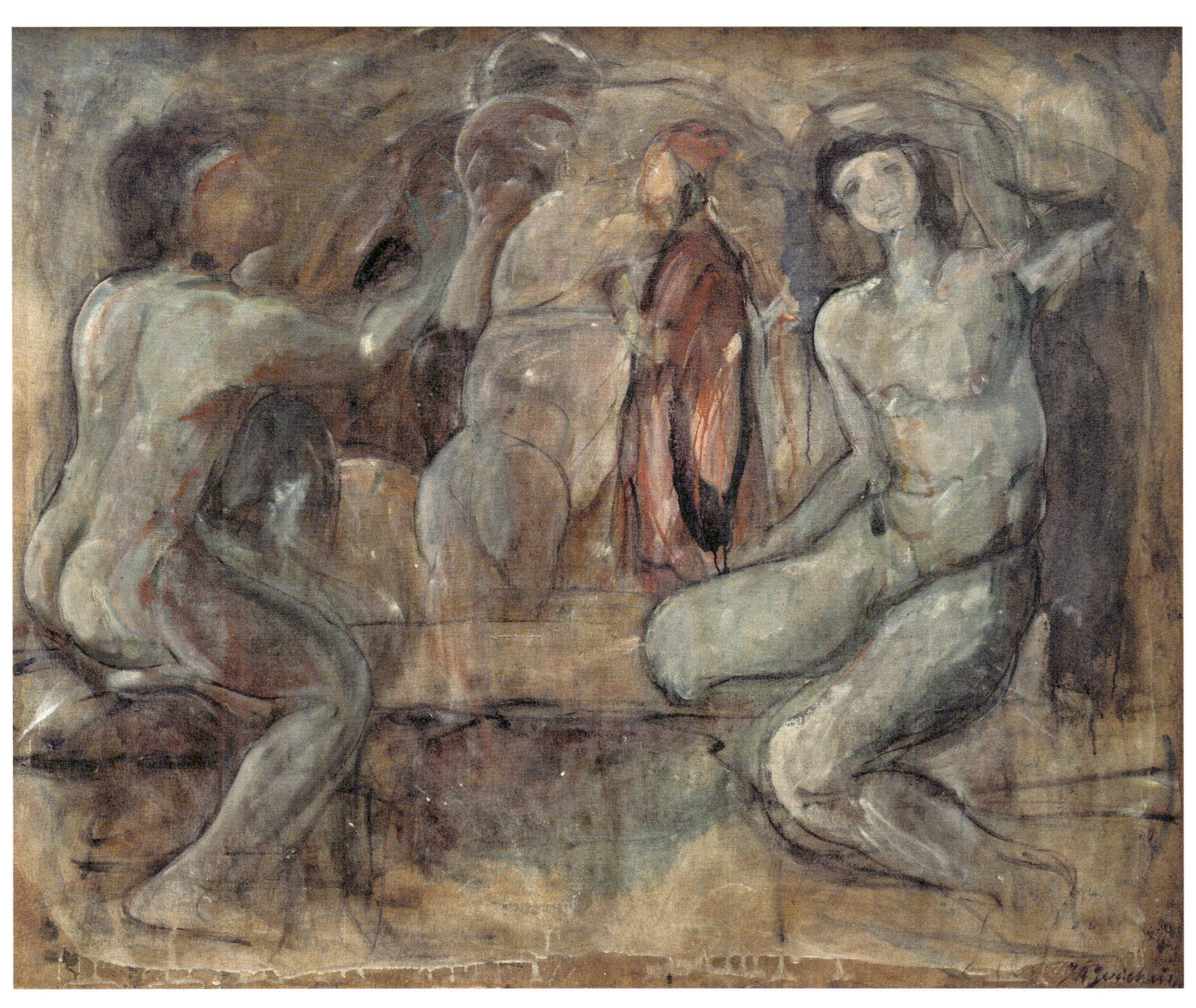

44 *The Resurrection. Tribute to the Renaissance. Symbols. Opus IV,* 1914-1915

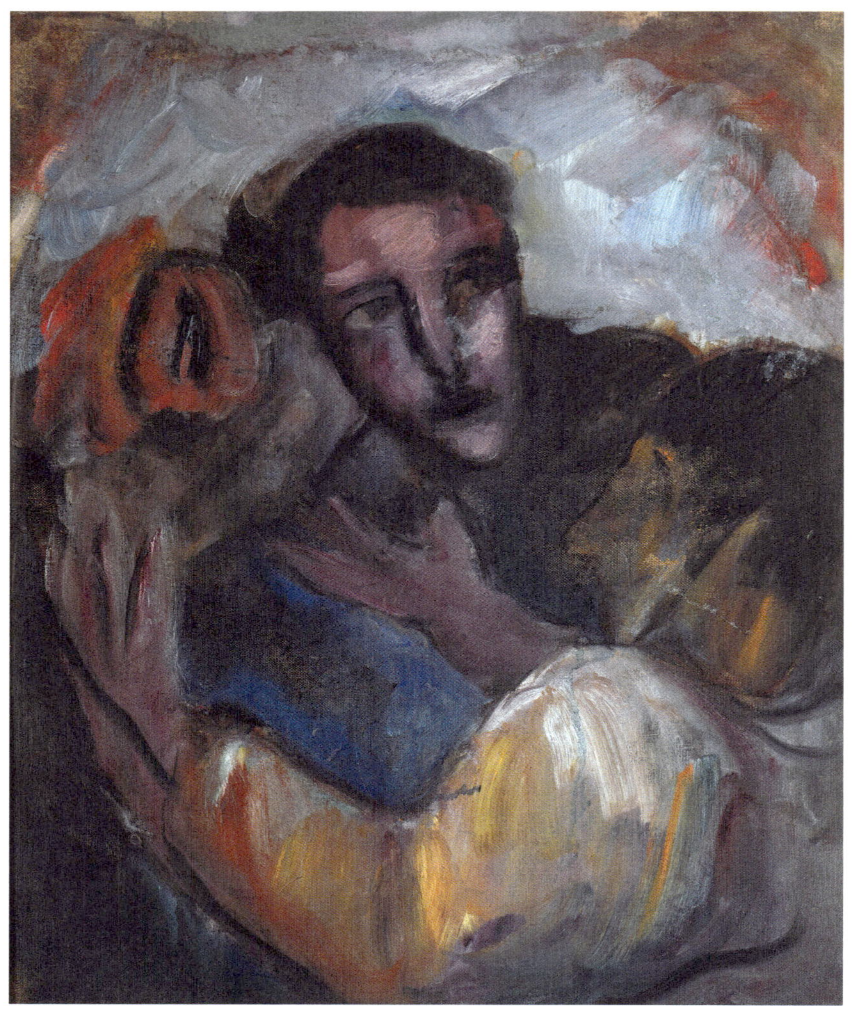

20 *Dante*, 1912

19 *Dante. Sketch*, 1912

Opposite page:
18 *Dante. Prophets, Opus I*, 1912

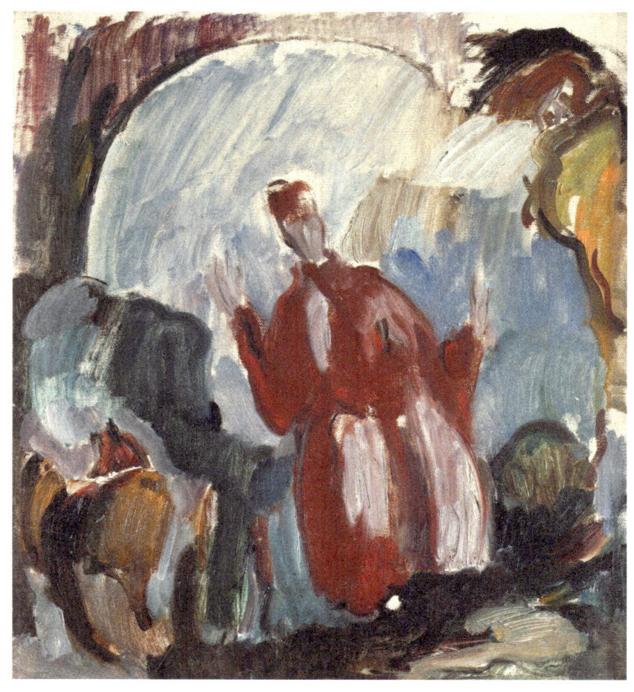

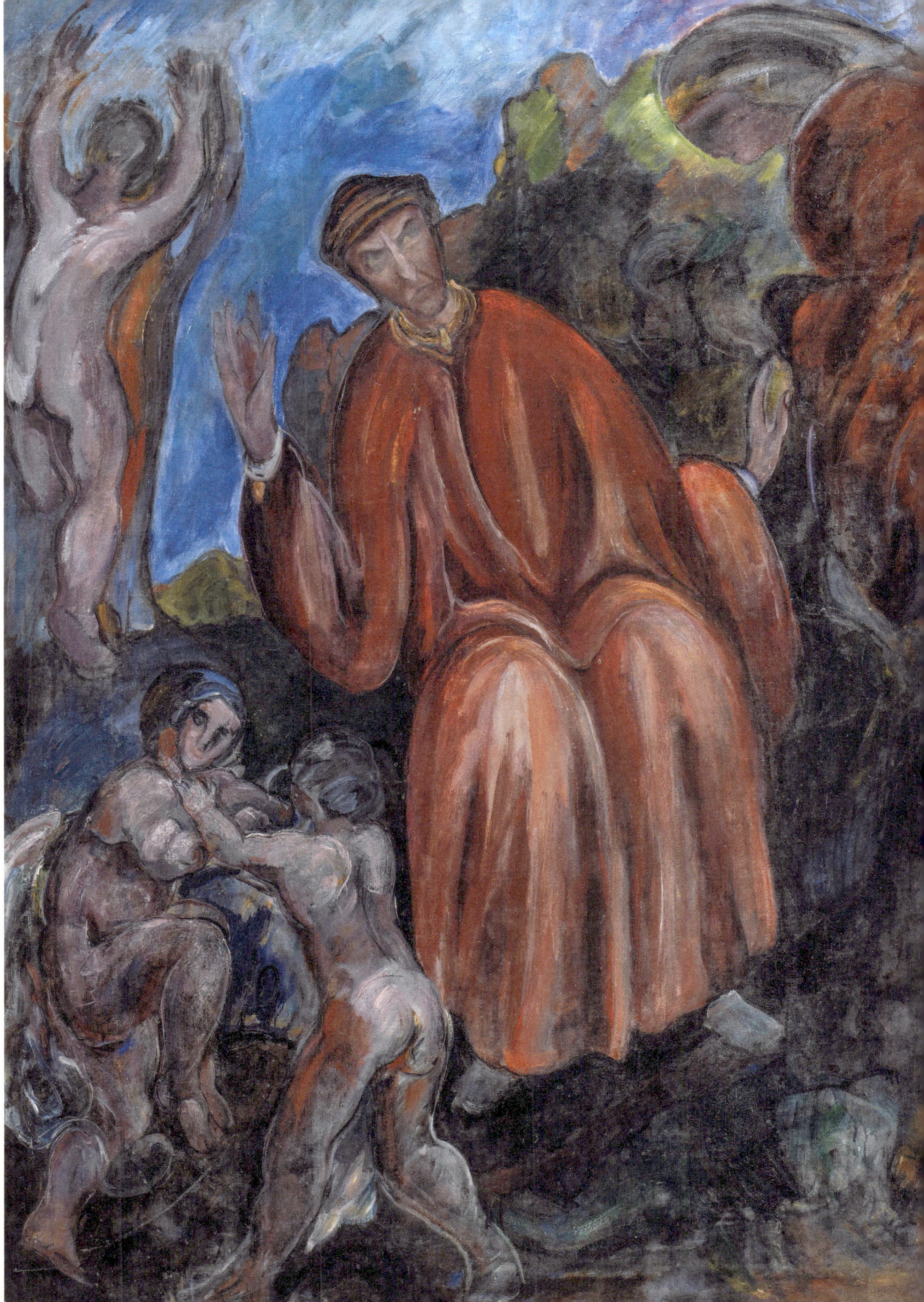

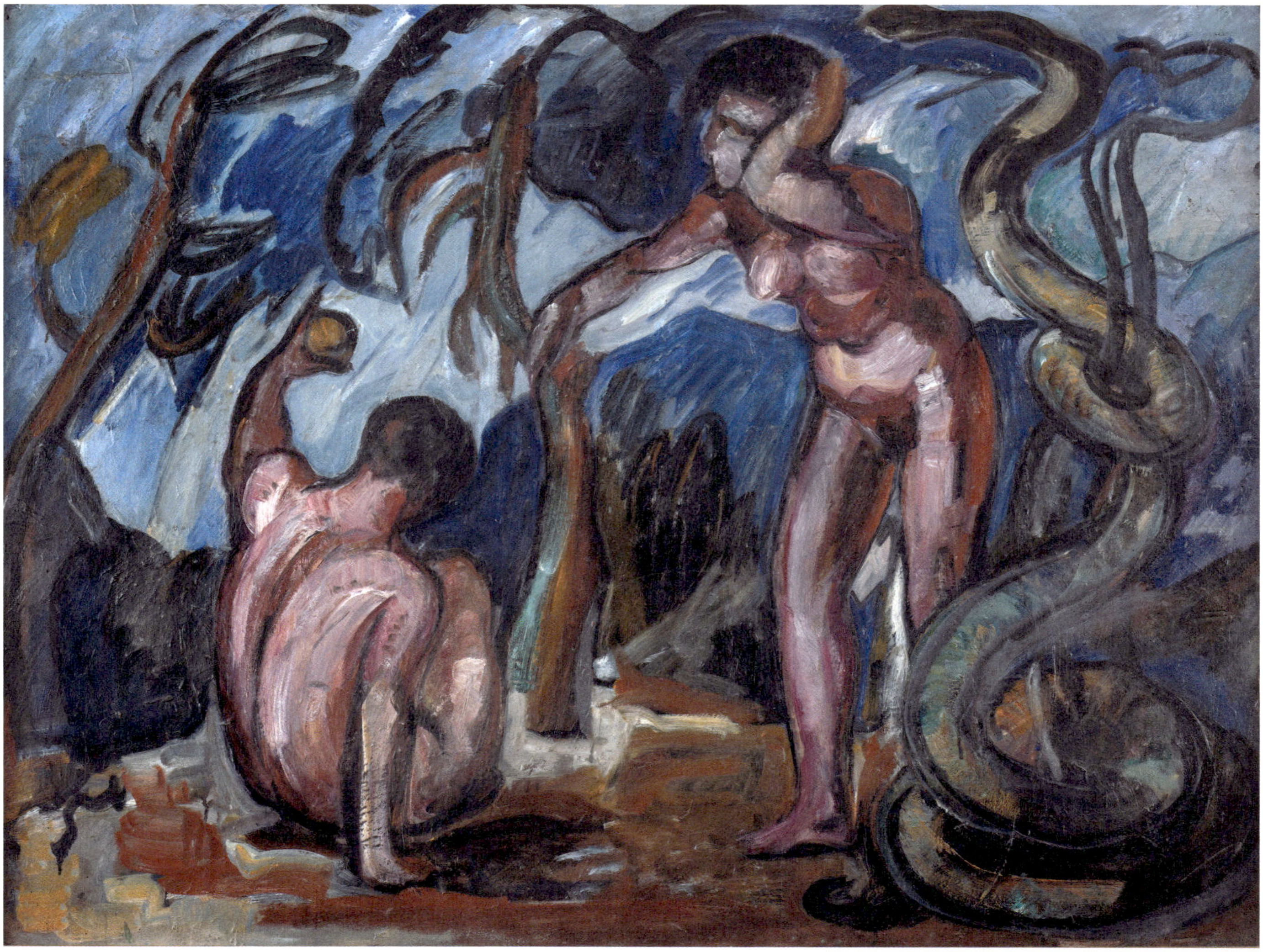

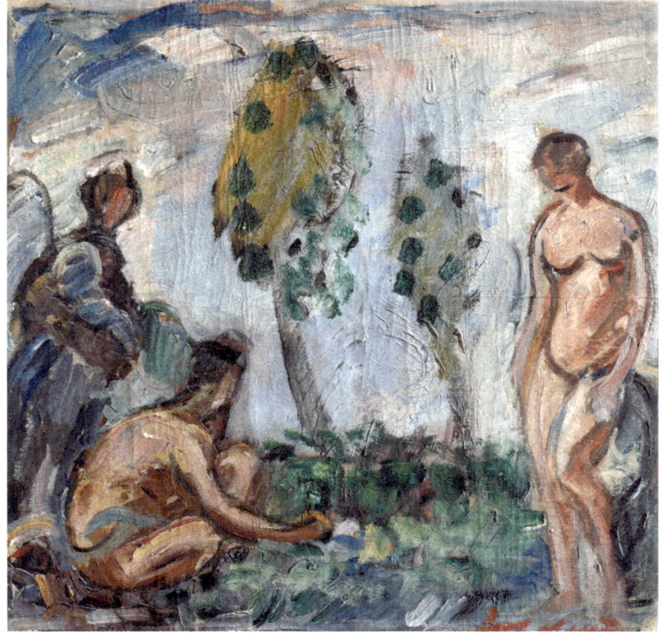

29 *The Serpent Tempting Eve*, 1913

40 *Adam and Eve*, 1914

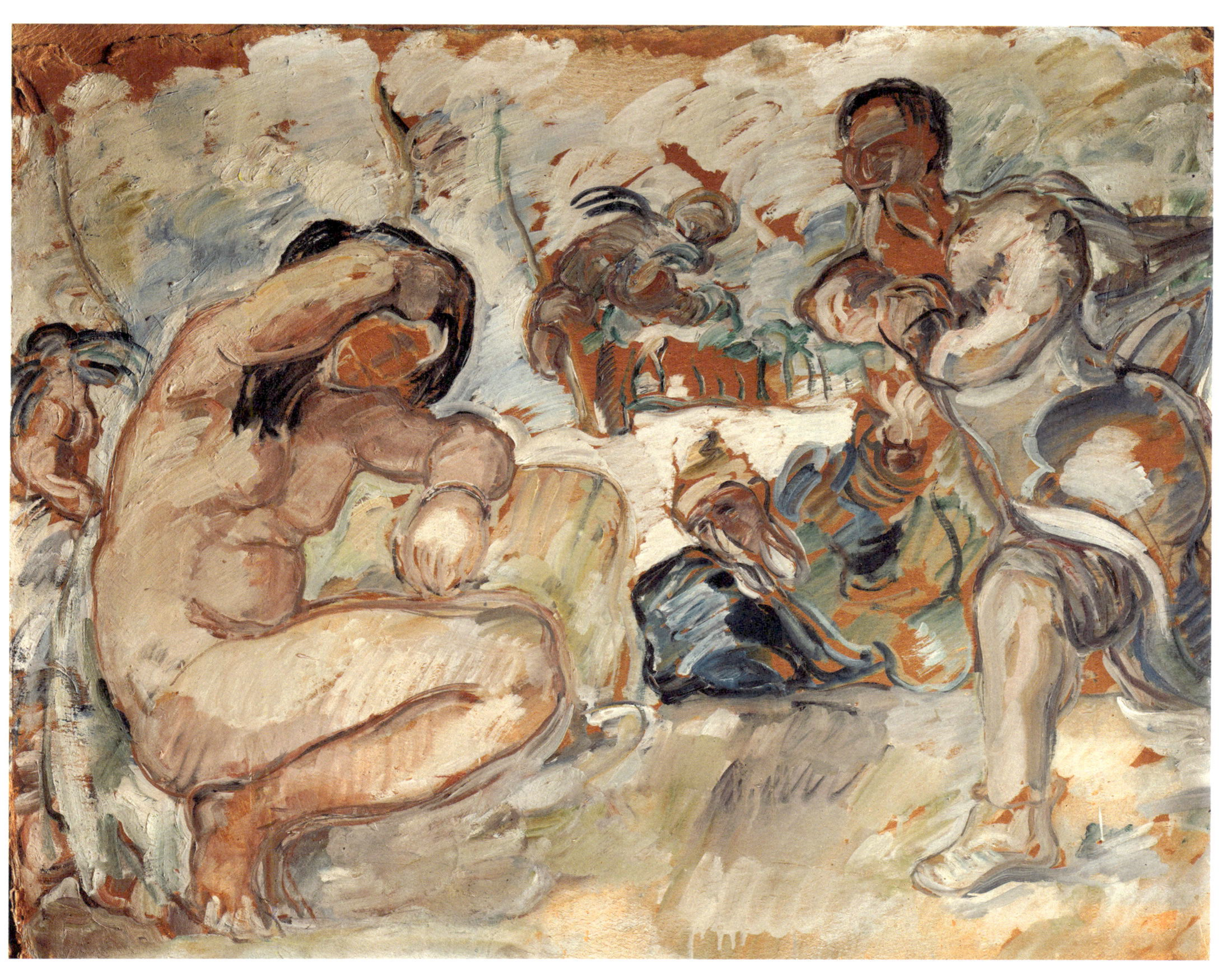

30 *Susanna Bathing*, 1913

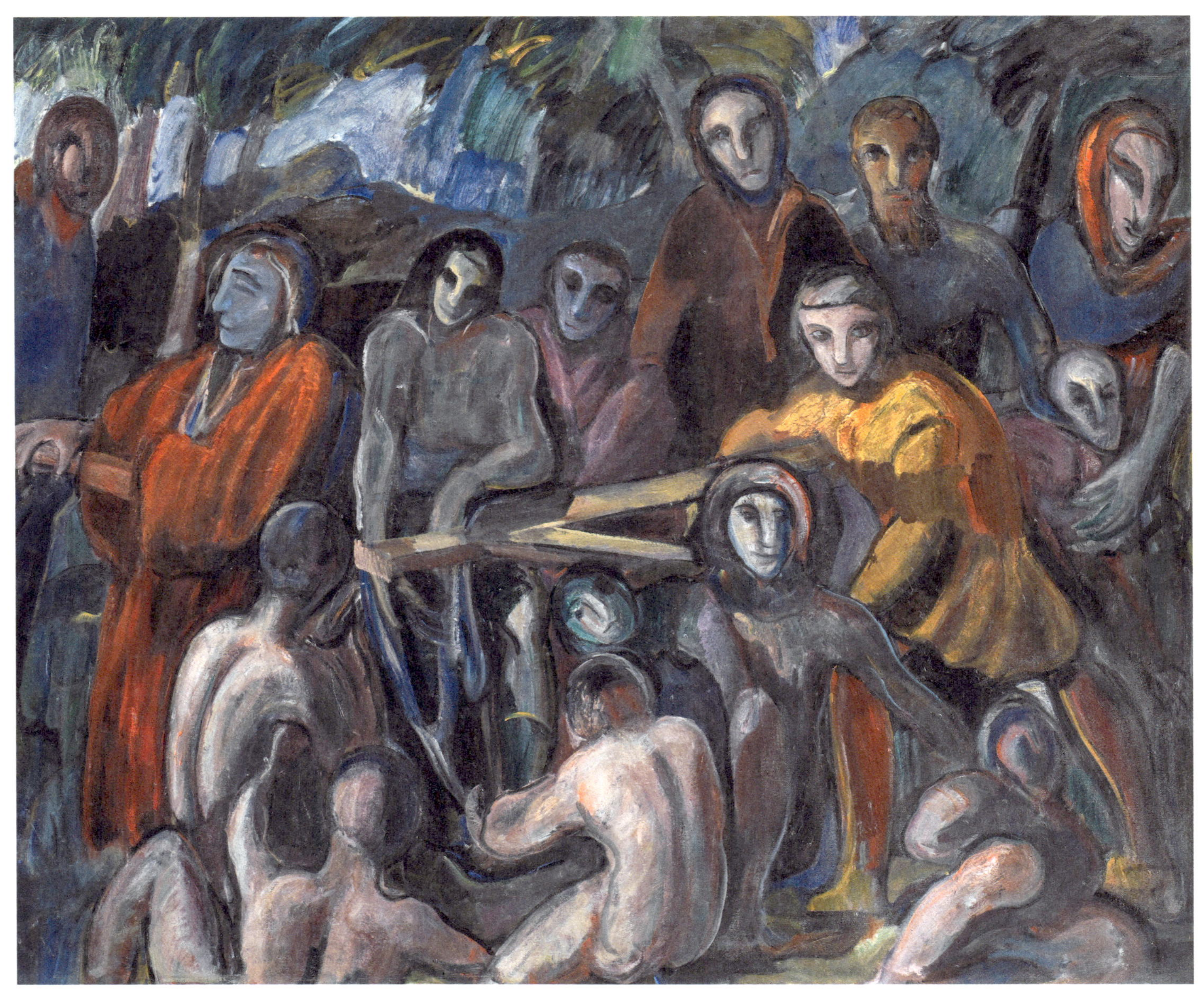

32 *The Road to Calvary*, 1913-1914

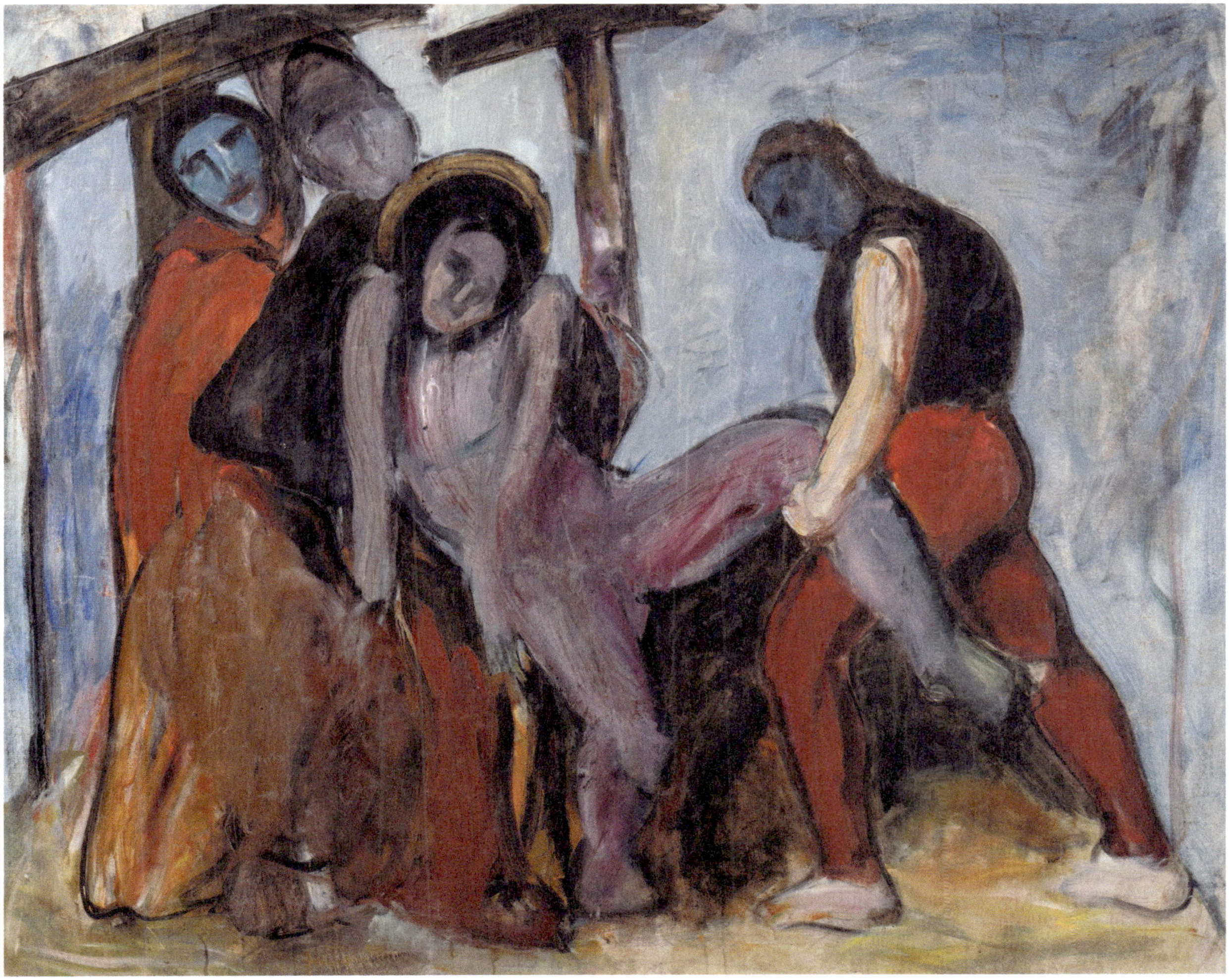

31 *The Deposition*, 1913

35 *Pietà*, 1914

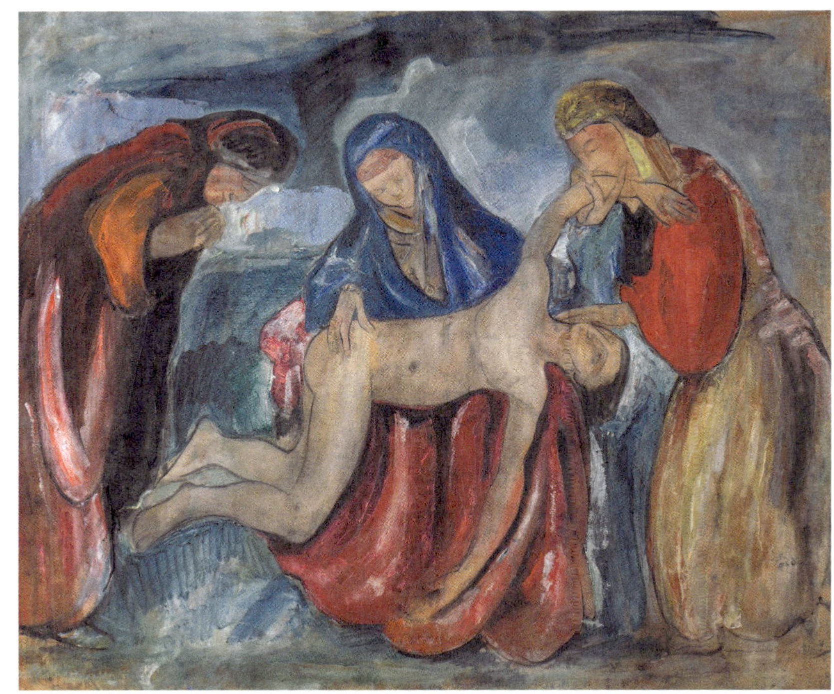

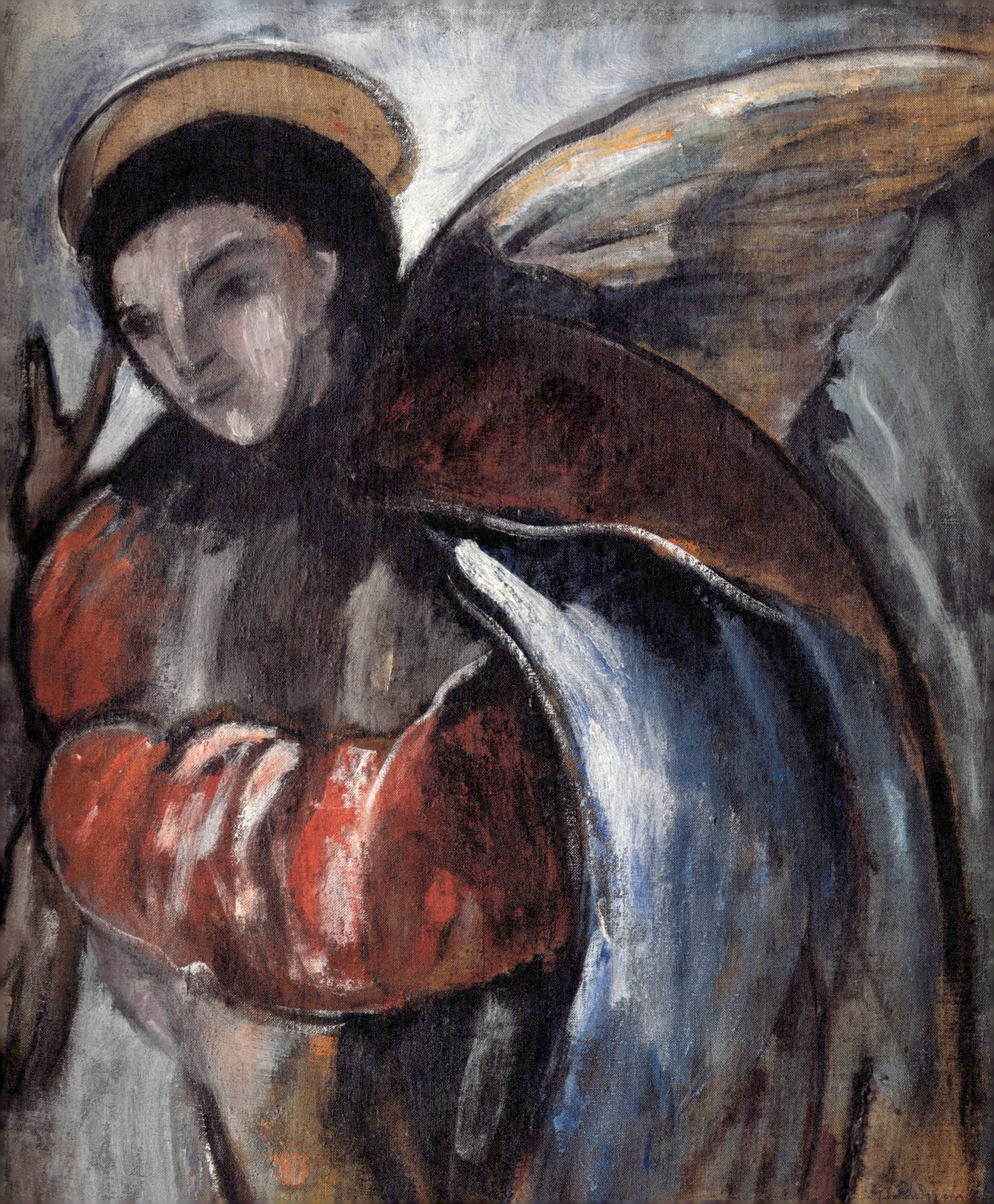

36 *The Angel (The Annunciation)*, 1914

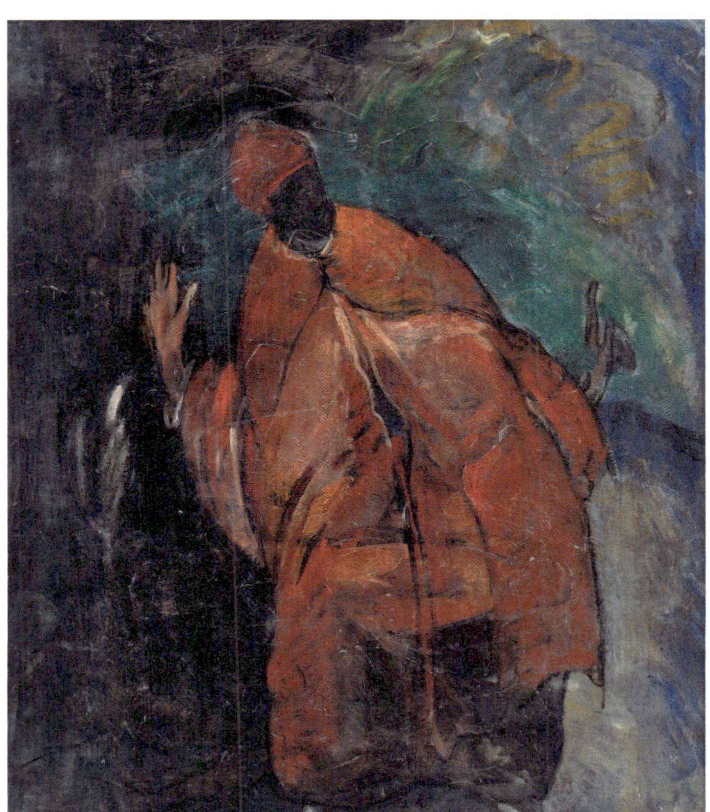

37 *The Black Prophet. Prophets. Opus II*, 1914

21 *A Bishop*, 1912

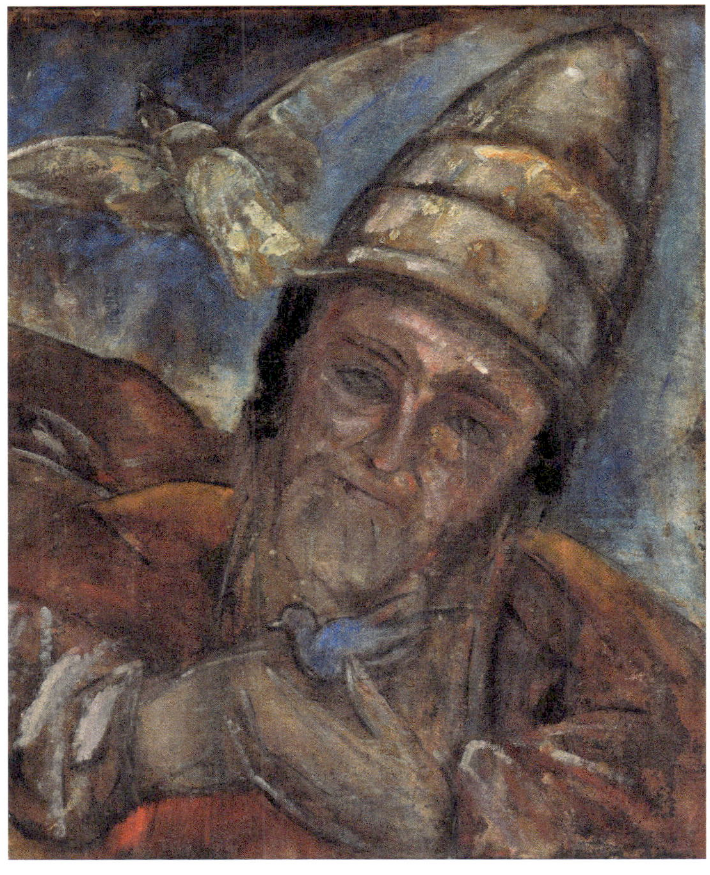

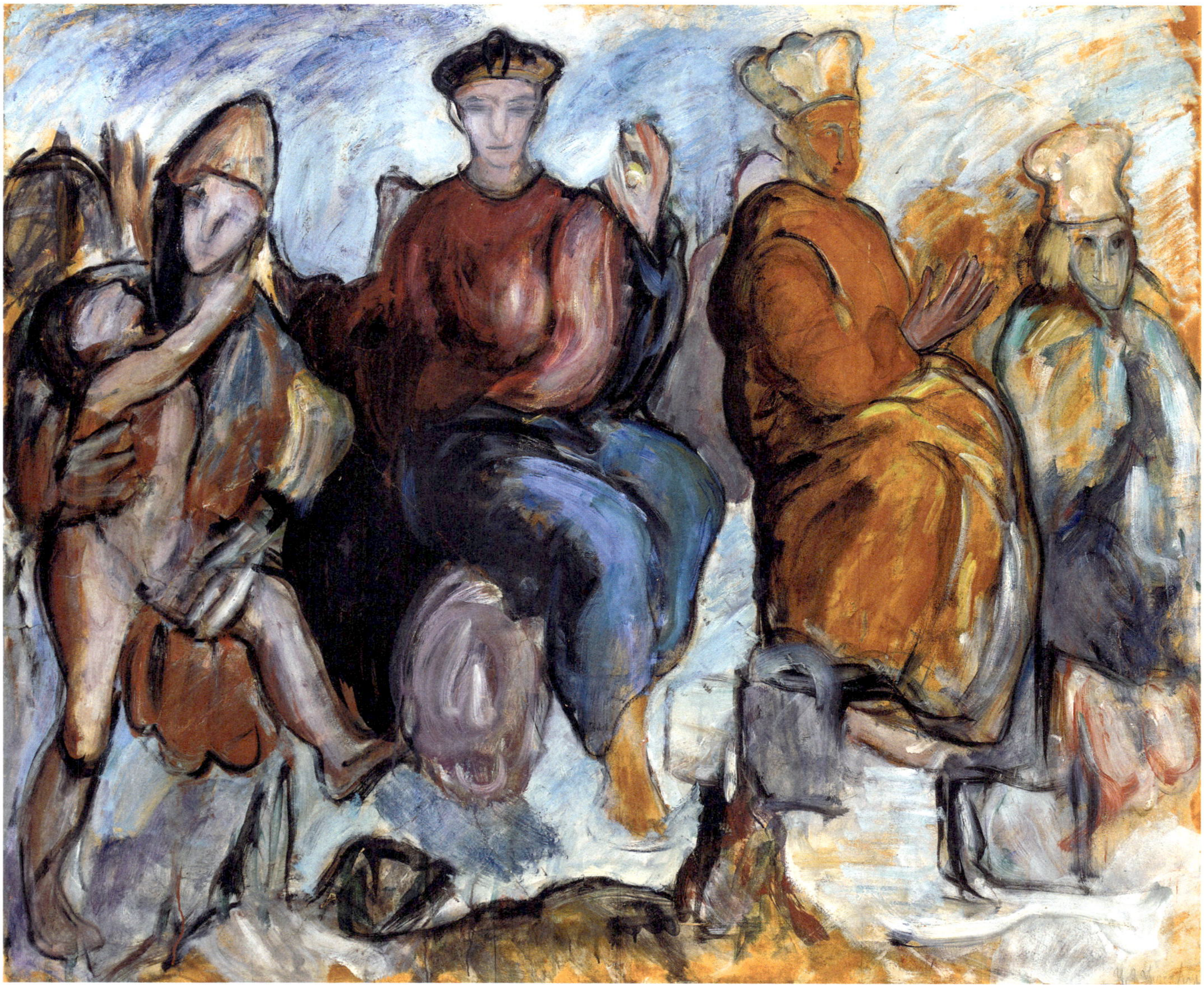

33 *The Magi and the Whore of Babylon*, 1913-1914

22 *The Judgement of Solomon*, 1912

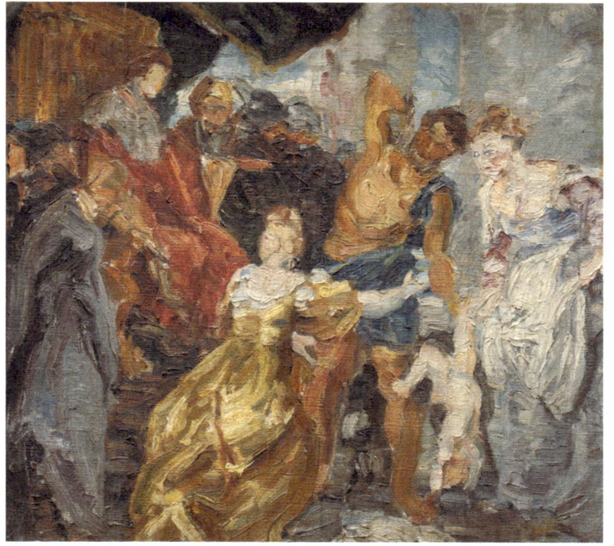

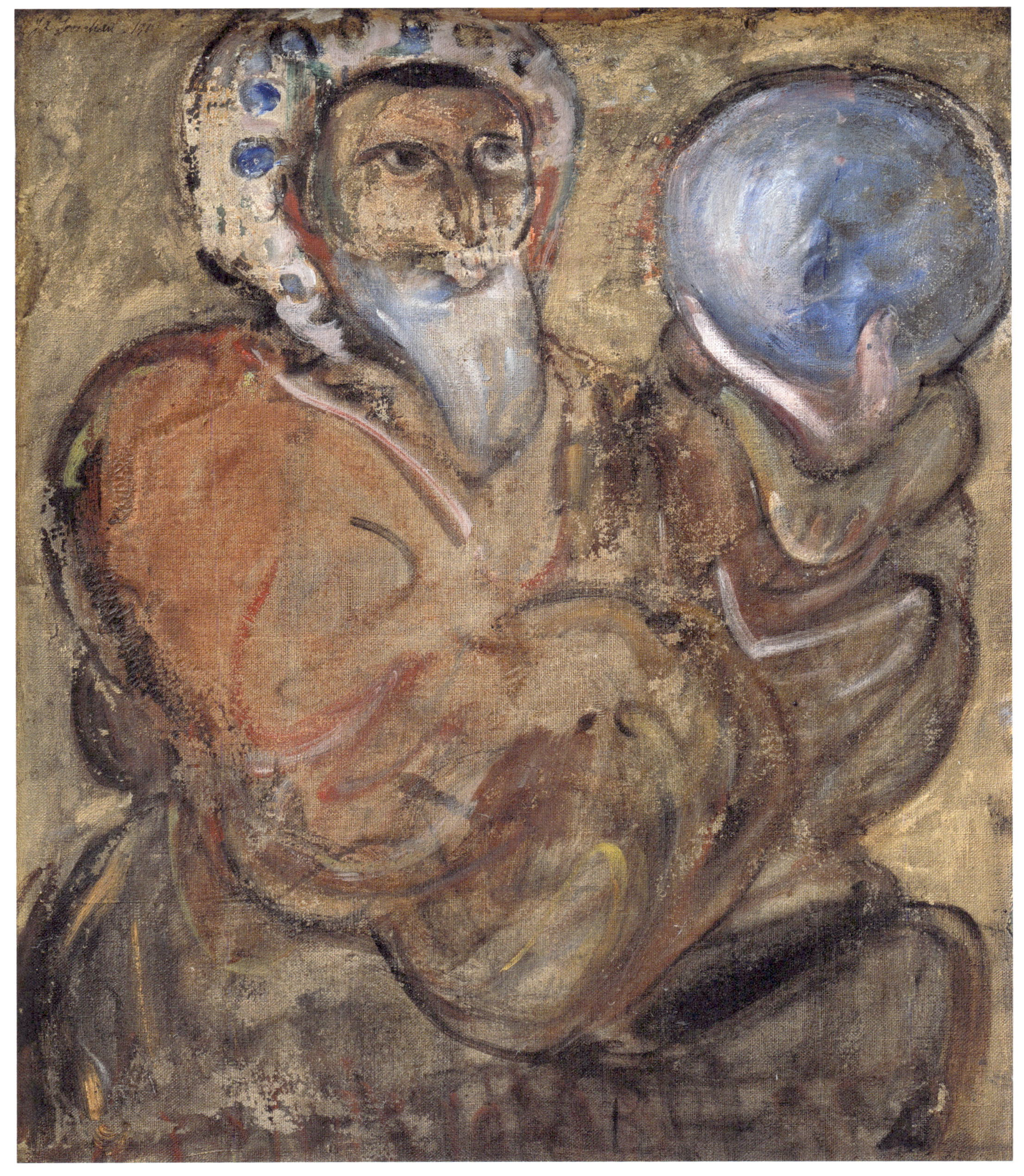

39 *A Babylonian Astrologer*, 1914

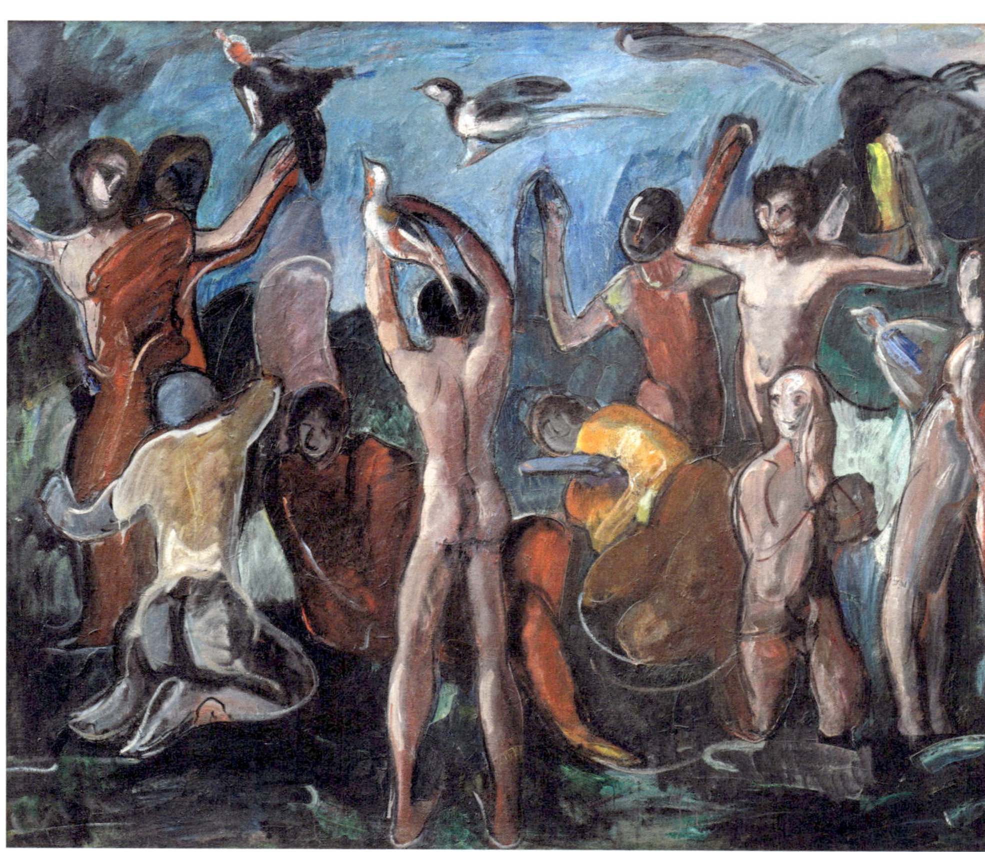

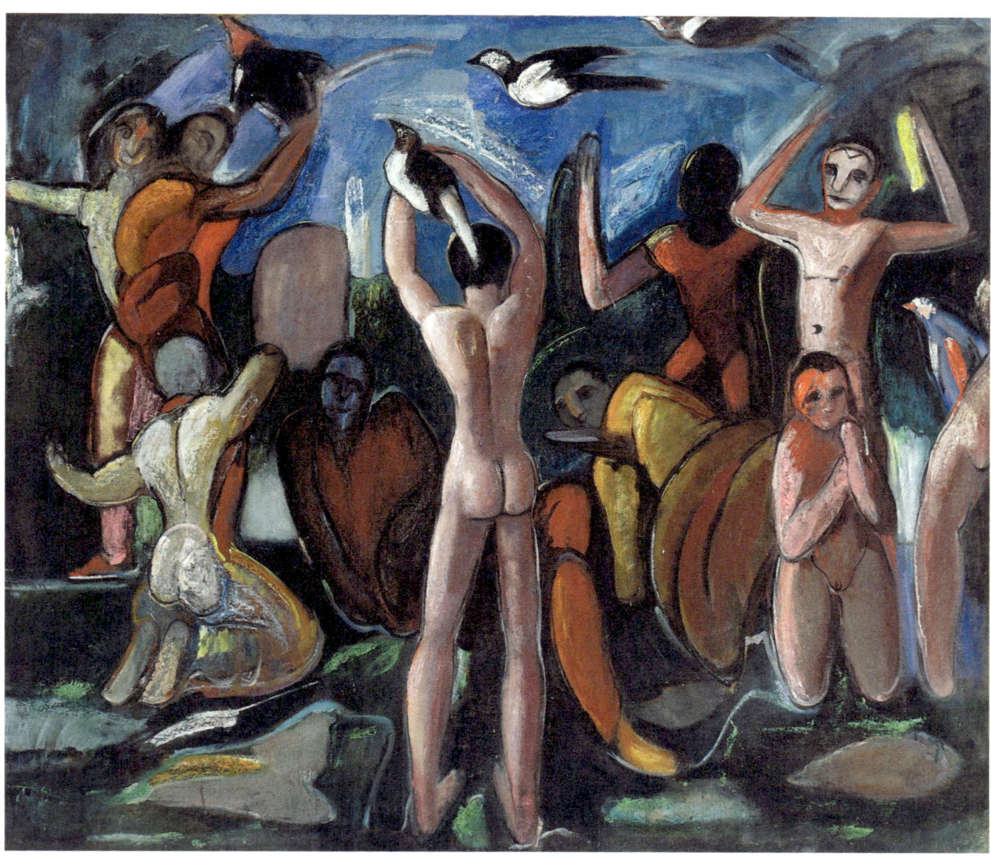

41 *The Sacrificial Feast. Man Seeking Omens. Opus I*, 1914

46 *The Sacrificial Feast. Man Seeking Omens. Opus II*, 1915

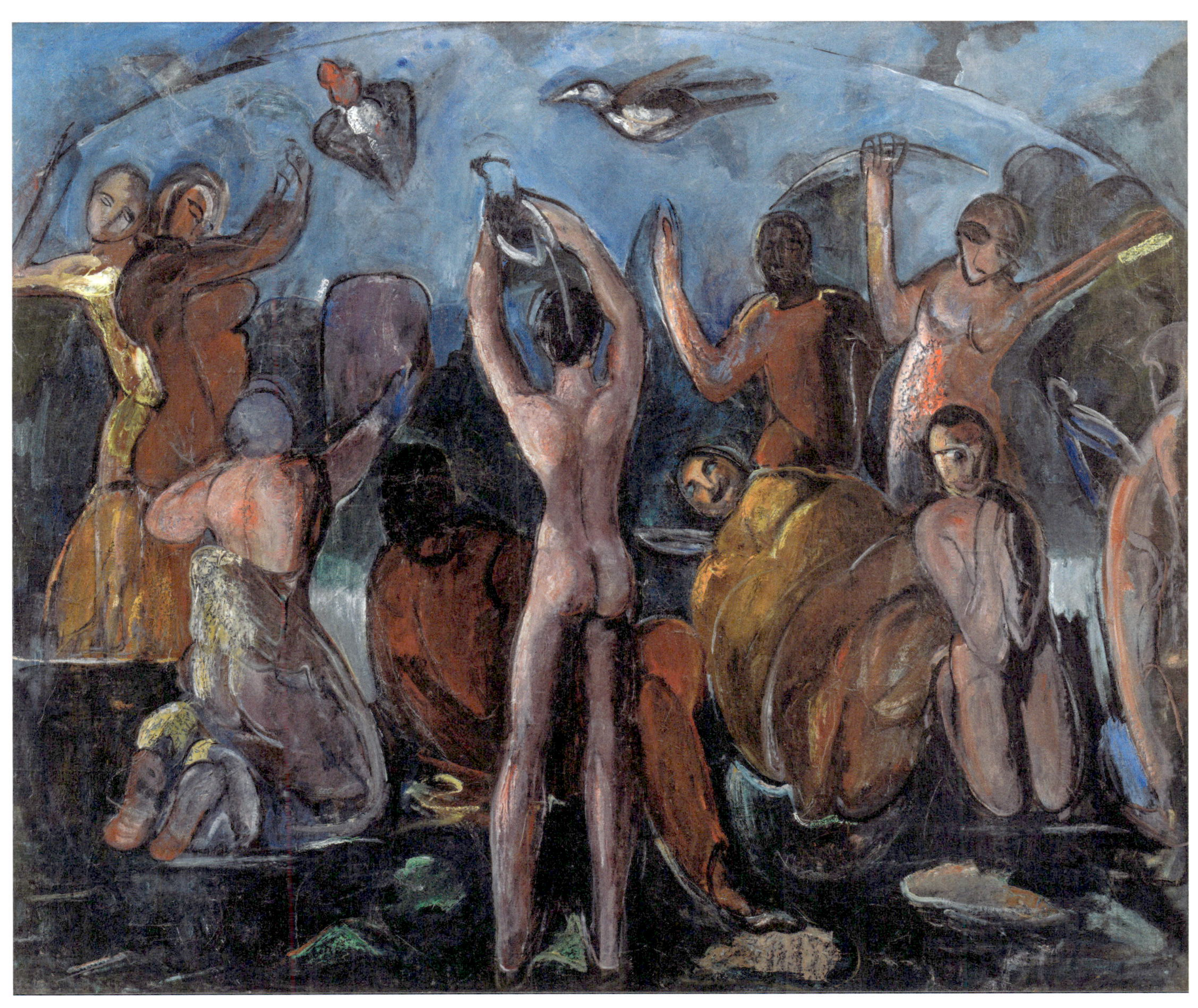

47 *The Sacrificial Feast. Man Seeking Omens. Opus III*, 1915

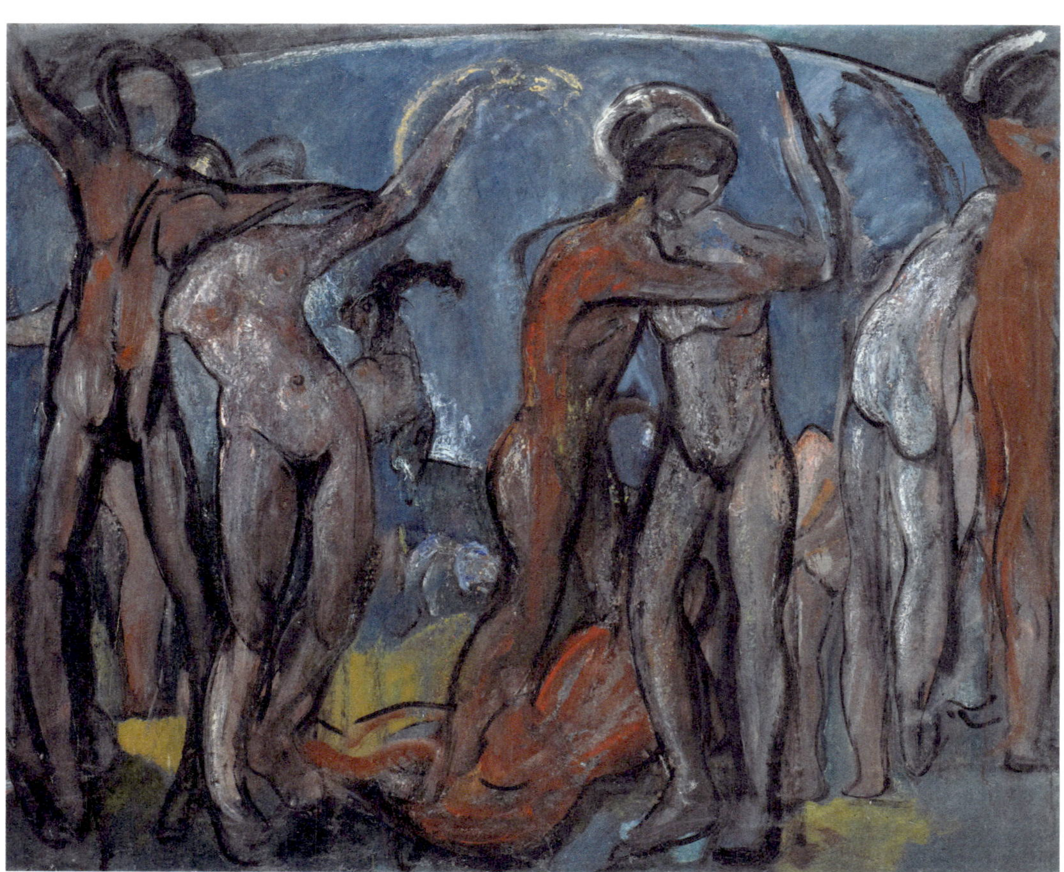

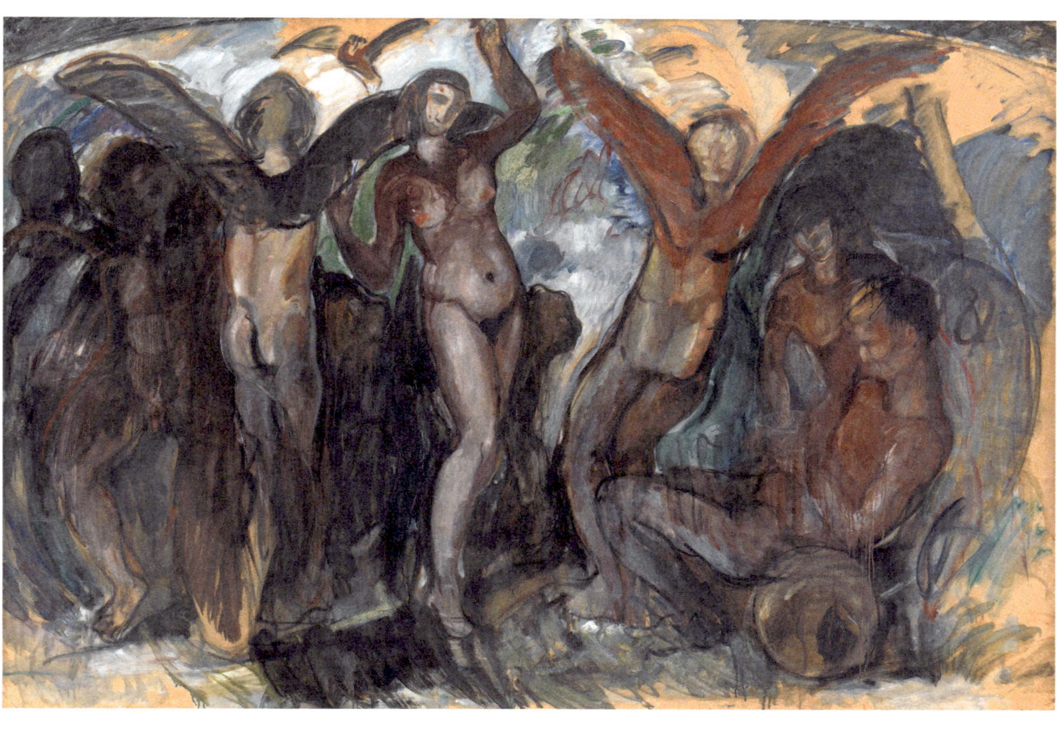

49 *Love. Bacchants. Opus I*, 1915

42 *Figure Composition with Bacchants*, 1914-1915

Opposite page:
27 *Figure Composition*, 1913

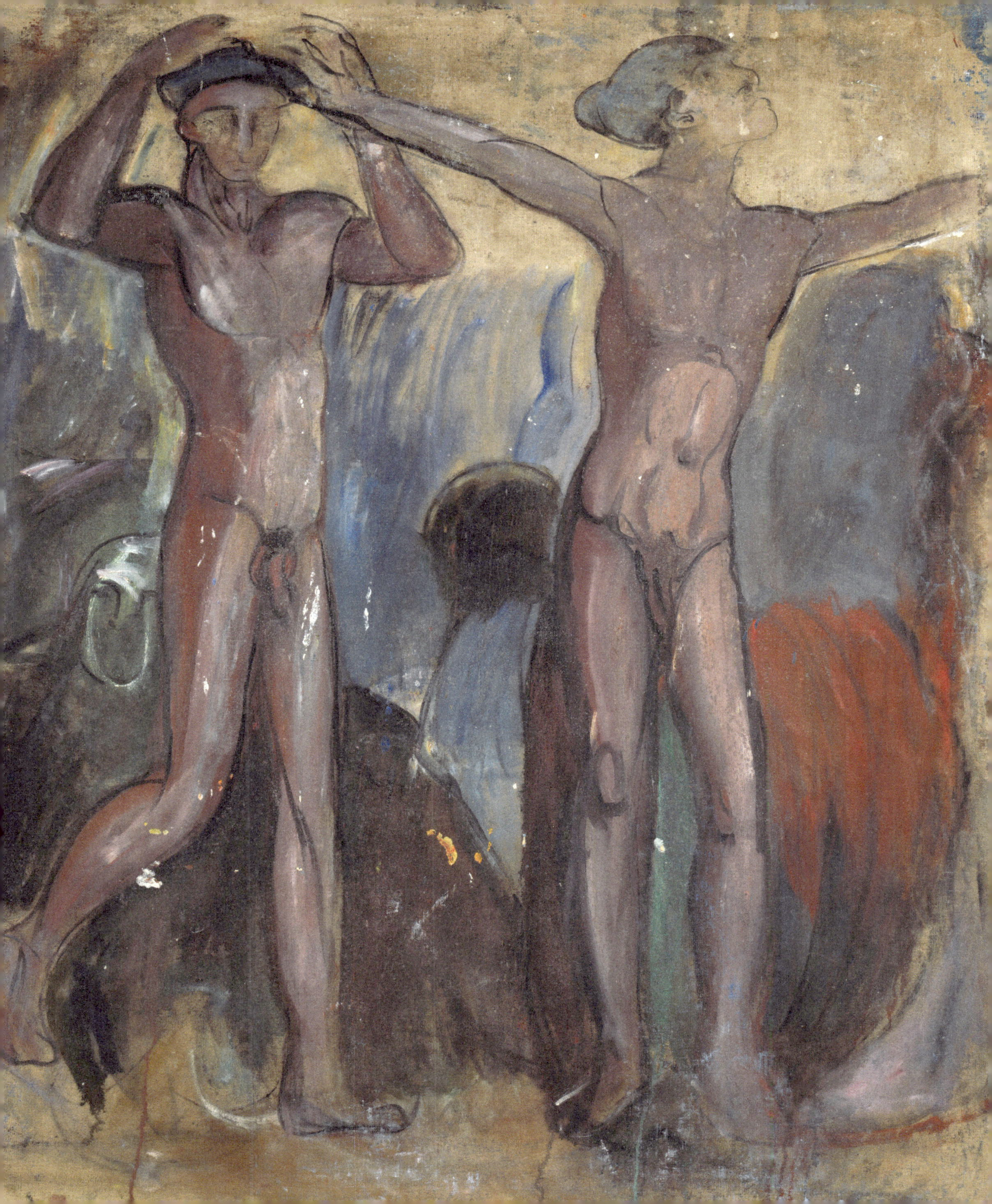

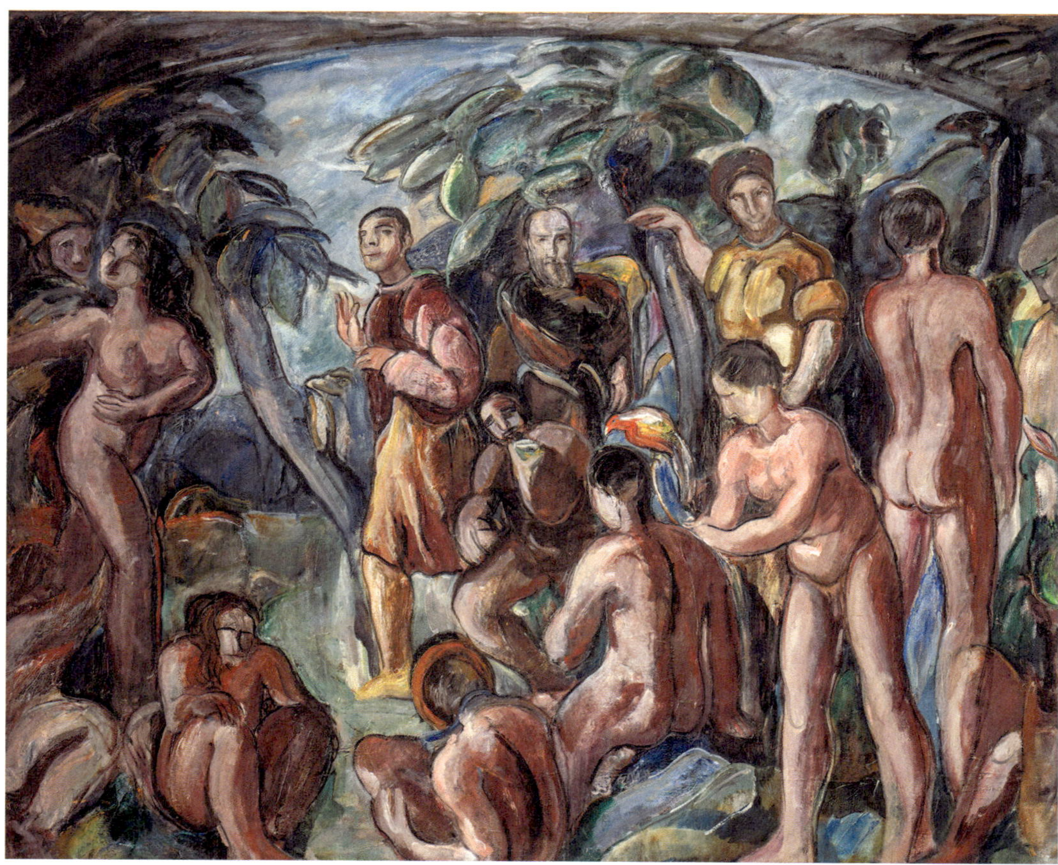

34 *The Golden Bird. From the Glorious Times of Ancient Greece. Opus I,* 1913-1914

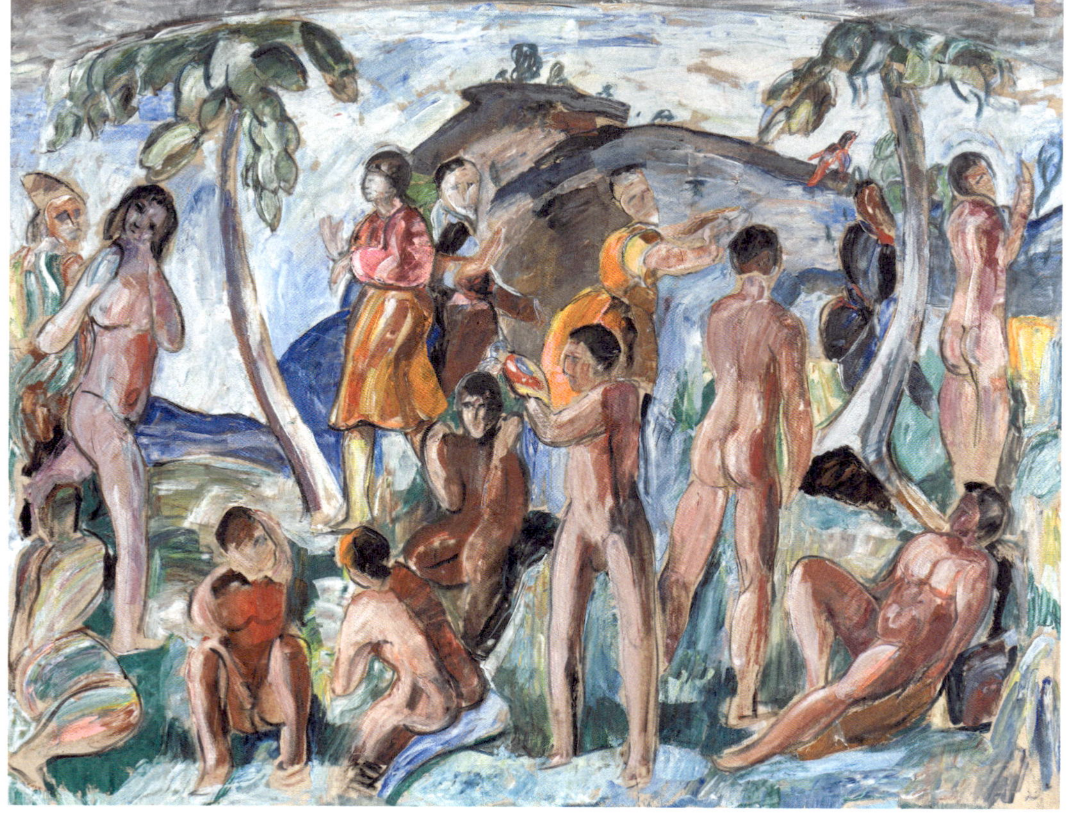

48 *The Arrival of Spring. From the Glorious Times of Ancient Greece. Opus II,* 1915

24 *The School of Athens. Copy after Raphael*, 1913

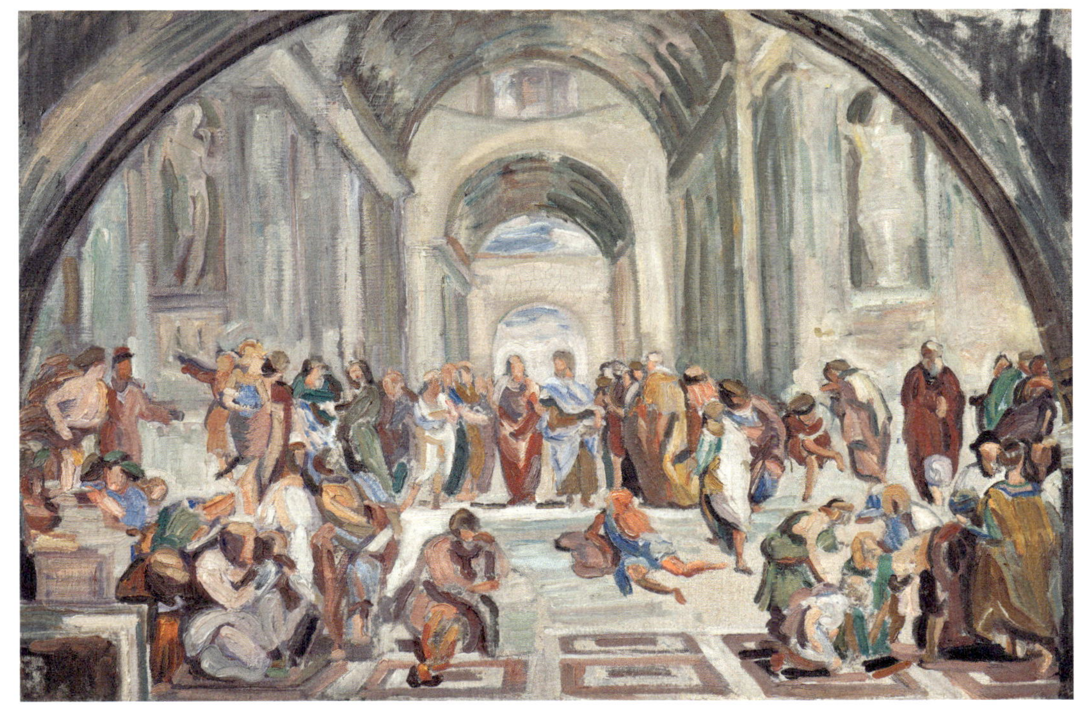

26 *Alcibiades*, 1913

23 *Socrates (Portrait of Vilhelm Wanscher)*, 1912

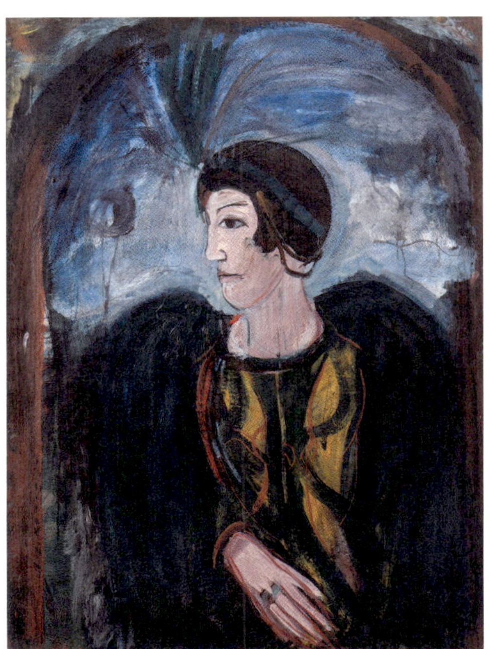

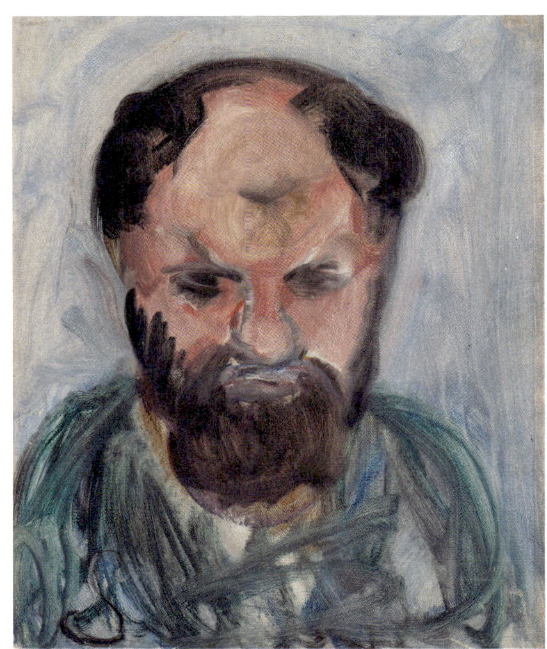

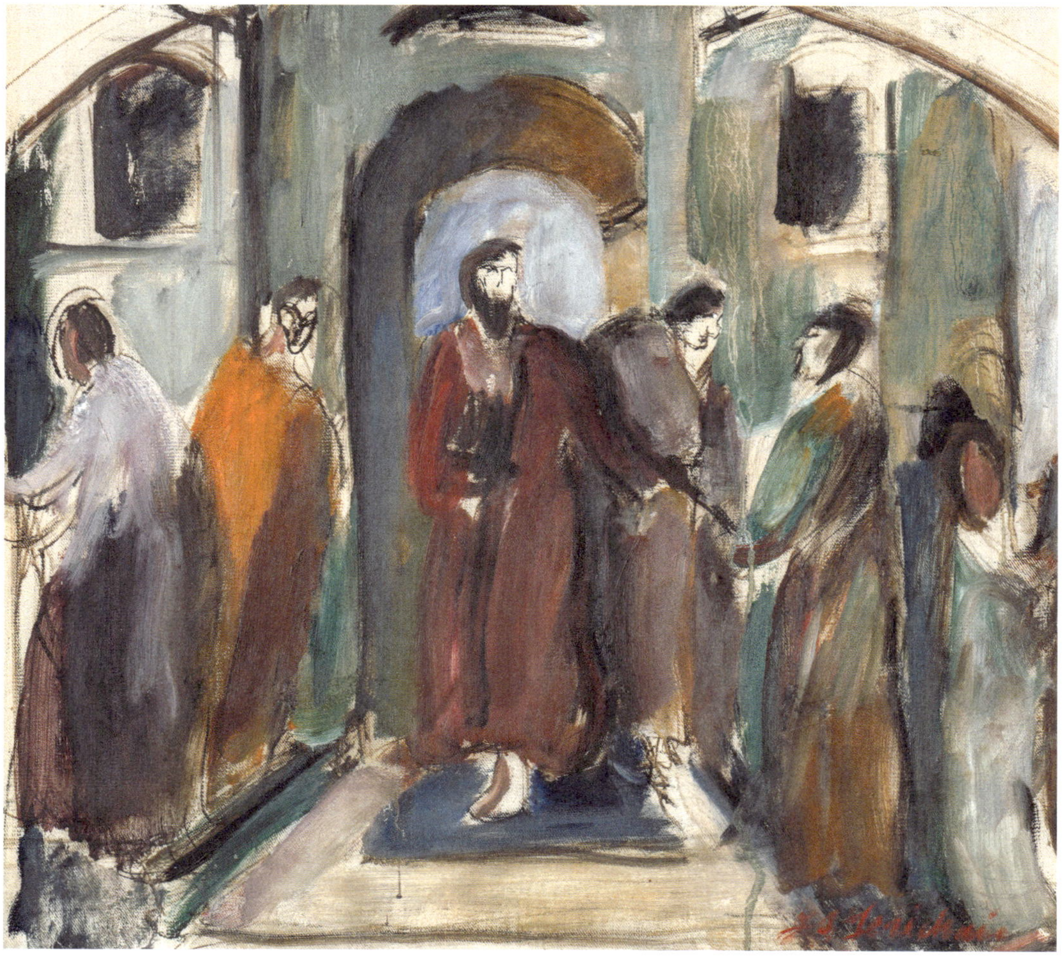

25 *Philosophers*, 1913

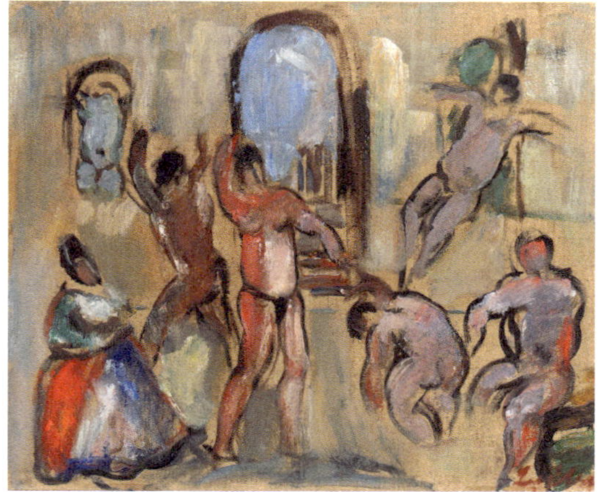

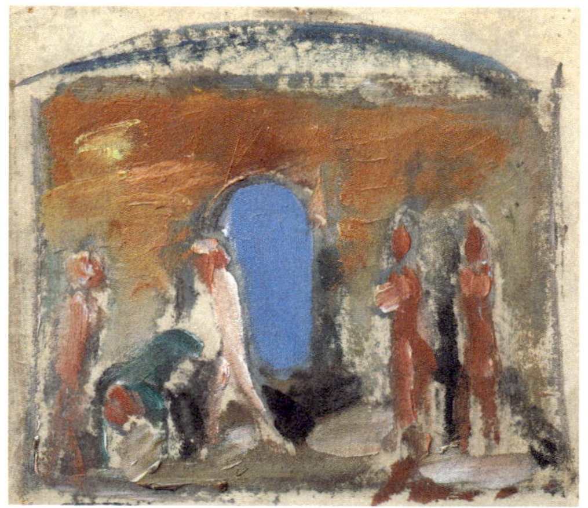

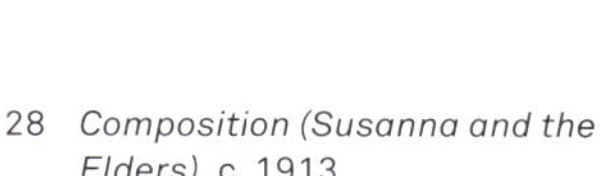

28 *Composition (Susanna and the Elders)*, c. 1913

38 *Susanna and the Elders*, 1914

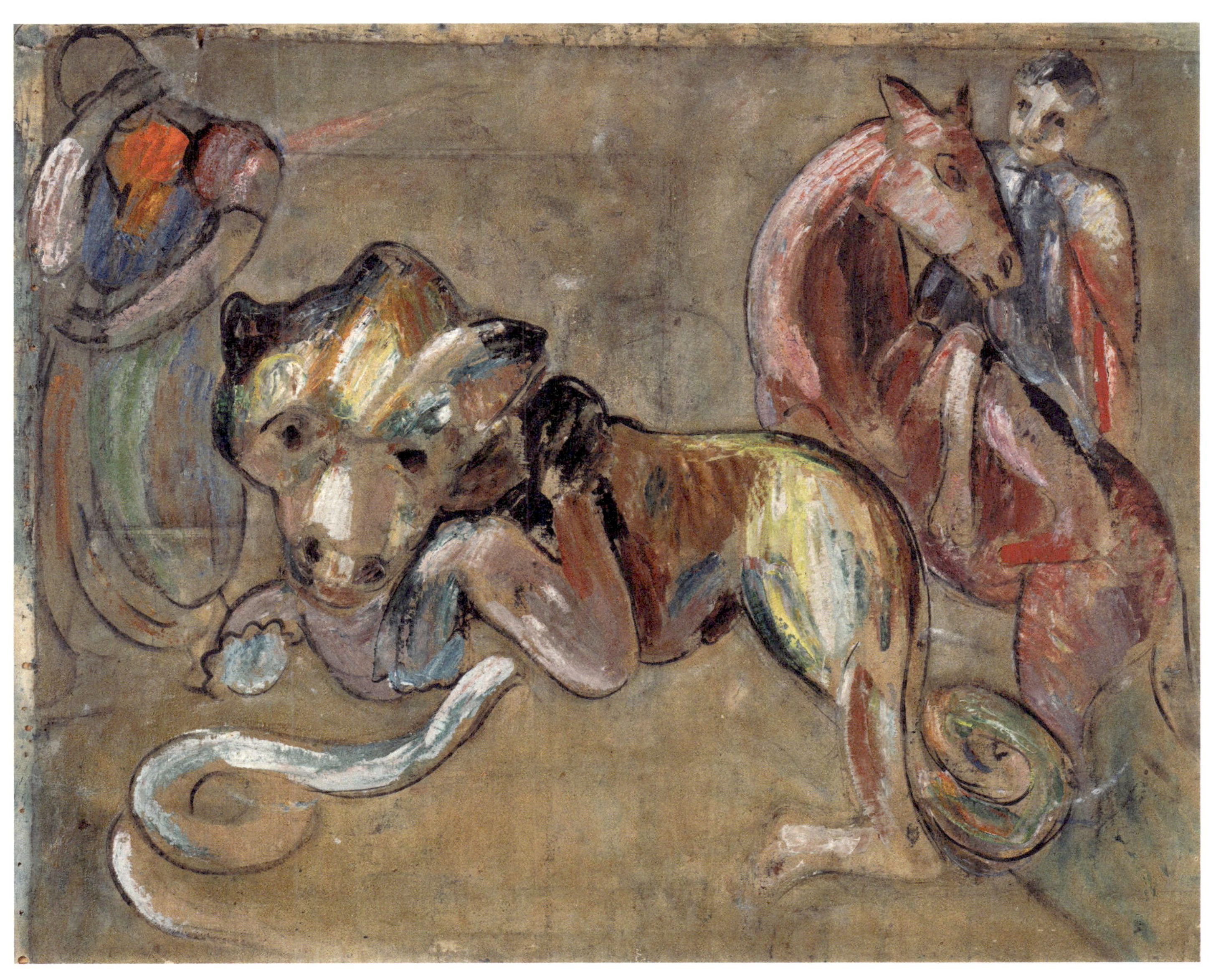

45 *Saint George and the Dragon Lion*, 1914-1915

Because I Want to Follow the Best in Me: Art and Love in Jerichau's Letters

Lise Villemoes Grønvold

On a Sunday in July 1910, Jens Adolf Jerichau sat down to write a letter to his mother and his aunt. He found a few empty pages in a sketchbook and wrote a draft, which is something he rarely did – he must have known that the letter would be hard to write. "Well, this time you won't be so happy about my letter, but you'll see, it's just a phase," he begins."I'll get right to it."[1] The matter at hand was Jerichau's relationship with an older man, the writer Aage Barfoed who lived openly as a gay man.

At the time, Barfoed had been an important part of Jerichau's life for the greater part of a year, and the two of them were planning a month's holiday in a small cabin in Rold Forest at the end of summer. Jerichau knew that his mother and his aunt would try to stop him from going. The letter was his attempt to assuage them, while he also wanted to start a conversation with them about his sexuality.

Jerichau was an 18-year-old architecture student when he met the 30-year-old Barfoed. An established author and playwright, Barfoed had travelled the world and seen his plays produced at the Royal Theatre in Copenhagen.[2] They met at a dinner party in November 1909 and were immediately fascinated by each other. As Jerichau wrote in his sketchbook afterwards, "Our eyes met in spiritual exchange, unconscious sympathy, understanding."[3] They agreed to meet a few days later at Barfoed's place, marking the beginning of a close relationship that lasted for a couple of years. Letters and notes left behind by Jerichau and Barfoed provide a fascinating look not only into early 20th century thinking about sexuality and queer identity but also into the provenance of the literary canon that became crucial to Jerichau's work.

Platonic Love

From Jerichau's detailed notes, we know that his first private conversation with Barfoed quickly turned to the nobleness of relationships between men. Barfoed told Jerichau about "the Belgian psychiatrist who defended homosexuality and believed that the heterosexual is really the perverse one."[4] Together they read Oscar Wilde and discussed the trials in which the Irish writer had spoken in praise of amorous relations between men, in particular the Greek *paiderastia*, "such love as Plato made the basis of his philosophy [...] this love of an elder man with his experience of life, and the younger with all the joy and hope of life before him."[5]

Whether Jerichau and Barfoed's relationship followed the "Greek model", we do not know, but we do know that Barfoed introduced Jerichau to many new things, not least in the realm of literature. It was also through Barfoed that Jerichau first encountered the progressive thinking about homosexuality (though mainly between men) that was slowly arriving in Denmark from Great Britain and the rest of Europe. Further along in their relationship, Jerichau recollected what took place in one of these first meetings in his diary:

> Had it now become really serious. I could only speak for the moment and the present, while Aage surely knew it was for eternity [...] He spoke about how he believed the ideal was to unite one's passion with one's love. He did, and he wanted to. How Woman was wicked, evil and bad, destructive for mankind. They think only about themselves, satisfying themselves. We talked back and forth about these questions which were very interesting and opened my eyes to many new things. I ended up spending the night with him and he saw me on my way in the morning, wonderful morning. I myself was in a daze.[6]

Jerichau omits certain details, but there is obviously something going on; something "really serious" for both of them.

Barfoed would become hugely important to Jerichau's career. Their conversations about art impelled Jerichau to drop out of architecture school and transfer to the Royal Academy of Fine Arts' painting department, in spite of his family's opposition. This incited an ongoing conflict where Barfoed and Jerichau's family each tried to pull Jerichau in opposite directions, both citing concern for him as their motivation. In a series of letters, Jerichau's mother repeatedly begged him to stop seeing Barfoed, whom she considered a bad influence, not least because of his sexuality. She was afraid that her son would ruin his reputation by consorting with Barfoed. Homosexuality was still illegal in Denmark, and after the Immorality Scandal of 1906-1907, where four Danish men were convicted of having sexual relations with other men, homosexuality had become reliable fodder for gossip in the Danish tabloids.[7] Being outed or suspected to be gay could have severe repercussions, as Herman Bang learned firsthand in 1907 when he had to leave Denmark after being accused of "Platonic love" (a code word for homosexuality) by his fellow writer Johannes V. Jensen in an opinion piece in *Politiken*, a Copenhagen broadsheet.[8]

Fight for Love

In a reply to his mother, Jerichau defends the importance of his relationship with Barfoed, describing him as "the only person who has ever fully understood me".[9] At the same time, Barfoed was encouraging Jerichau to break with his family, as he himself had done to live the life he wanted as a writer and as an out gay man.

While Barfoed's letters are undeniably declarations of love, much still had to be written between the lines. Anything directly pointing to amorous relations could be entered as evidence in court, as had happened in the case of Wilde. In a note Jerichau made after a night at Barfoed's, he writes that they discussed "homosexuality which gave so much occasion for whispers and dissimulation."[10] "Whispers" or not, the intensity of their relationship is evident from their letters. In a letter to Jerichau, Barfoed writes,

> Jens Adolf, I do not fight to win you for myself – or to have influence over you – or to use my love to coax something out of you that does not exist – I fight for your personality. I am taking myself out of play – my sorrow and my joy is up to me – but one thing, one single wish has grown from my love for you. The wish to protect you. I stand alone against so many, against the others who clutch on to you with invisible claws and bind you with little, hidden ties. [...] The two of us are free with each other, there is nothing that ties you to me – I at least will not hear of any ties – but from me to you leads a road of love, straight and clear and free – *truer than any other road by which people seek you* – for I fight for your personality, that it may live and not be killed. Were I to venture nothing here, you would die, your innermost self, your soul, your talent, everything, all in this world that solely and only makes *a Man*.[11]

Love and art become merged, as Barfoed argues that Jerichau has to liberate himself from his family and society's expectations in order to realize his art. The same conjunction is found in Jerichau's own letters from the period, when he describes his decision to become a painter as part of a process where "the steady core of all this is the eternal search, eternal longing for love, eternal love, that is, happiness, eternity, eternal life".[12] As in the writings of Dante – another writer Barfoed and Jerichau likely read together, and a recurring motif in Jerichau's paintings – love is the road to divinity and eternal life.[13]

In Barfoed's letter, we recognize some of today's interest in identity and its role for the artist. Finding and expressing your own truth, in particular when it comes to sexuality, is closely linked with the ability to create great art. At this time, however, early on in his relationship with Barfoed, Jerichau still had his doubts, not least as to whether his truth was really the same as Barfoed's.

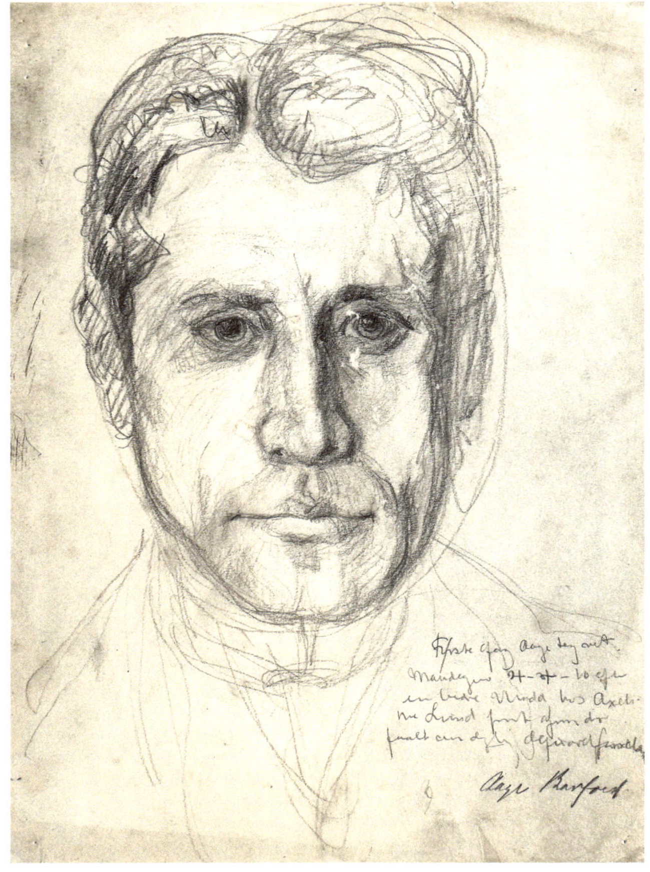

Jens Adolf Jerichau: Sketch of Aage Barfoed, "Aage drawn for the first time", 1910

An As Yet All But Unsolved Riddle

In the previously mentioned draft letter to his mother and his aunt, Jerichau openly discusses his sexuality. He writes that he does not think he is gay, at least when it comes to feeling physical attraction. However, as the following excerpt reveals, he suggests that a certain affinity with same-sex attraction could stem from his having been gay in a previous life:

> That two *men*, as well as *man and woman*, can love each other is a historical fact that cannot be denied. So the people whose houses and homes might be closed to me, as you write – imagine, because I live with a person for a fortnight or so who is a homosexual – no, those people I would rather be without. *I* am quite at ease going over there now, simply because *I am not a homosexual*, if being so (as I understand it) means *preferring to live together with men* instead of women.
>
> I have never in a sexual regard been attracted to men. However, in a spiritual regard I have most often felt at home with men – a union or a separation of these two conditions is for me an as yet all but unsolved riddle, and I do not wish to have it finally solved. I assume that homosexuality as well as heterosexuality is inborn. *So, dear Mother*, if I had happened to be the former, nothing in this world would cause me to change. Since you would have found that horrific, *rejoice*, for, as mentioned, to *my* awareness *I am not*. However, I do believe (I have become a bit of a Theosophist) that I was in a past life. It is in any case quite natural to understand homosexuals.

Jerichau denies being "a homosexual," if homosexuality is defined as preferring men to women, and he describes his attraction to men as "spiritual" rather than "sexual". Jerichau's defence of homosexuality not only shows that he was well versed in the thinking that circulated in the queer intellectual milieu at the time. It hints at something other than heterosexuality. His letter states that he is attracted to both men and women, but in different ways, which fits with his mentor Vilhelm Wanscher's description of him as "possessing an erotic duality", i.e., being bisexual.[14] The letter draft also contains several discrepancies, indicating that Jerichau was either trying out different explanations to see if they were convincing or had not made up his mind about what to tell his mother and his aunt. First, he writes that his stay will last a month, then a few lines down he says that they will be living together for "a fortnight or so". And despite the fact of his fervent defense of homosexuality in the above passage, he backtracks a bit at the end. "About Rold," he writes, "after all, no one really needs to know, right? At least there is no reason to particularly trumpet it about."[15]

Grand, Eternal Emotions

When Jerichau wrote the draft letter, he had decided to go on holiday with Barfoed, whatever the cost. "It is because I want the truth, because I want to follow the best in me," he writes about his decision to go, underscoring the significance of their relationship to him.[16] He had hesitated too long, however. Barfoed had grown impatient. In a letter a few days later, Barfoed tells him that he thinks they should cancel their trip to Rold, which had already been postponed. "Had you been able to see how much, how deep and great it all was, you would, in spite of your family, in spite of everything and everybody, have bowed out of the two rather pointless months in Funen [...]. Vacationing and viewing scenery is so trivial when you have the greatest and only thing of value in this world: a person who *means* something to you!"[17] He goes on to write that he is beginning to doubt that Jerichau reciprocates his feelings: "*I am as I am*, and in your innermost self you would have to be *like me* to be able to follow the paths I tread. [...] I have long realized that the truth is not like that – in other words, that you in your innermost are different than, at some moments and in some words, you have led me to believe."[18]

But Jerichau's reaction to the letter tells a different story. Underlined passages and question marks pencilled in the margins indicate frustration and disbelief. In one passage, where Barfoed writes that although they need each other and are fond of each other, they should perhaps just be friends, two drops have fallen on the page, smudging the ink. As Barfoed's next letter implies, a despondent Jerichau replied that he wanted to give it another chance. Could the two drops on the page be Jerichau's tears?

Jens Adolf Jerichau, Hjørring, 1908

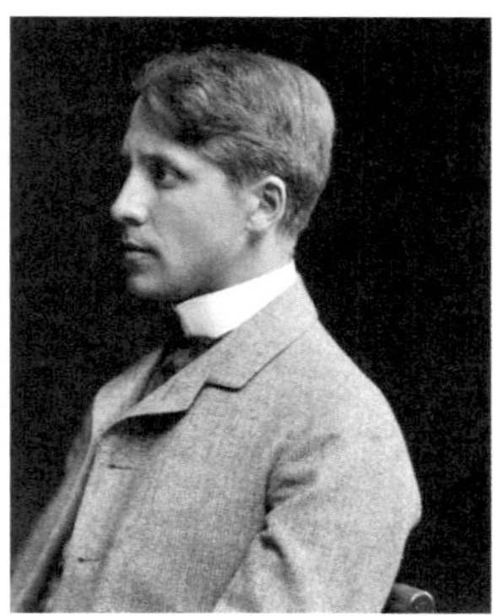

Aage Barfoed, c. 1910

"If it is anything but caprices and moods", Barfoed next writes to Jerichau, in a tone implying that he is happy to have received Jerichau's words of confirmation but still feels hurt, "then come on up here [to Rold] [...] You owe it to me to show that you are an adult and that Aage Barfoed is not a degenerate."[19]

As far as we know, Jerichau never made it to Rold that summer. After this time, Jerichau (or his family) saved fewer of Barfoed's letters. We do know, however, that Jerichau and Barfoed kept seeing each other over the next year and a half, while the literary influences that Barfoed introduced Jerichau to became recurrent motifs in his art. Plato, Socrates, Dante, Michelangelo, Goethe and Wilde kept appearing in Jerichau's pictures and writings as some of his greatest sources of inspiration.

Boundlessly Unhappy and Happy

Whether their love only had a spiritual dimension or also had physical dimension, the period of Jerichau's relationship to Barfoed provides the best window into the artist's love life, thanks to the many surviving letters and notes. Jerichau later had a relationship with Sigrun Schalburg. A divorcée and the mother of four children, she was the sister of Jerichau's academy friend Jean Hakon Schalburg, with whom he had toured Southern Europe in 1912. Much less is known about their relationship. A few mentions in letters to others show that he intended to marry her, but nothing exists of their correspondence beyond a single letter that Jerichau wrote to her after she broke up with him.

After his relationship with Barfoed, Jerichau kept his emotional life private, with the exception of cryptic passages in his notebooks and fragments found among his papers, all addressed to boys. To one, he writes, with thinly veiled erotic undertones, "We have become as close as two can, gorgeous boy, your lance you have thrust nobly and you have struck me right in the heart. [...] We have met, met, met, as very few or no one meets."[20] Likewise, among the last things he wrote in Paris shortly before his death, are the words to a person whose identity we do not know, "I know she will be a mother to you because I have loved you, darling, darling boy. [...] You, boy, I have given all. You alone I have given all. You could wield the most. And you could receive the most. You are the one who understood me most closely. O God, you have understood me."[21]

Stories about Jerichau's life tend to highlight the circumstances of his tragic fate: depression and mental illness, heartbreak, suicide. These aspects are evident in his letters. But there are other sentiments that take up space, too: profound happiness, deep infatuation, wild ambition and ecstasy at his own art and genius. Clearly, Jerichau had a zest for life, even if it sometimes knocked him down. As Salto writes in a memorial tribute, Jerichau was a person who "bravely bit of the fruit from the tree of knowledge even when it left an acrid taste in his mouth".[22] In some of his letters, Jerichau insists that life should be embraced, in art as well as in love. A few days after receiving Schalburg's letter breaking their engagement, Jerichau writes to his mother,

> What do we humans know, we are like specks of dust. [...] We are actually so abjectly small, while at the same time grand and eternal emotions and wills lie in us, and therein I think is the natural explanation for how we can be at once boundlessly unhappy and happy. Hence it does not trouble me. I know it must be so. Such is life, especially if you really seize it and live it, and that I think is the right thing to do.[23]

Jerichau insisted on pursuing "grand and eternal emotions and wills" and made a point of knowing life, in joy and in misery.

Why read an artist's love letters, over a hundred years after his death? Jerichau wanted all his letters and "unnecessary papers" to be destroyed after his death, according to a will he wrote in Paris shortly before dying by suicide.[24] But Jerichau's family chose to defy his last will and save many of his letters and papers, most likely because of what these lovely, tender and, at times, dramatic writings say about the person who wrote and received them. We can be grateful for that today, when these texts add nuance to Jerichau's story and open a window into the emotions and experiences that lay at the root of his art.

Lise Villemoes Grønvold is a doctoral candidate in literature at Birkbeck, University of London, and served as assistant curator of the Louisiana Museums's Jerichau exhibition.

Drops – possibly teardrops – on the page of the letter. Aage Barfoed's letter to Jens Adolf Jerichau, 25 July 1910, Skagen

1915
Bandol

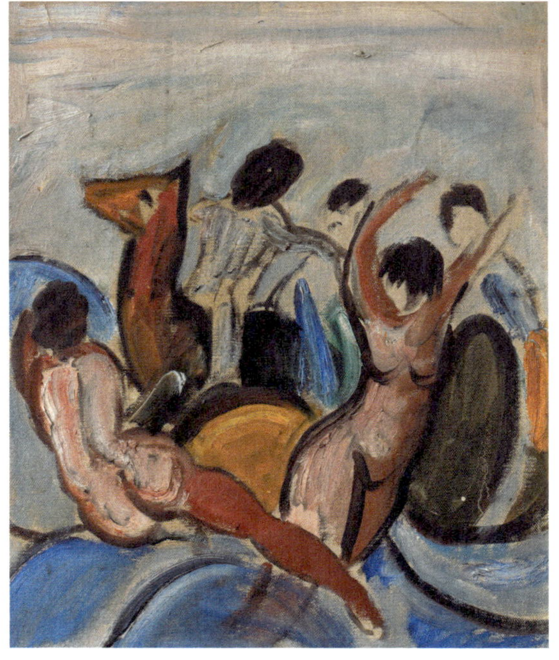

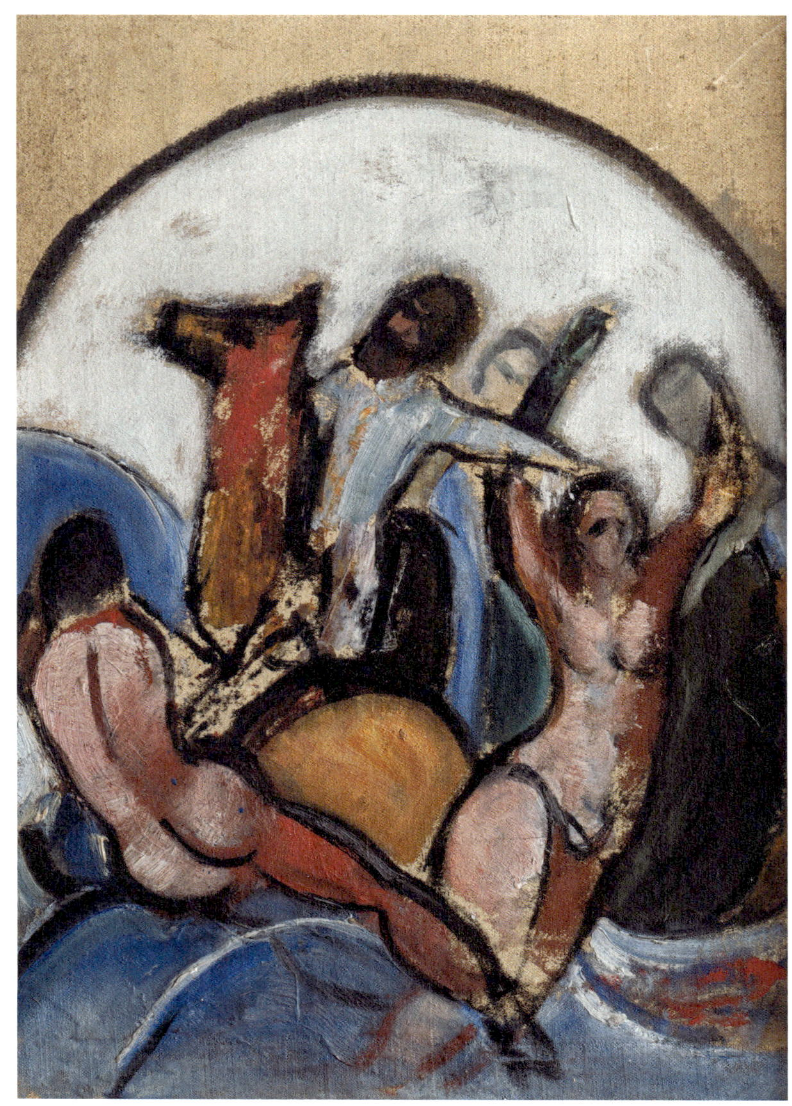

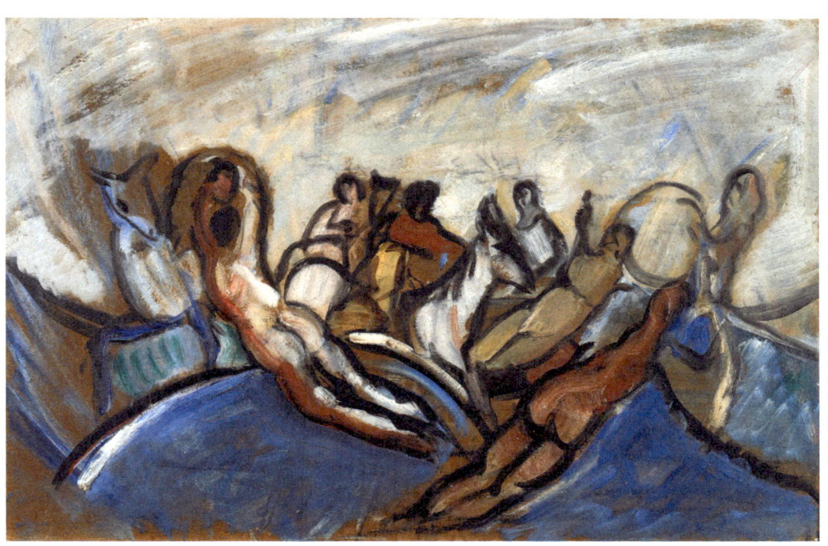

66 *Sea Deities. Sketch*, 1915

67 *Sea Deities. Sketch*, 1915

68 *Sea Deities. Sketch*, 1915

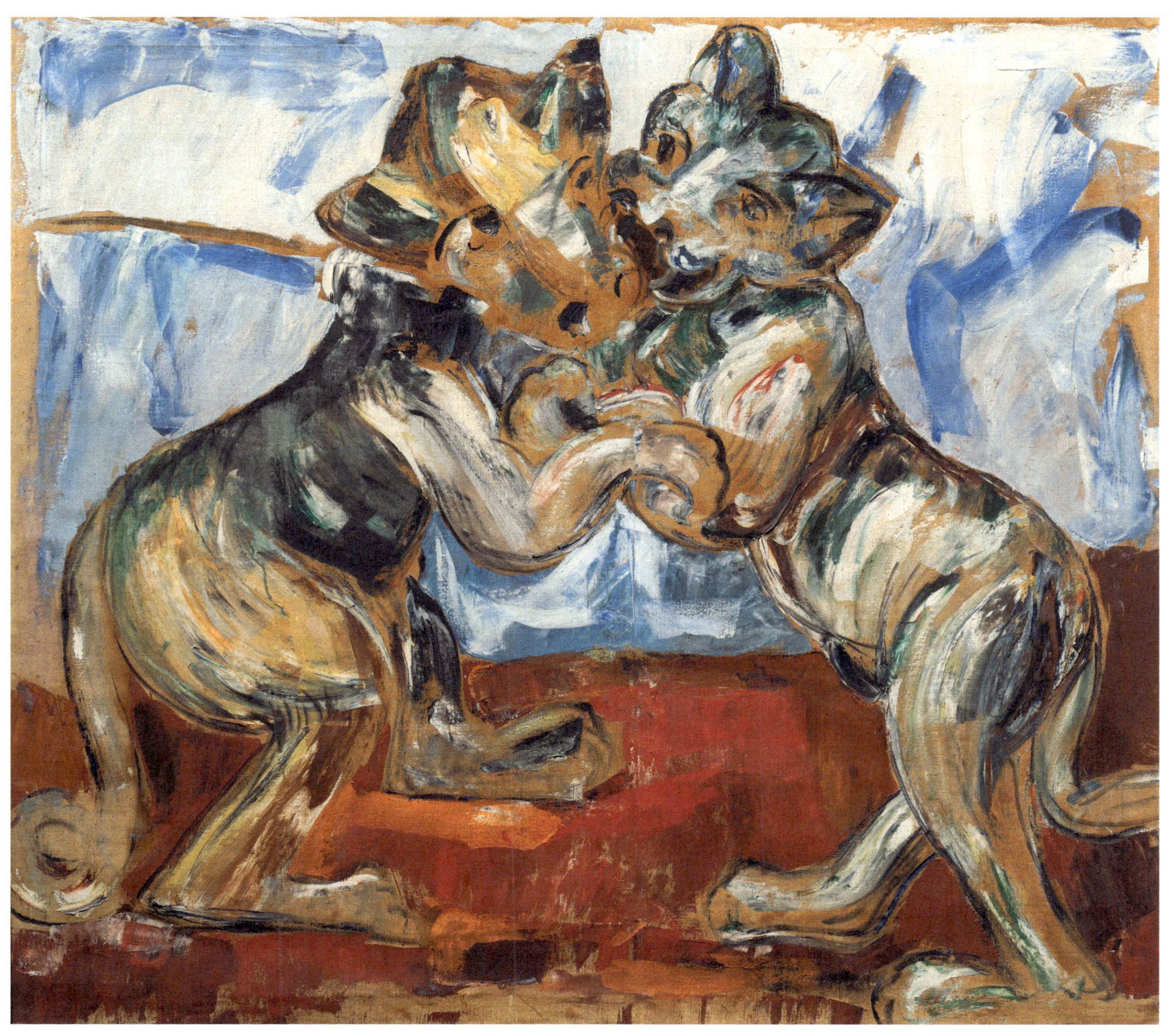

69 *Dragon Lions*, 1915

53 *The Quay*, 1915

56 *The Large Crier*, 1915

57 *The Beach*, 1915

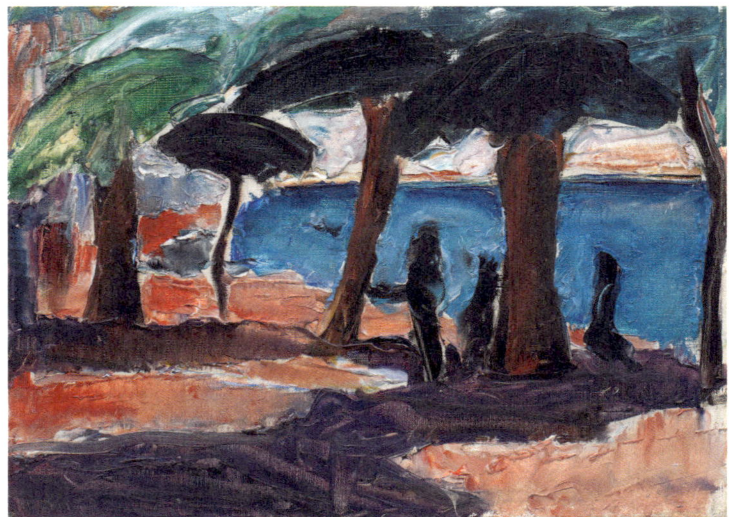

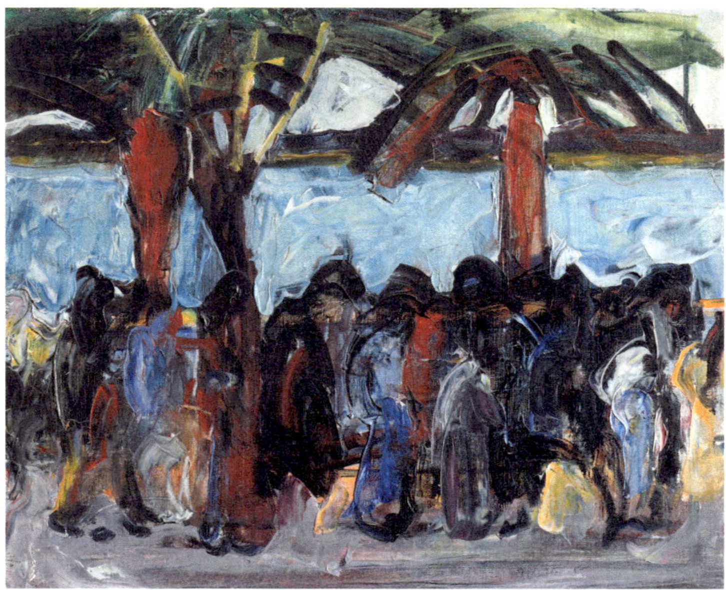

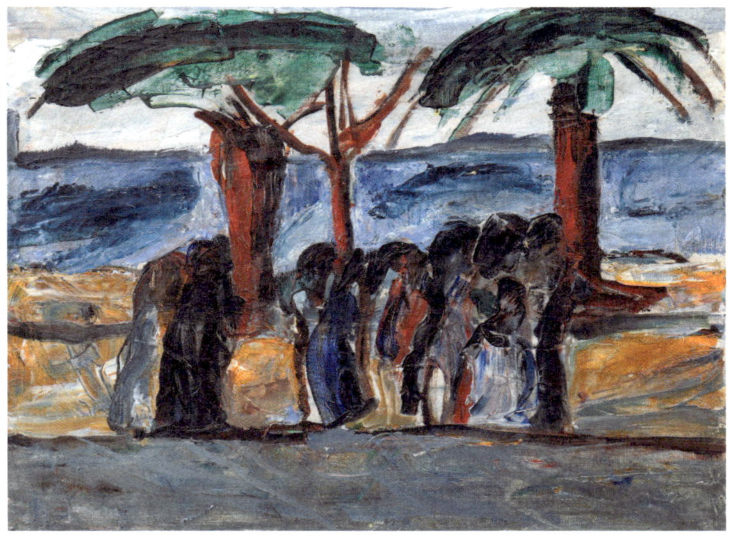

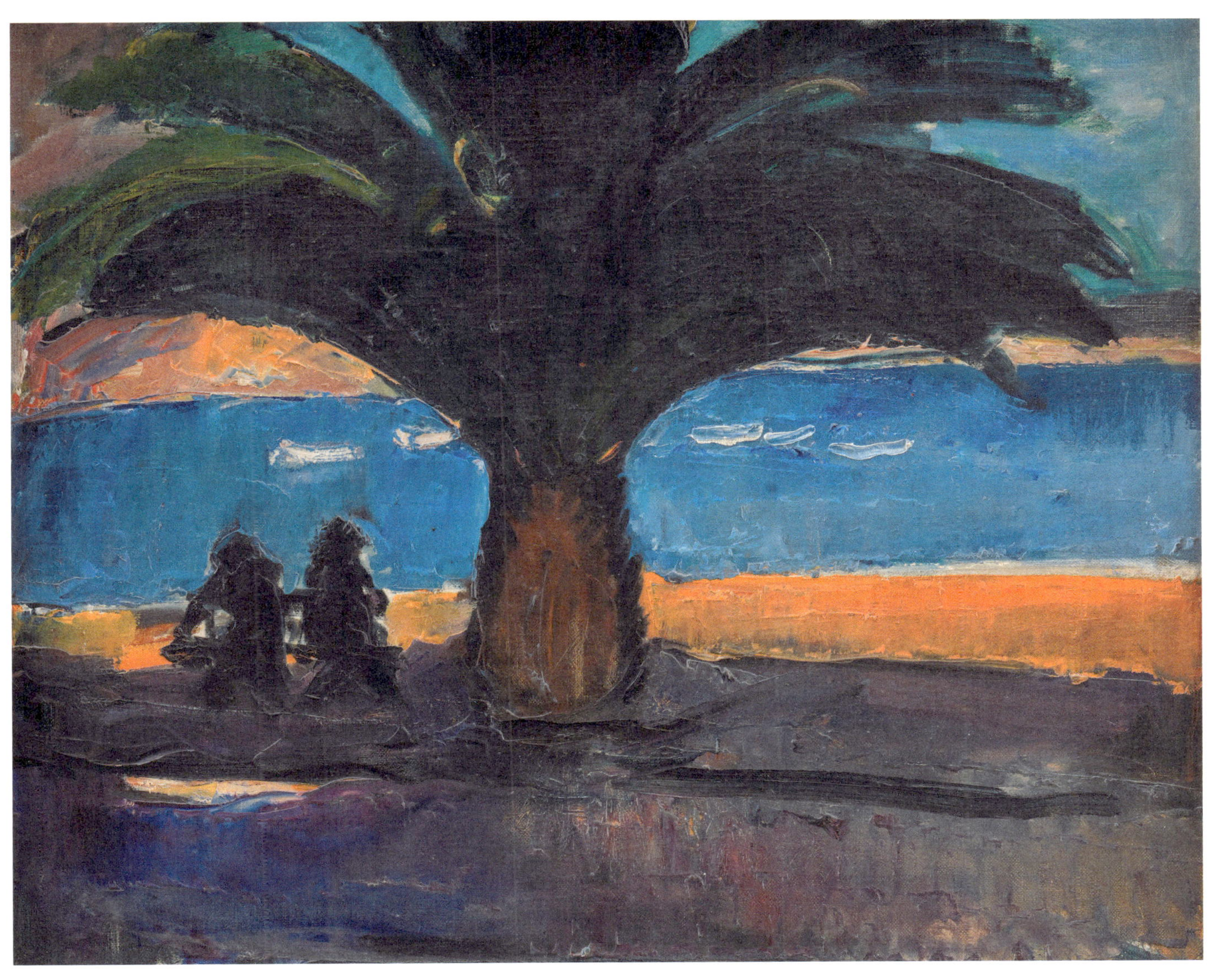

50 *The Thick Palm Tree. View from Villefranche*, 1915

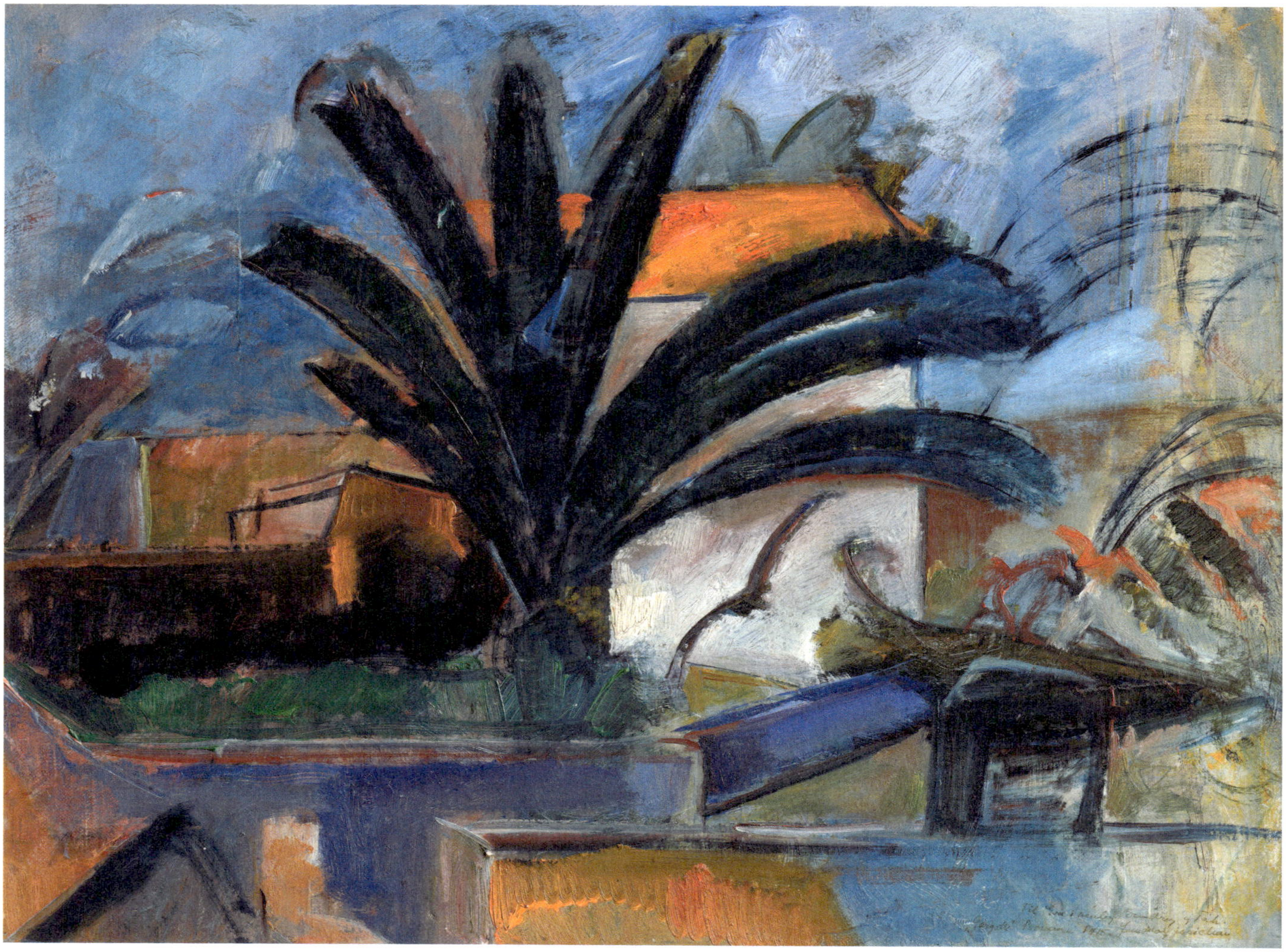

52 *Gorgette's Large Palm Tree,* 1915

51 *The Palm Tree, View of St. Sir,* 1915

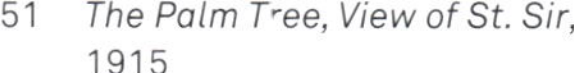

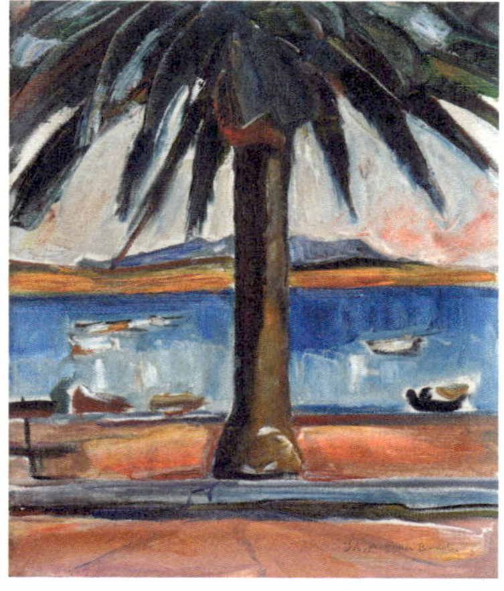

59 *The Small Bay*, 1915

55 *View of the Mediterranean*, 1915

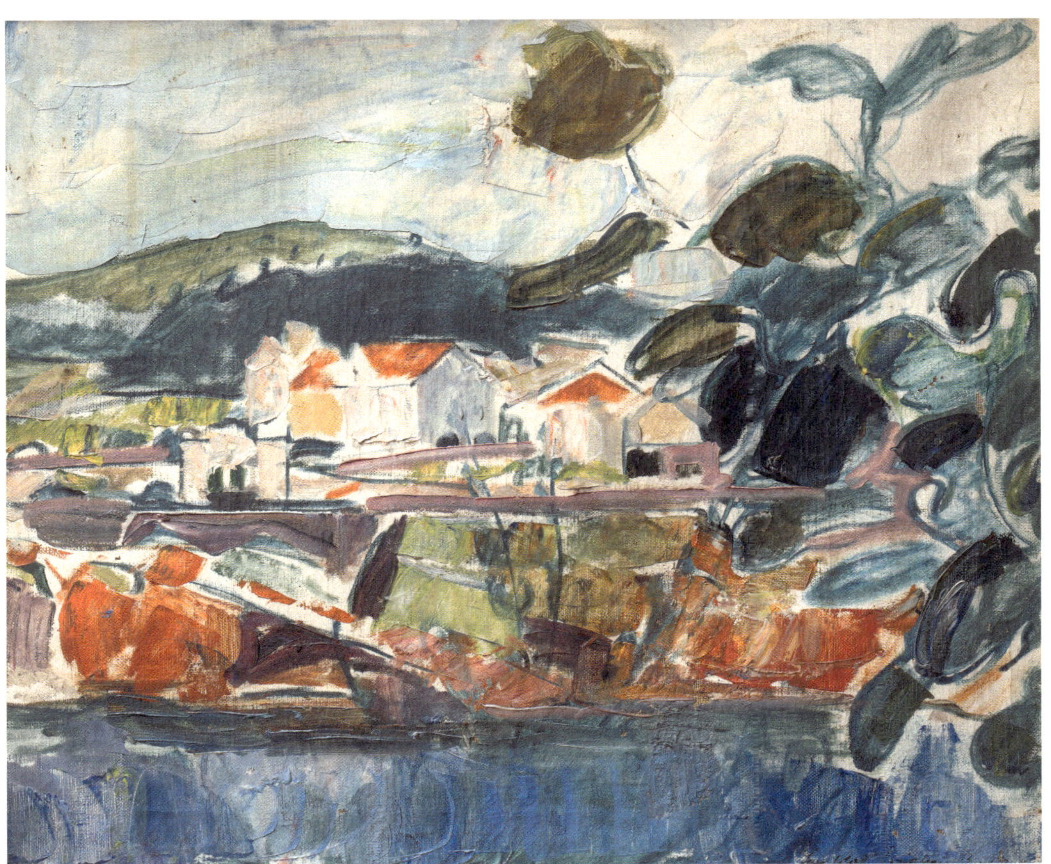

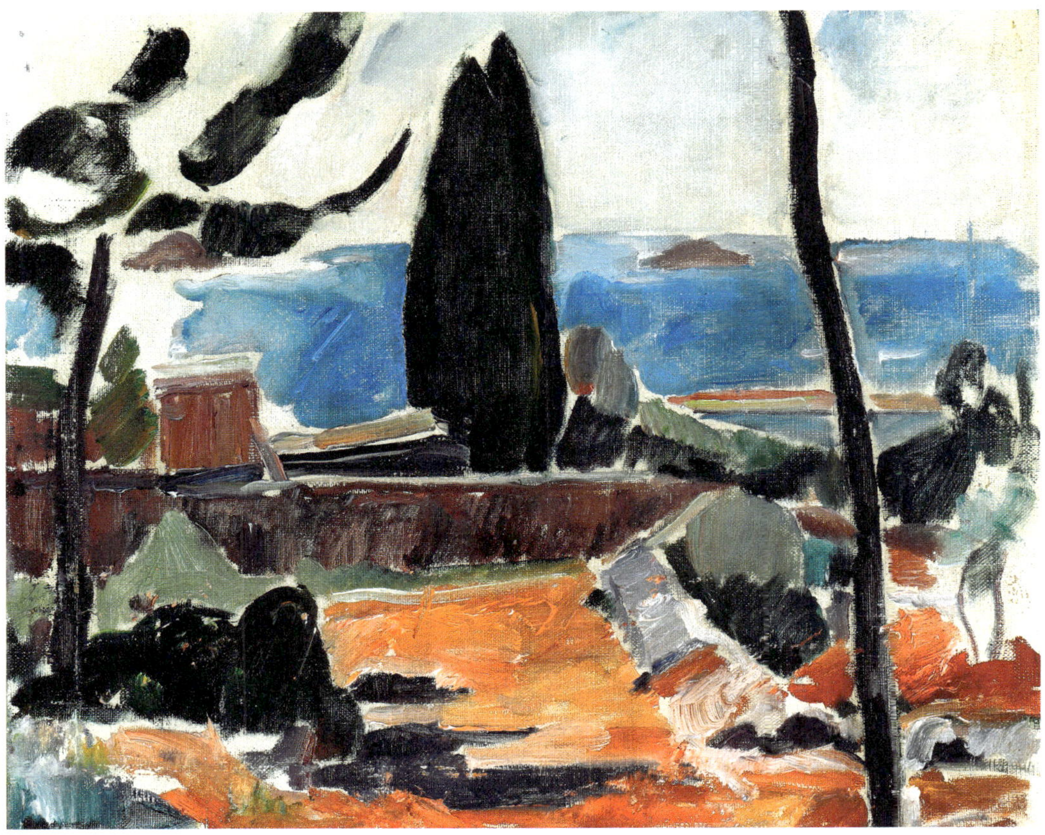

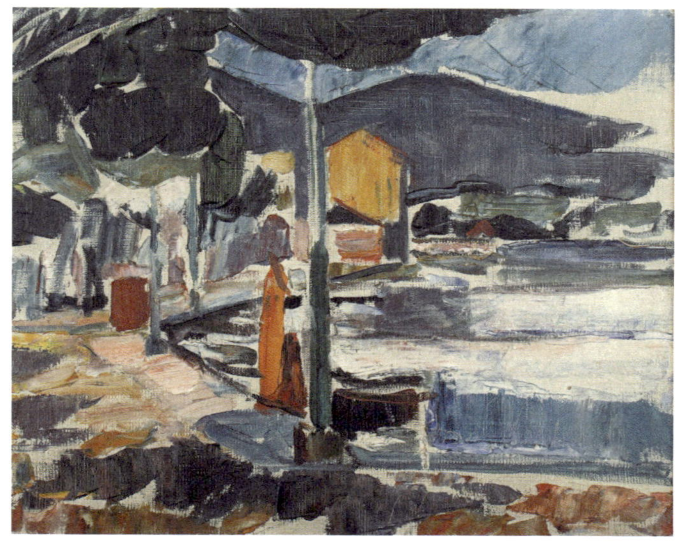

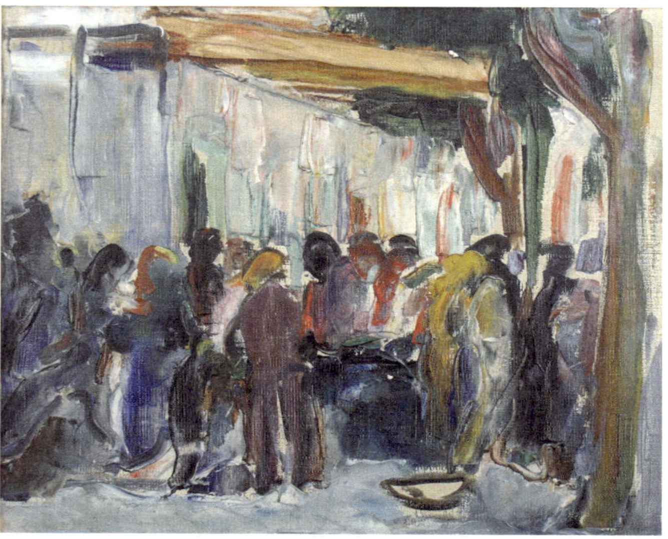

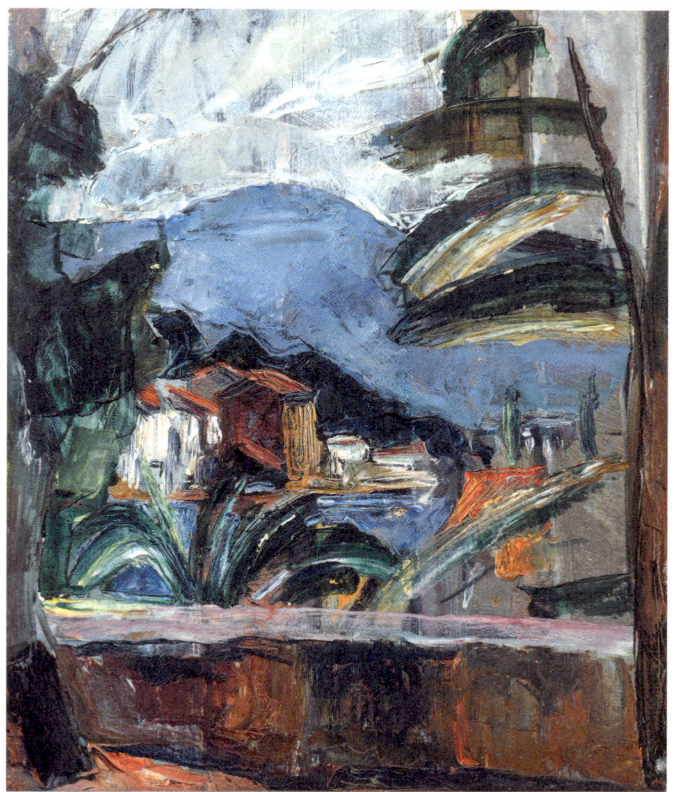

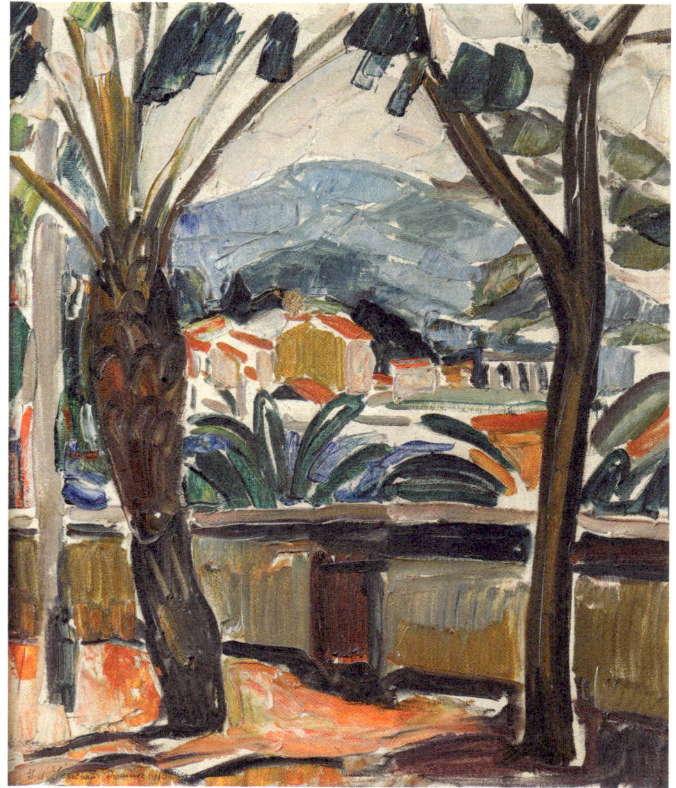

54 *The Quay*, 1915

64 *The Blue Mountain*, 1915

58 *The "Small Crier"*, 1915

63 *The Blue Mountain*, 1915

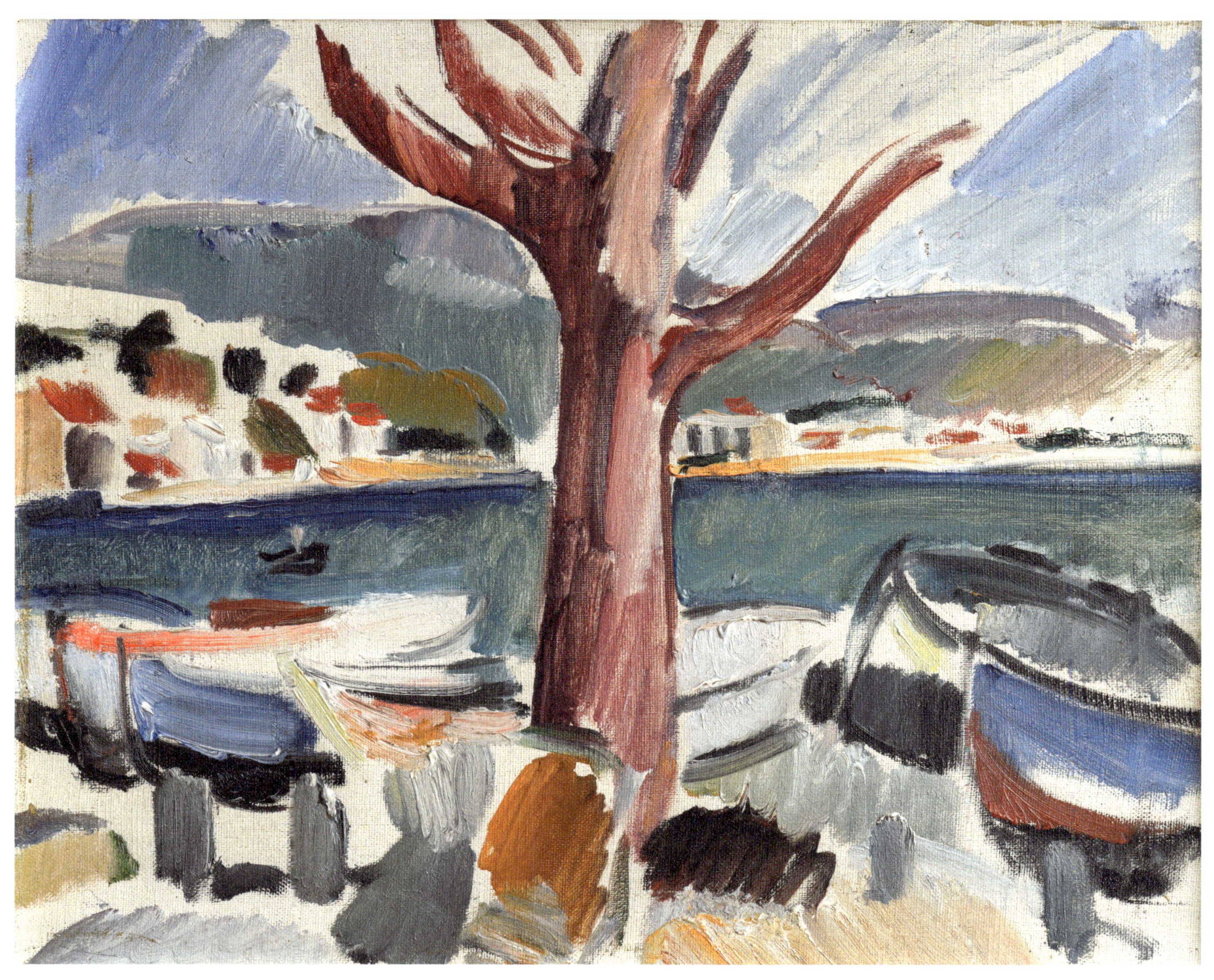

60 *Tree by the Beach*, 1915

61 *Street in Bandol,* 1915

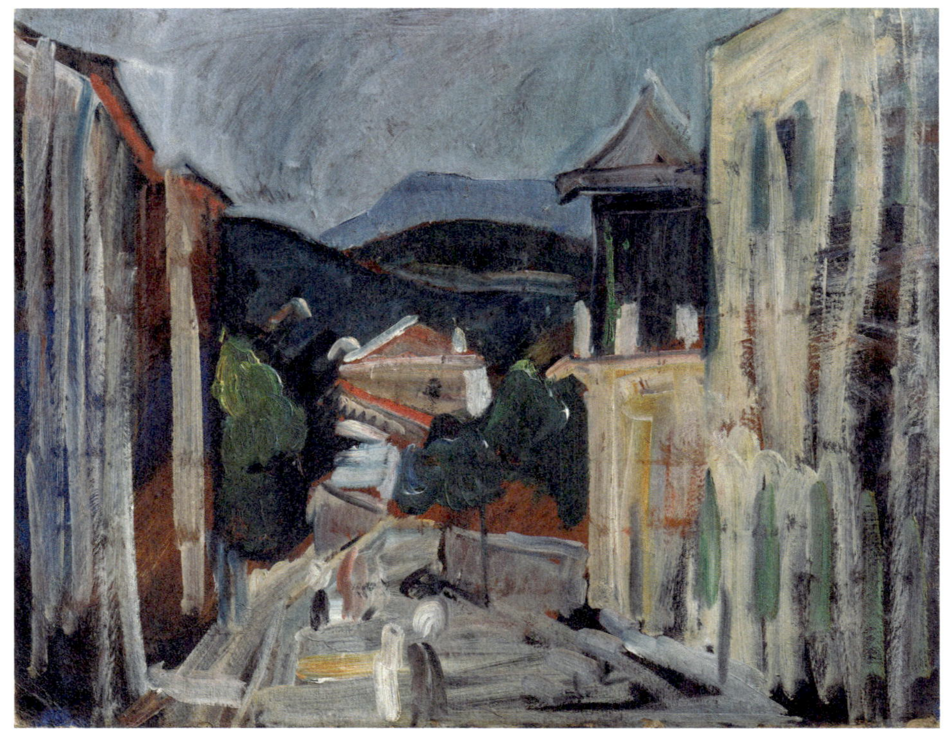

62 *Street in Bandol,* 1915

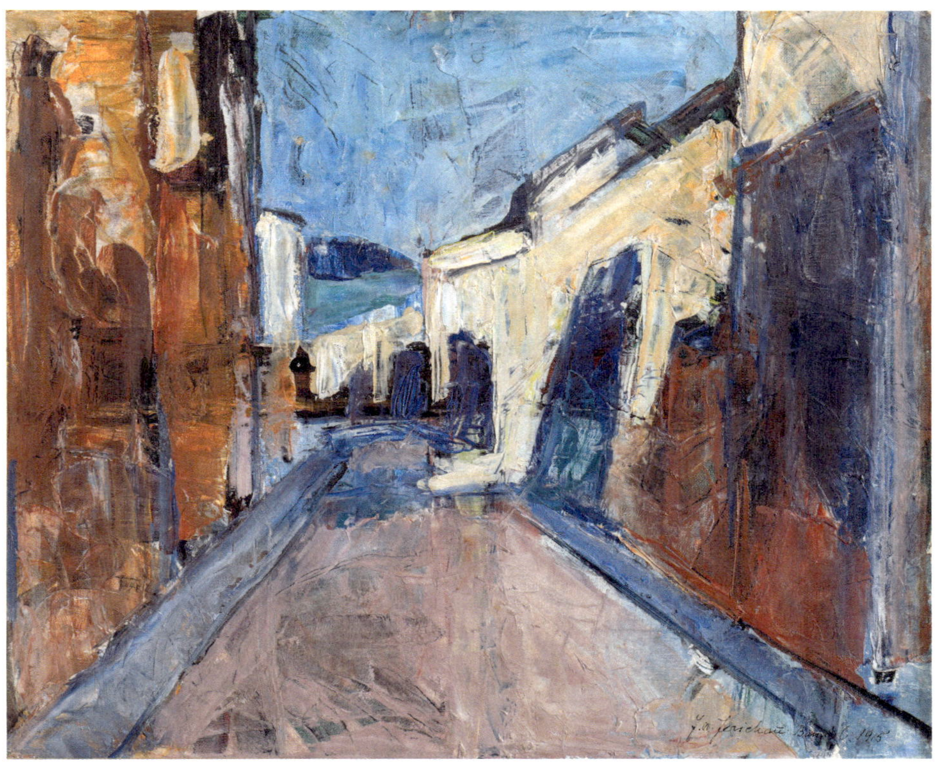

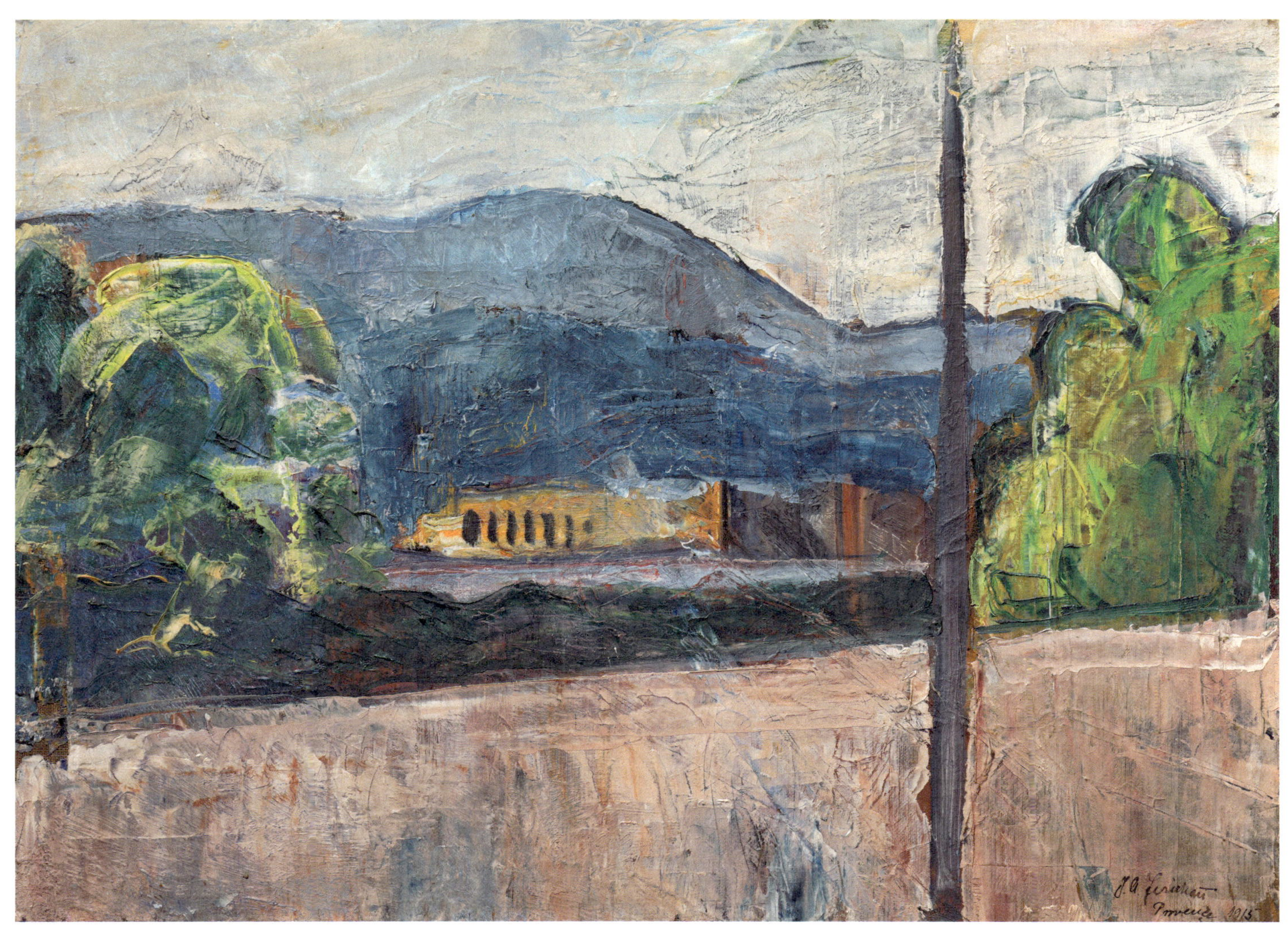

65 *From Provence*, 1915

Letter about J. A. Jerichau

In 1962 Asger Jorn wrote a letter to Troels Andersen in reply to an article Andersen had written earlier in the periodical *Signum*. Jorn's letter appeared in *Hvedekorn* no. 6, December, 1962. We are publishing Asger Jorn's letter.

Dear Troels Andersen,

I have just received the new issue of *Signum* (no. 1, 1962) and read your article about Jerichau with great interest. I think you have hit the problem head on by pointing out that Jerichau's pictures are images of states of mind. But I regret that you have not dealt further with this as the essential thing, for a state of mind is neither an ideal *à l'italienne* nor a pure and fixed imagining, a symbol (*nature morte,* icon). Out of sight, out of mind. *Mind* in German is *gemüt* – mood or temperament. Images of states of mind are images of moods, and as such ambivalent. This is the connection with Max Ernst. I have written an article on the ambivalent interpretation in a book by Serber. Unfortunately he forgot to print the basic diagram. But here I think the connection with Carl Nielsen is clear. All folk songs must be ambivalent since anyone is able to express his special gemüt by singing the same poem. That you have not clarified this along the lines indicated by Jerichau's ability to turn the back of one composition into a quite different one has the effect, first, that you lose yourself in a detailed comparison with the details of Raphael's picture, which reduces Jerichau's contribution with-out explaining and liberating it. So when you place Jerichau's work in a context you can no longer respect it, because you put it in a *wrong* context that you respect too much.

Despite everything you have seen rightly in emphasizing the connection with Weie. But you have forgotten that there is also a connection with Kandinsky's first period and with Kokoschka's Romantic compositions, although Jerichau's development has been quite independent of that.

You have thus fallen into two pitfalls, in the first place that of the Italian Renaissance as ideal, and in the second that of *Symbolism*, by going into the details of the Dante symbolism. The non-essential in Jerichau's production is his use of the classical visual motifs – Greek, Christian and Nordic (Loki). The most important thing is his use of the great dramatic compositions, his work in the Grand Style, and in this case the essential thing is what reaches out beyond the classical compositional forms towards more free, new compositional forms. In that sense the direct connections are the Skovgårds, Poul S. Christiansen, Larsen Stevns, Giersing, Weie with Willumsen's strong presence felt in the background. You should formulate an explanation of and connections in this quite independent Danish context with a new article that supplements the first one – penetrate even deeper into the problem, which is Danish art's close connections with and independent development of what is happening elsewhere. I will even include Jens Søndergård as well as Olivia Holm Møller, who is perhaps the most direct further development of the line to which Jerichau gives a new formulation – even Carl Henning Pedersen I think is in reality an explanation of something I consider very important in Jerichau. *Omens* in art, *warnings* and *forecasts* as landmarks for the future, are incomprehensible if one wants to be too specific – unclear in meaning because one must extract one's own value, one's personal message from the picture.

This is not Greek, this proverbial approach which cannot be expressed in words. but which is and remains *images of moods*; this is perhaps a visual development that we have special reason to be proud of having created in the North. Here I am also thinking of Munch, Josephson and Isaksson, who must not be forgotten in relation to Jerichau, Weie and Poul S. Christiansen.

The essential thing about *the image of the state of mind* is that it builds on the mood, the being moved, the emotional affect. Therefore Lundstrøm has a limited place here (his 'crumpled' pictures) and in all essentials Lundstrøm is static, an icon painter, a *nature-morte* painter like Bille.

Jerichau's *Hecuba* also has links with Matisse's dance and flute-players. They are products of the Muses. The triumph of Cubism was the defeat of this art in Paris. There was only Soutine. He also belongs together with Modigliani, but not with the Futurists. He is not an idealist-realist. He is a fantasist with a past who forces himself into the present – that is, Scandinavian.

As for myself, my closeness to Jerichau lies perhaps most in the actual *method* of painting, the rather dry character that form and colour scheme often take on as a result of doubt as to whether it is correct – reworkings, but interrupted by other works that cross over into the spontaneous. Poul S. Christiansen can also have a rather chalky character. My interest in the mental imagery and the extensive compositions also lies along these lines, perhaps most in a wheel-of-fortune picture (from 1953). In the battle with the big compositions I see a number of failed gambits from Skovgård onward in Danish painting, but throughout all these determined efforts, some of which by Larsen Stevns must be said to have succeeded, a feeling of great Danish art is building up. When this will really arise I do not know. But this determined will is something very interesting. I am not familiar with Wanscher's theories, more and more I want to look at Julius Lange's theories of form and compare them to Wanscher's and all the more recent ones.

Yours sincerely
Asger Jorn

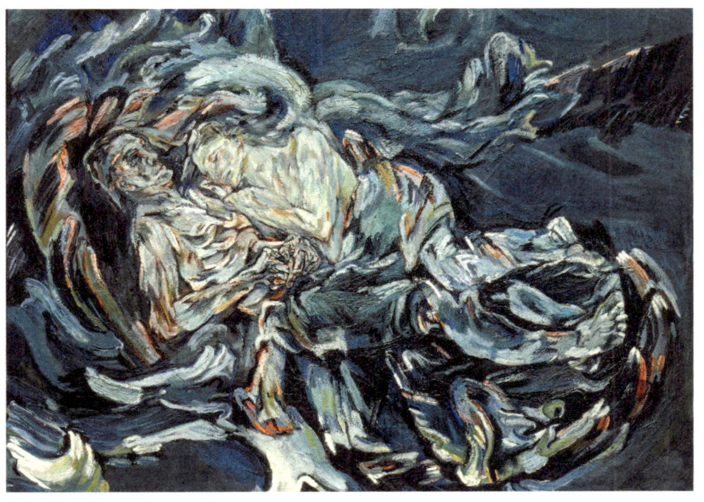

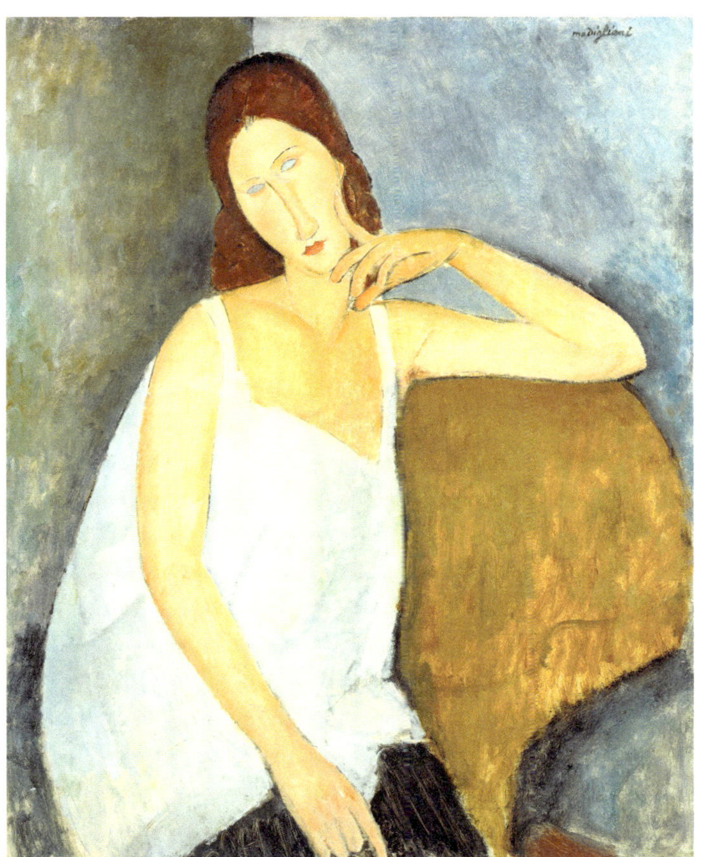

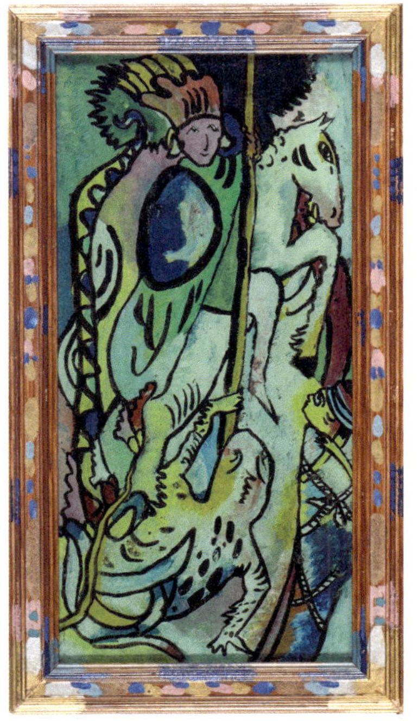

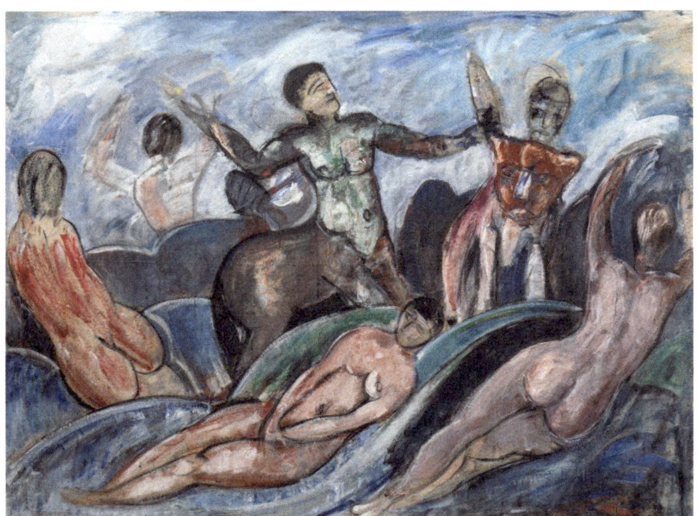

Oskar Kokoschka: *The Bride of the Wind*, 1913-1914
Oil on canvas, 181 cm × 220 cm. Art Museum Basel

Wassily Kandinsky: *St. Georg II*, 1911
Reverse glass painting, 30 × 15 cm
Städtische Galerie im Lenbachhaus und Kunstbau München, Gabriele Münter Stiftung 1957

Amedeo Modigliani: *Jeanne Hébuterne*, 1919
Oil on canvas, 91 × 73 cm
Metropolitan Museum of Art, New York

Jens Adolf Jerichau:
Sea Deities, 1916 (92)

1915
Barcelona, Madrid, Toledo

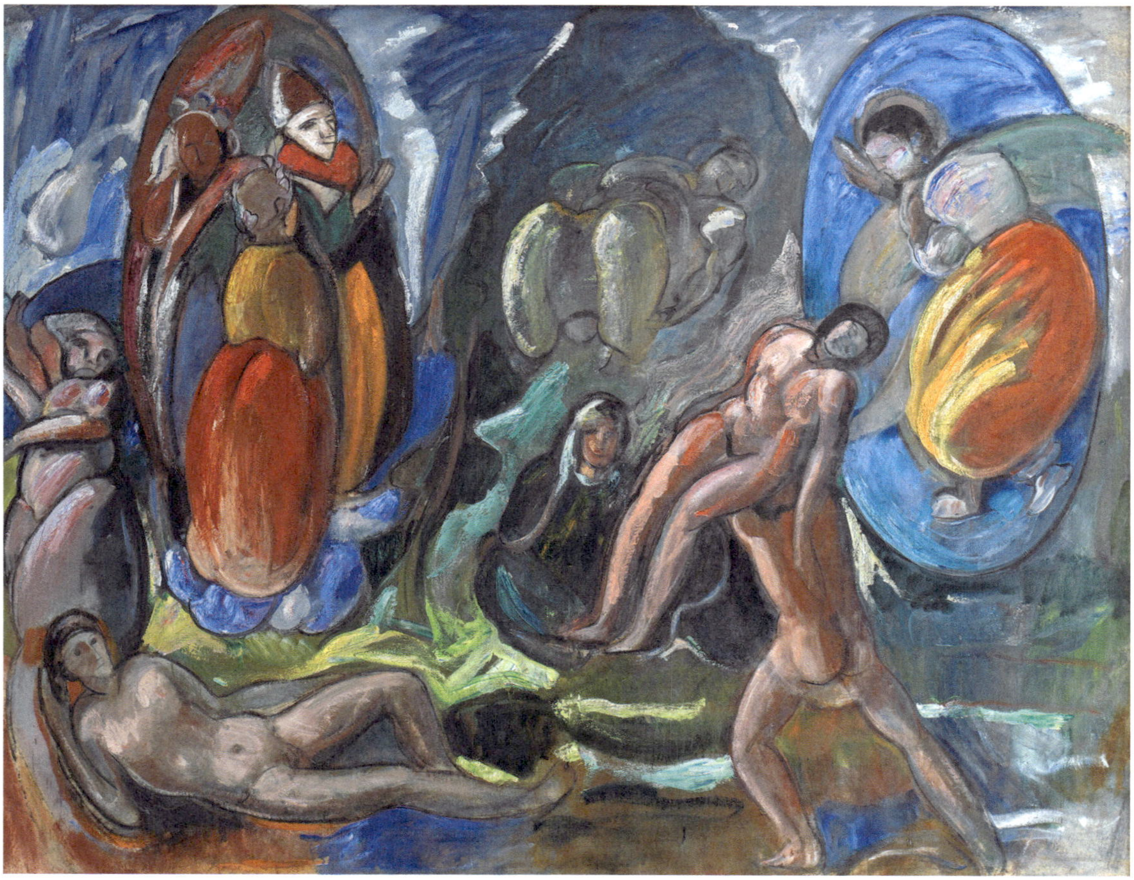

75 *The Creation of Eve. Composition. Opus II*, 1915

77 *The Spinners. Madrid (Copy after painting by Velázquez Las Hilanderas)*, 1915

Opposite page::
76 *The Great Cardinal. Opus III*, 1915

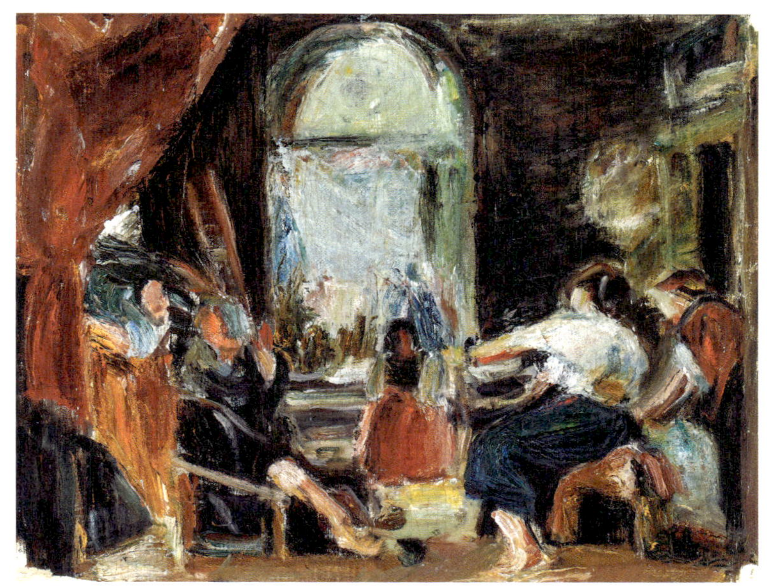

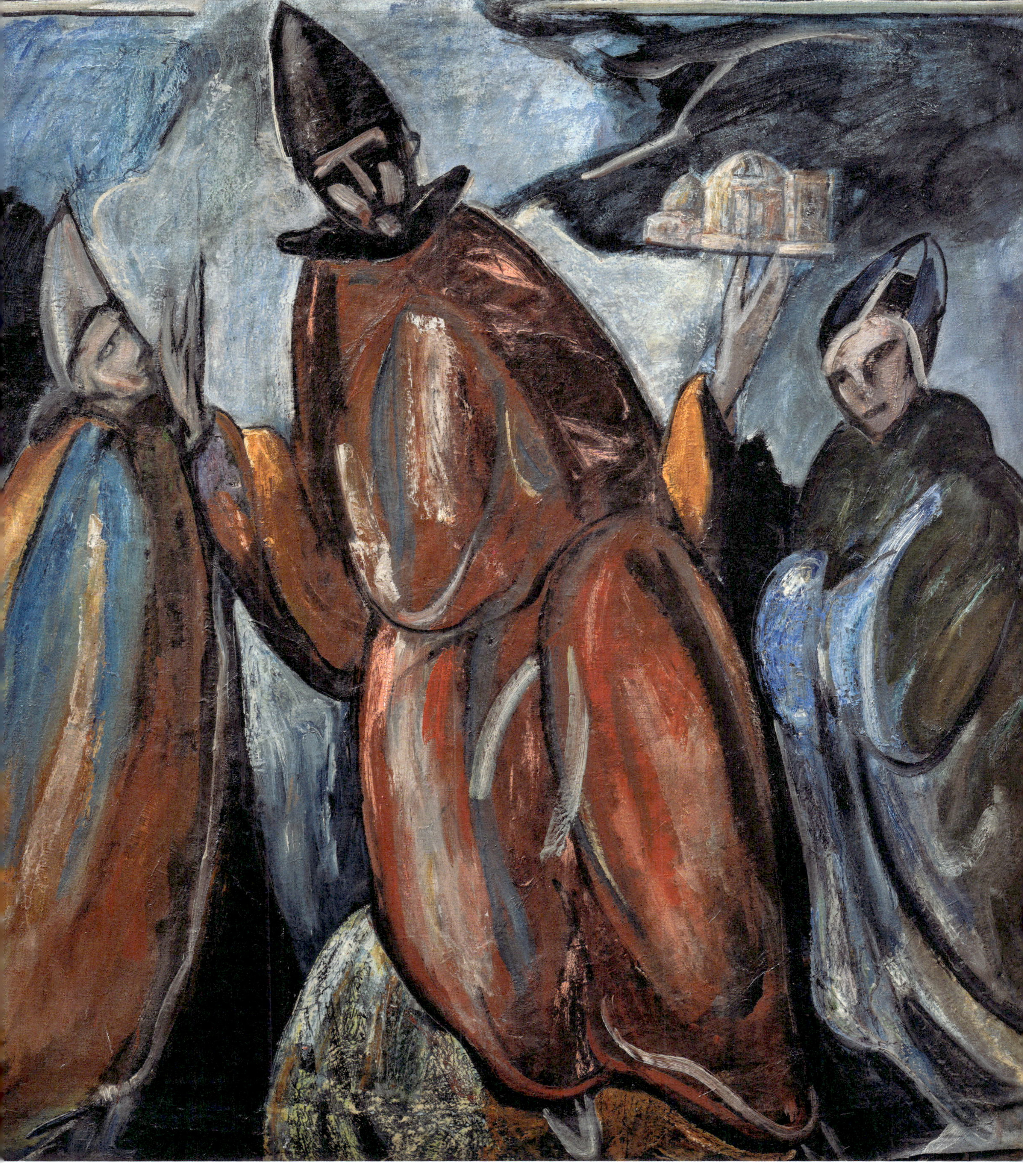

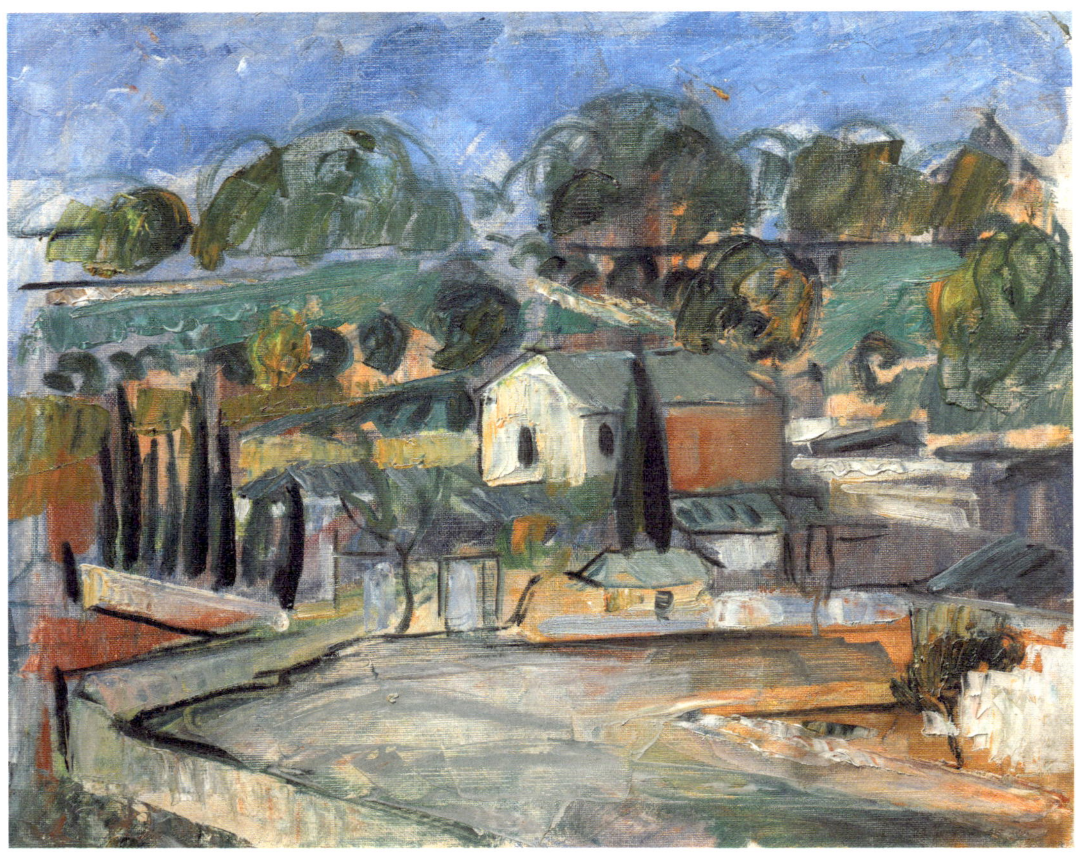

71 *View of the Monastery of Cristo de la Vega*, 1915

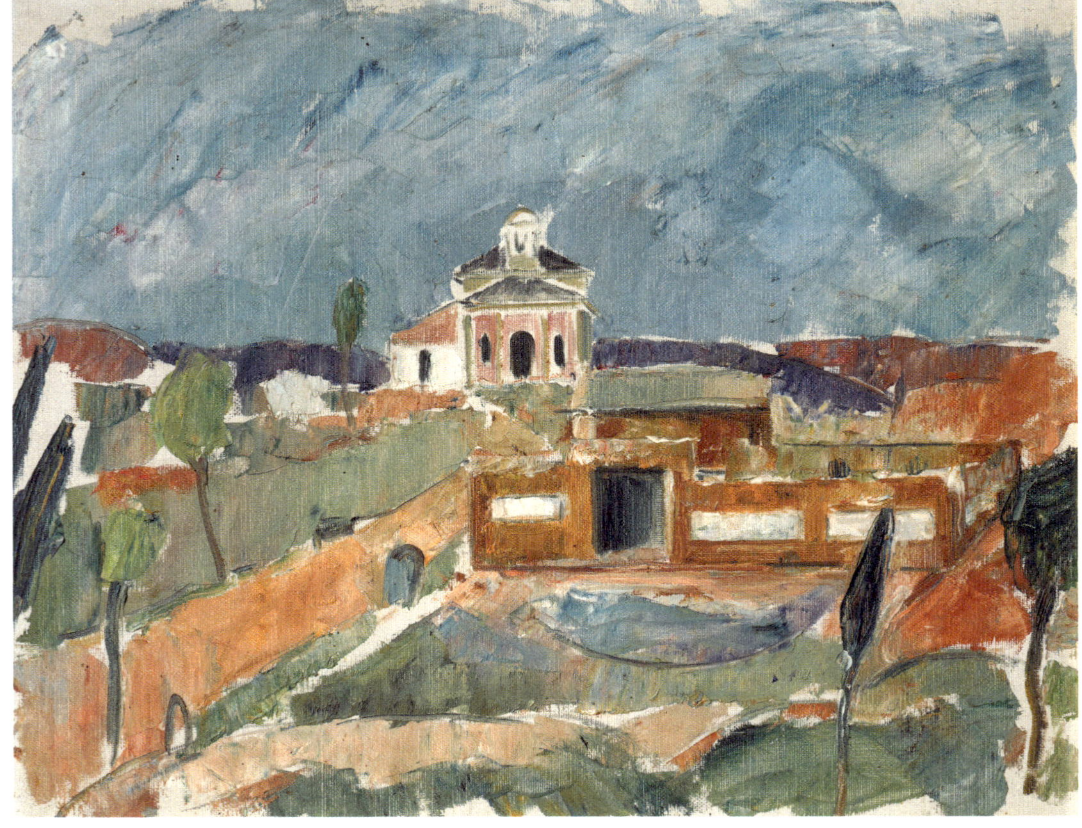

72 *The Chapel of St. Lawrence*, 1915

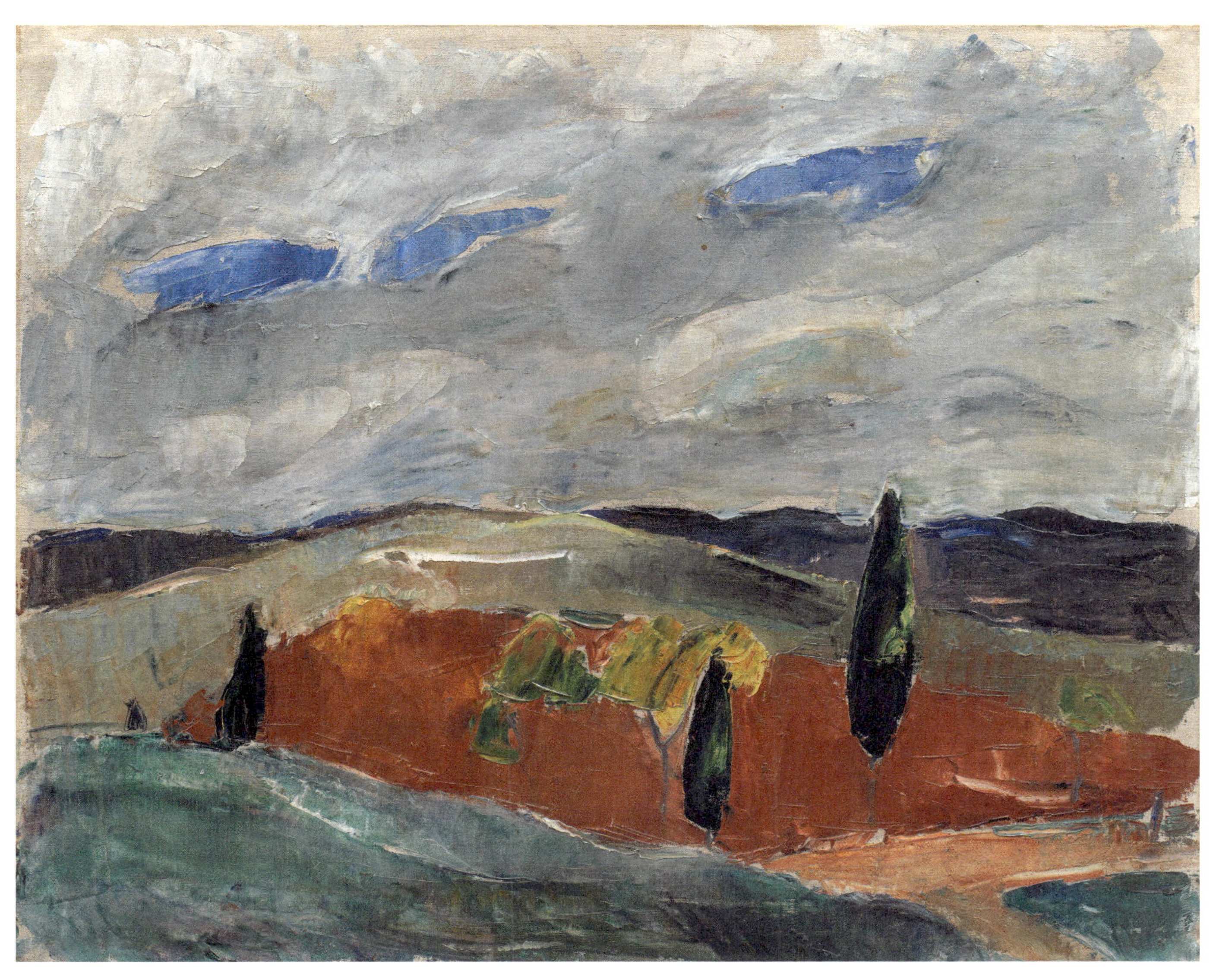

70 *The Cemetary Road in Toledo*, 1915

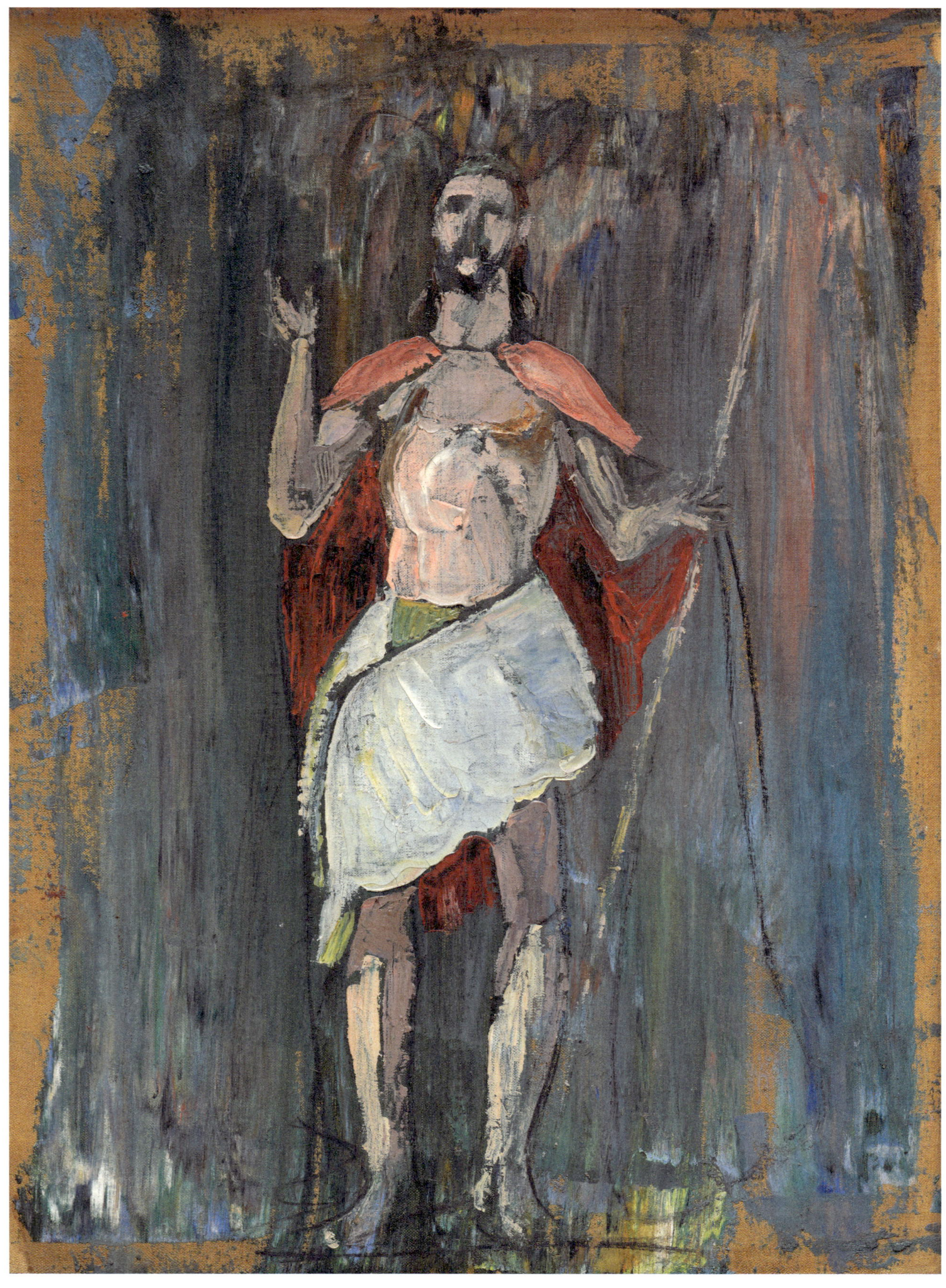

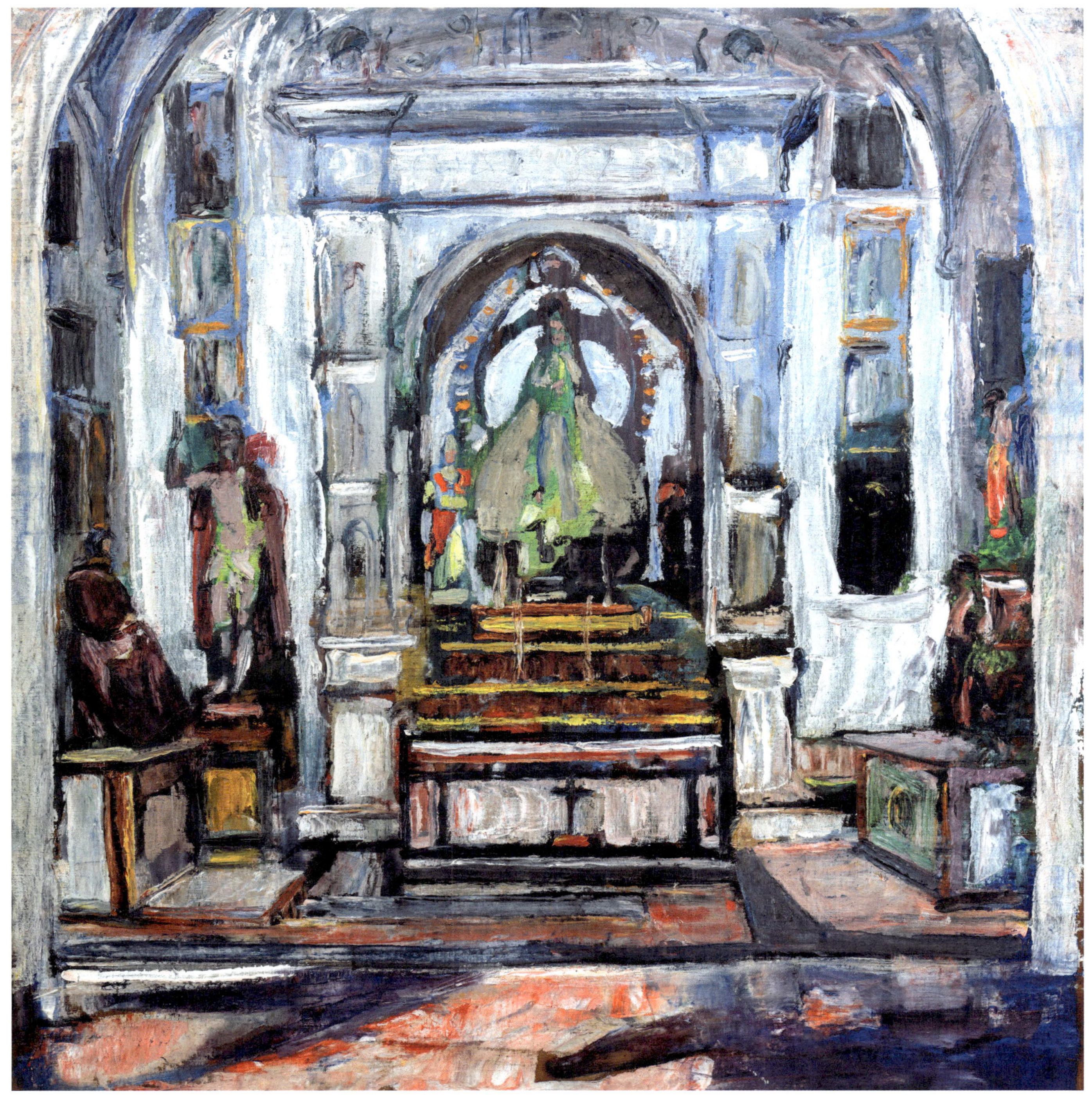

73 *From Domus Gothika*, 1915

74 *Dressed Figure of Christ in Wood*, 1915

Art and Artists in Wartime Paris

Marilyn McCully

France and Paris are the heart from which all the new ideas come or, at least, are promoted. Indeed, I am glad I now realize what Paris and all that means. I didn't understand earlier, and you will see that when I have got my thoughts together, I shall soon be able to work well and make good pictures.

Jens Adolf Jerichau[1]

During the first World War, the city of Paris's reputation as a welcome haven for artists and writers continued to thrive, with an influx of foreigners dominating much of the art scene. Because the theatre of war for the French army was principally in northern France, it was possible for soldiers to return home from the battlefields, as Paris itself remained relatively unscathed. Many artists and writers, including French painters André Derain, Fernand Léger and Georges Braque – to name just a few – had been called up for duty, and others, although not French, volunteered, such as the poet Guillaume Apollinaire and the writer Blaise Cendrars. As well as those who came back to Paris during wartime to recover from their wounds, others were allowed to leave the front for short periods of time for "rest and relaxation". Many foreigners also worked in hospitals, the ambulance service or provided social assistance, such as Americans Gertrude Stein and Alice B. Toklas, and the Russians Serge Férat and Marie Wassilieff. In this context, the enjoyment of Parisian café culture as well as gatherings in artists' studios offered plenty of opportunities during wartime for artistic exchange.

As far as the focus of innovative artistic activity in Paris was concerned, a notable shift had occurred during the years just before the outbreak of war in 1914, with many painters and writers moving from the Bohemian quarter of Montmartre high above the city to more bourgeois Montparnasse on the left bank. Apollinaire claimed that Montmartre had become a haunt for "fake artists, eccentric industrialists and devil-may-care opium smokers," while Montparnasse was the place where the "real artists" could be found.[2] Moreover, the French state had allowed a "free zone" to develop in Montparnasse, with little police intervention and an acceptance of unconventional behaviour. "The police kept the area free of the unsavoury elements that had invaded Montmartre: brothels and organized prostitution were not allowed, and criminal elements were kept away."[3]

In Montparnasse many artists lived in one of several districts that offered affordable studio space. La Ruche, for example, which had opened in 1902, was located at number 2, passage Dantzig, and by the time of the war, housed almost 200 tenants. The main rotunda of the complex, which gave the place its name as the "hive", had originally been the wine pavilion at the 1900 *Exposition Universelle*. This building had been reinstalled in Montparnasse, and studios radiated out from the circular structure like "wedges of brie";[4] small studios were also dotted around the garden. The Italian artist Ardengo Soffici remembered that over the years among the residents at La Ruche were "Frenchmen, Scandinavians, Russians, Englishmen, Americans, German sculptors and musicians,"[5] as well as fellow Italians. Amedeo Modigliani lived there briefly in 1911 and 1912 and returned in 1915 or 1916.[6] He had also lived for a time on the boulevard Raspail (in 1913), but he changed domiciles frequently and often painted in the studios of his friends.

Another popular area where artists and writers lived in Montparnasse was around the rue Notre-Dame des Champs, just off the boulevard Raspail. The collector and critic Wilhelm Uhde had an apartment there before the war, but like every other German in the art world, including the dealer Daniel-Henry Kahnweiler, he had left France. Anti-German sentiment was pervasive throughout the war and was a feature of the content of many illustrated journals, such as *Le Mot*. This large-format periodical was edited and illustrated by Jean Cocteau and Paul Iribe and ran from late 1914 through summer 1915. The covers and pages were filled with their drawings as well as those of other artists, including Raoul Dufy and Albert Gleizes. The

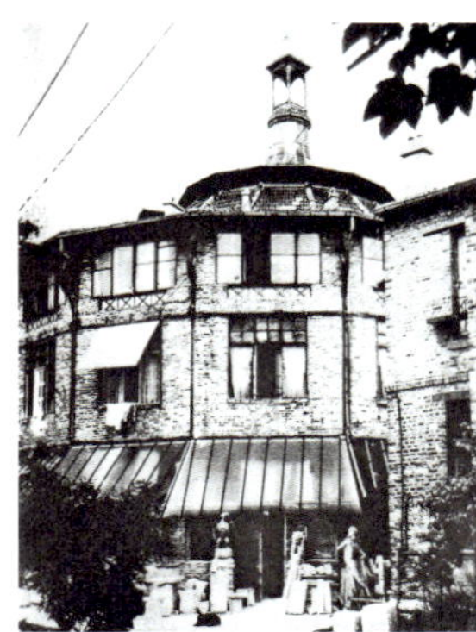

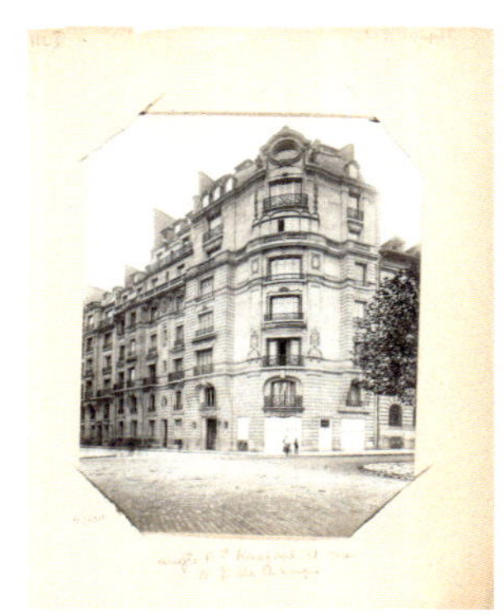

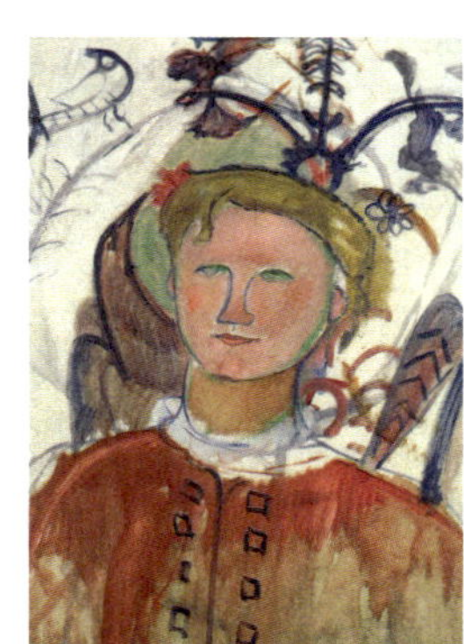

From the left:

The building complex La Ruche in Montparnasse, Paris, 1918

The corner of boulevard Raspail and rue Notre-Dame des Champs, 6th arrondissement, Paris, 7 November 1917

Amedeo Modigliani: *Marie Wassilieff*, c. 1918

elegant but vitriolic images that characterized *Le Mot* were usually aimed at the Germans and the consequences of war. Another of the journals that focused on war-related topics was *La Baïonnette*, which featured a marvellous drawing of Guillaume Apollinaire in uniform on the cover of the issue dated 8 March 1917. This image was created by the Danish artist Gerda Wegener, who had lived in Paris since 1912 and had become a friend of the poet, when he came back from the front in 1916.[7]

Among the Scandinavians who lived on rue Notre-Dame des Champs in 1915-16 was the Norwegian Walther Halvorsen, who would himself become an art dealer after the war. Halvorsen was well connected in Paris. He had been a student in the Matisse academy and not only was he a painter but he also often bought works from his fellow artists.[8] Others who lived on the same street were the Danish couple, printmaker and ceramicist Axel Salto and artist Kamma Salto. They were joined in the summer of 1916 by their fellow countryman Jens Adolf Jerichau. Salto recalled that "we lived above each other in a house that was set back from the street and had a little garden out front."[9] Jerichau wrote, "at last I am settled fairly inexpensively in a studio for which I pay 80 Fr. a month – which is reasonable in Paris – in a charming place here on the Montparnasse side not far from the Luxembourg Garden. Lis [Jerichau's sister] will probably describe the little garden etc. for you. I eat my meals in little restaurants in the neighbourhood and now and then I walk over to the right bank. Now I must economize in earnest if it is not to go all wrong [....] Nevertheless, I am working well at present, I think, and I am happy about that – otherwise I take no absolute pleasure in existence, nowhere do I find peace or calm."[10]

Jerichau and the Saltos apparently spent much time together: "We walked around Montparnasse by day and by night," Salto recalled. "Our conversation wandered through mystical labyrinths. [...] We played cards on the banks of the Marne for half the day and saw the summer clouds come and go. [...] Over meals, Jerichau could charm anyone; even [the dealer Ambroise] Vollard, who was so aloof, had to give in to his warm enthusiasm."[11] The compatriots could also frequently be found at the Café du Dôme or the Café de la Rotonde, around the corner at the intersection of the boulevard Raspail and the boulevard du Montparnasse. The Germans, whose regular occupation of the café led to them being known as the "Dômiers", had already left the French capital, but in spite of their absence, the Russian writer Ilya Ehrenburg recalled that at the Rotonde "from early in the morning the four or five tables in the hot, stuffy, smoke-filled back room would be full of Russians, Spaniards, South Americans, Scandinavians, people of many other nationalities, all exceedingly poor, oddly dressed, and hungry, who argued about painting, declaimed poetry, discussed likely sources for borrowing five francs, quarrelled and made up; someone would always get drunk and be thrown out."[12]

Finding enough money to eat and pay for a studio would be a constant problem for many artists and writers during the war, with dealers, collectors and publishers scaling down their business activities. There was also a curfew for cafés and restaurants, making it difficult to find a cheap meal at night, so that the artists' canteen that Marie Wassilieff set up in the impasse at 21 avenue du Maine was always crowded. The police considered her establishment to be a private club and allowed it to stay open late, so every night the canteen was full. Not only were meals served but impromptu musical performances and other artistic events often took place. According to the Swedish artist Gunnar Cederschiöld, "the walls were hung with paintings by Chagall and Modigliani, drawings by Picasso and Léger, and a wooden sculpture by Zadkine in the corner."[13] To celebrate the discharge from the army of the wounded Georges Braque, a banquet was organized in January 1917 in his honour at the canteen and was attended by many of the artist's closest friends, including Pablo Picasso and other Montparnasse regulars. Although he was not invited, Modigliani crashed the party and caused a commotion, but after Picasso and Henri Matisse intervened and the Italian was locked out, the evening continued happily without incident.

The American artist Walter Pach, who had come to Paris to make arrangements for a Matisse show in New York, recalled that opportunities to see art were limited during the war: "Paris was very quiet, even cheerful. [...] The Louvre being closed, knots of men and women would stand in front of art-dealers' windows to look at the pictures, which were still a necessity (even more than usually, for they were a symbol of the France men were fighting for)."[14] The occasional exhibitions that did take place were sometimes held in alternative spaces. The architect Amédée Ozenfant, for example, organized three group exhibitions in the showrooms of the dressmaker (and Ozenfant's girlfriend) Germaine Bongard, sister of the couturier

From the left:

Paolo Picasso: The painting *Girl with Bare Feet* in the artist's studio at rue Schoelcher, Paris, 1914. Photograph, 12 × 9 cm
Musée national Picasso-Paris

Gino Severini: *Armored Train in Action*, 1915
Oil on canvas, 116 × 88 cm
Museum of Modern Art, New York

Cover for the exhibition catalogue for Lyre & Palette's second exhibition, November-December 1916

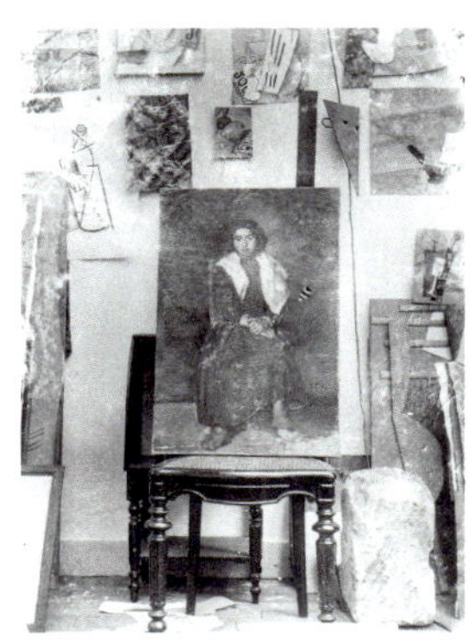

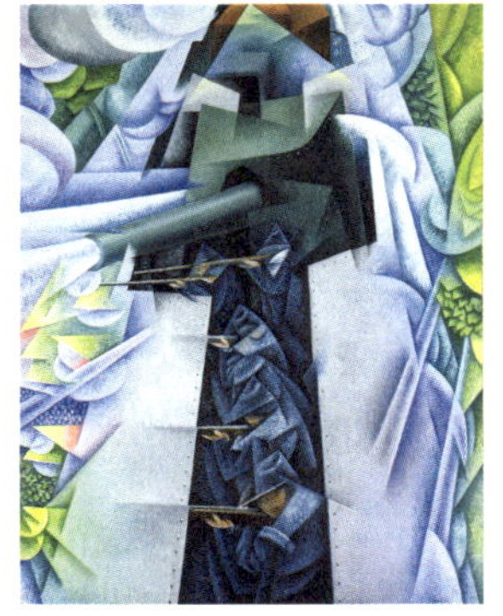

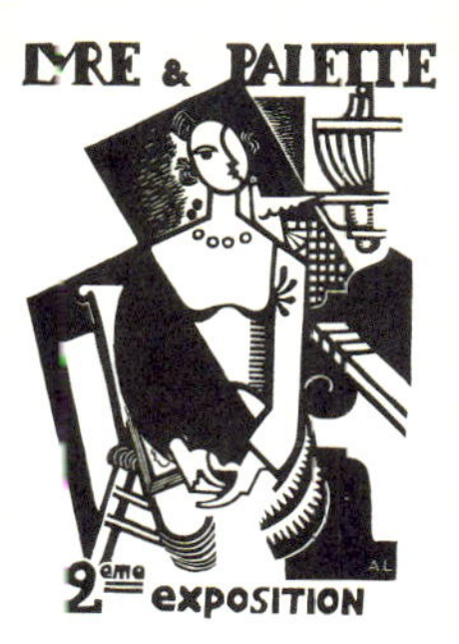

Paul Poiret, at 5 rue de Penthièvre, near the Elysée Palace. The first show, which closed on 18 December 1915, included works by Raoul Dufy, Derain, Roger de La Fresnaye, Auguste Herbin, Moïse Kisling, Léger, André Lhote, Matisse, Paul Signac, Picasso and Maurice de Vlaminck.[15] This was followed in April 1916 by an exhibition of drawings by Max Jacob, the sculptor Jacques Lipchitz and Matisse, among others. The last of the three shows at Bongard's (29 May – 15 June 1916) was devoted to painting, and the opening was marked by a musical evening featuring compositions by Erik Satie and Spanish musicians.[16]

A few gallery shows were also organized, including, at the beginning of 1916, the so-called *First Futurist Exhibition of the Plastic Art of War* at the Galerie Boutet de Monvel (18 rue Tronchet, near the Madeleine), where the Italian Gino Severini showed some of his recent work. As Kenneth Silver has pointed out, "Severini's exhibition was the most famous and most public demonstration of putting pre-war style (whether we call it Futurist or Cubist) to wartime use." Nonetheless, "the most striking effect of the show was [...] that he did not sell a single work from his war pictures."[17] Silver concludes that a changing attitude to recent artistic trends was becoming increasingly evident as a result of the war. In his review of the *Triennale salon* exhibition that was held at the Jeu de Paume in the spring of 1916, the critic Jacques Vernay predicted that there would be a reactionary wave in the arts in favor of classical tendencies that countered the excess of certain pre-war trends.[18] Cubism itself came to be regarded with suspicion, in part because of the pre-war success of its wide dissemination by German dealers among collectors in Austria and Germany, and therefore an affront to French taste.

Another of the spaces where various cultural events took place, beginning in June 1916, was the Salle Huyghens, which was located at 6 rue Huyghens in the studio of a Swiss painter named Emile Lejeune. "[The Salle Huyghens] was the high point of the Montparnasse adventure, and everyone, who has a name today in painting, literature, poetry, and music, made his debut in the basement located at the end of the courtyard. [...] Worldly Paris mingled in these sessions with artists in sweaters, who had come from the Rotonde and the Dôme and made a smoke screen with their pipes around these elegant people. There were, in this dingy, badly-heated studio, moments of rare artistic quality of a kind that occurs but several times in a century."[19] At the beginning, Lejeune arranged a series of concerts and showed the work of a number of Montparnasse artists, including Modigliani.

The collective known as Lyre et Palette[20] sponsored various events, including poetry readings by Jean Cocteau and Blaise Cendrars, at the Salle Huyghens, where the skylight in the middle of the roof had to be covered during blackouts. The dealer Paul Guillaume curated an exhibition for the Lyre et Palette, which took place at the Salle Huyghens (November-December 1916) and represented the first time that contemporary European, African and Oceanic art were shown together on an equal footing.[21]

In addition to organized exhibitions and cultural events, visits to the studios of Matisse and Picasso, who were both present in Paris during most of the war, were made by artists of different nationalities who were eager to track the progress of the two leaders of the avantgarde. The Spaniard Picasso was a non-combatant, while Matisse, who was forty-four when war was declared, had reported for service but had been rejected. Apart from some months spent in the south of France, Matisse continued to work in the studio he had set up in Issy-les-Moulineaux (a southwestern suburb of Paris, lying on the left bank of the Seine). There he opened his studio for weekly gatherings of artists, including the Mexican Diego Rivera, a number of Russian emigrés, as well as the Spaniard Juan Gris, whom Matisse had befriended in the south and who had followed him back to Paris.

In 1916, when Jens Adolf Jerichau and Axel Salto were spending time together, they made a pilgrimage to visit Matisse in Issy-les-Moulineaux. Salto recalled that in the house they saw the painting, known as *The Moroccans*, on an easel in the middle of his living room. According to Salto, Matisse discussed with his guests how it had been created: "The painter showed us how the individual parts of the composition were assembled, transformed and reworked to form a whole totality whose effect was purely decorative yet at the same time solidly based on observation and studies from life ..."[22] He then took his visitors to his studio at the back of the garden, where he was at work on the large composition known as *Bathers by a River* (Art Institute of Chicago). "Stricter, purer in style, in sympathy with cubist theories," Salto later wrote, "Matisse works here with greater and greater powers surrounded by the luxuriance of nature, which provides him with rest and renewal."[23] In the hallway, they observed one of Matisse's relief sculptures showing the back of a nude.[24]

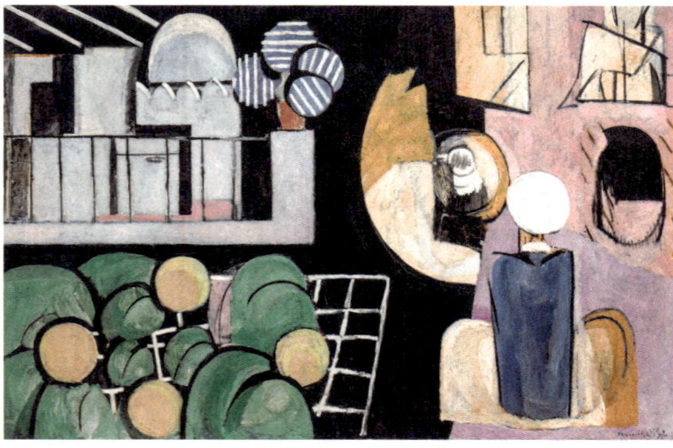

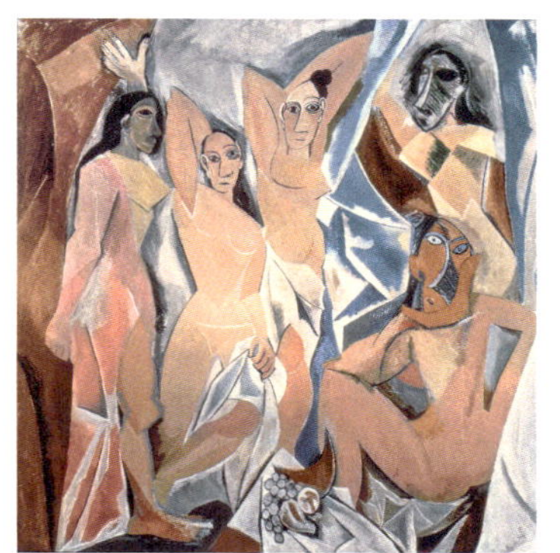

From the left:

Henri Matisse: *The Moroccans*, 1915-1916
Oil on canvas, 181 × 279 cm
Museum of Modern Art, New York

Pablo Picasso: *Les Demoiselles d'Avignon*, 1907. Oil on canvas, 244 × 234 cm
Museum of Modern Art, New York

Picasso had moved from Montmartre to Montparnasse as early as 1912, to the boulevard Raspail, although he stayed there for only a year.[25] He then moved to an impressive Art Nouveau building on the rue Schoelcher, overlooking the Cimetière du Montparnasse, and it was there that Axel and Kamma Salto visited him at the beginning of May 1916. Salto later published an account of this encounter in his journal *Klingen*. He describes the artist "as amiability itself" and that he showed them all of his possessions, including his collection of paintings by Le Douanier Rousseau, Derain and Matisse, as well as his own painting *Girl with Bare Feet* (Musée national Picasso), which he had done in A Coruña when he was only 13. Significantly for art historians, Salto also describes seeing *Les Demoiselles d'Avignon*, hanging in the studio: "Form is simplified, without appearing inorganic or degenerating into arabesques."[26] He goes on to relate the figures in the painting "to Javanese stone reliefs and Negro carvings. Modern French art has turned towards these new forms (Maillol, Matisse) and the artists of other countries come to them indirectly, through the French."[27]

At the time of the Saltos' visit, Picasso was experimenting with assemblage techniques and non-fine arts paints and other materials. "On an easel in the middle of the room," Salto writes, "among pots of Ripolin enamel paint, there hung a square box without a lid, containing some bits of wood fixed at an angle to the bottom and sides; another piece of wood, like the handle of an awl, was fastened so as to cast a shadow on the inside of the box. This produced an interplay of light and shade, angles and planes, in the little world within; here and there the effect was varied with stuck-on sand or bits of newspaper. This work had been created by Picasso with the utmost *objectivity*, taking precise account of the character of the materials and the balance of planes in relation to one another. His method of work, in which German aestheticians are so interested, is marked by a determined attempt to establish as concretely as possible the extent of the decorative elements of a picture, their material value and location in space."[28] One has the impression that Salto clearly recognized in Picasso's wartime work the emergence of a particularly innovative phase in his art. He concludes: "One feels that the possibilities are as manifold as combinations on a chess-board."[29]

As a result of the meeting with Picasso, Axel and Kamma Salto were invited, along with Jerichau, to the *Salon d'Antin* exhibition (also called *L'Art moderne en France*) in which *Les Demoiselles d'Avignon* was exhibited publicly for the first time. This show had been organized by the writer (and close friend of Picasso's) André Salmon at the Galerie Barbazanges in the right-bank *hôtel particulier* that belonged to the couturier Paul Poiret, who was also the sponsor. The exhibition, which ran from 16 to 31 July, included 160 works by 52 artists including Giorgio de Chirico, Raoul Dufy, Max Jacob, Kisling, Léger, Matisse, Severini, and Marie Wassilieff. The purchase of a caricature puppet of Picasso that she had made was probably made by Jerichau at the show.[30]

On 12 August 1916, a group of illustrious friends gathered outside the Rotonde, and Jean Cocteau, who had brought his mother's camera, took a memorable sequence of photographs of the assembled group. One photograph shows the Chilean painter Manuel Ortiz de Zarate, Marie Wassilieff, the writer Henri-Pierre Roché, Max Jacob and Picasso, while other photos included André Salmon, Modigliani, Kisling and Picasso with his girlfriend Pâquerette (one of Poiret's models). Spirits were high, and the group spent most of the day together. Roché, who would become an art adviser and screenwriter in the 1920s, wrote in his diary: "Lunch with Picasso, Max Jacob, Mme. Wassilieff and Jean Cocteau, whom I met for the first time on the *terrasse* of [the restaurant] Baty. The conversation was too witty and tired me out."[31] Four days later, Jerichau and Axel Salto had breakfast at the Rotonde, followed by a drive through the Bois de Boulogne. In the evening they dined together and attended a show, and then returned to their studios on the rue Notre-Dame des Champs. Shortly after they parted ways, Salto heard a gunshot from Jerichau's room, and climbing the stairs to the studio above, he discovered that Jerichau had committed suicide.[32] A memorial service was held on 20 August, attended by some of Jerichau's family, as well as Kamma and Axel Salto, Ortiz de Zarate, Kisling and Picasso. Their shared grief contrasted the gaiety of the gathering just days before on the boulevard du Montparnasse. Salto paid tribute to his friend on the opening pages of the first issue of *Klingen*, which he published in October 1917.

Marilyn McCully is a writer and has a Ph.D. in art history from Yale University. She has written extensively on Picasso and has organized exhibitions of his work all over the world.

From the left:

Marie Wassilieff's caricature puppet of Picasso

Manuel Ortiz de Zarate, Max Jacob, Moïse Kisling, Pâquerette and Picasso at Café de la Rotonde, Paris 1916. Photo by Jean Cocteau

Cover of the first issue of the journal *Klingen*, October 1917

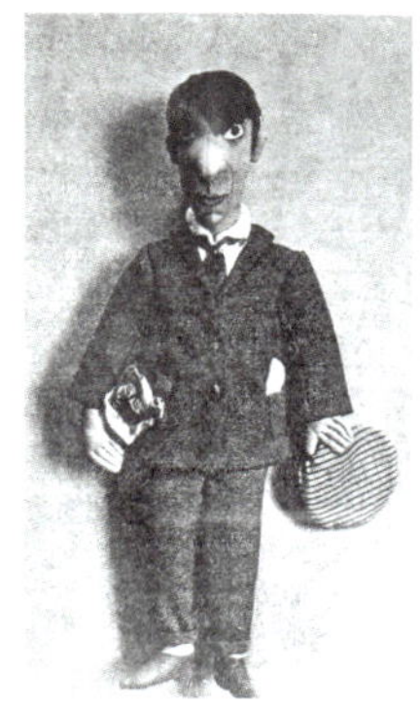

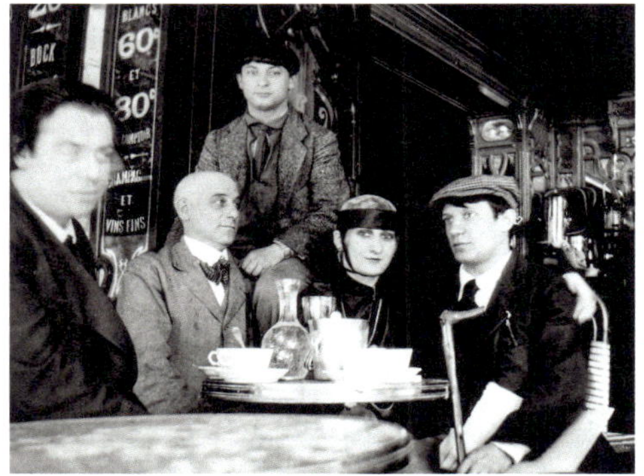

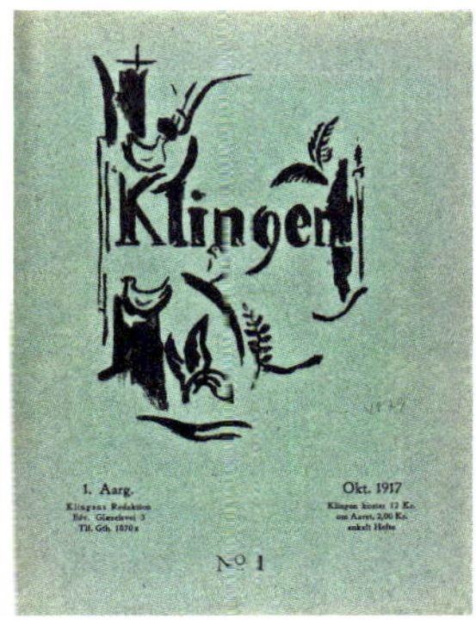

1916
Paris

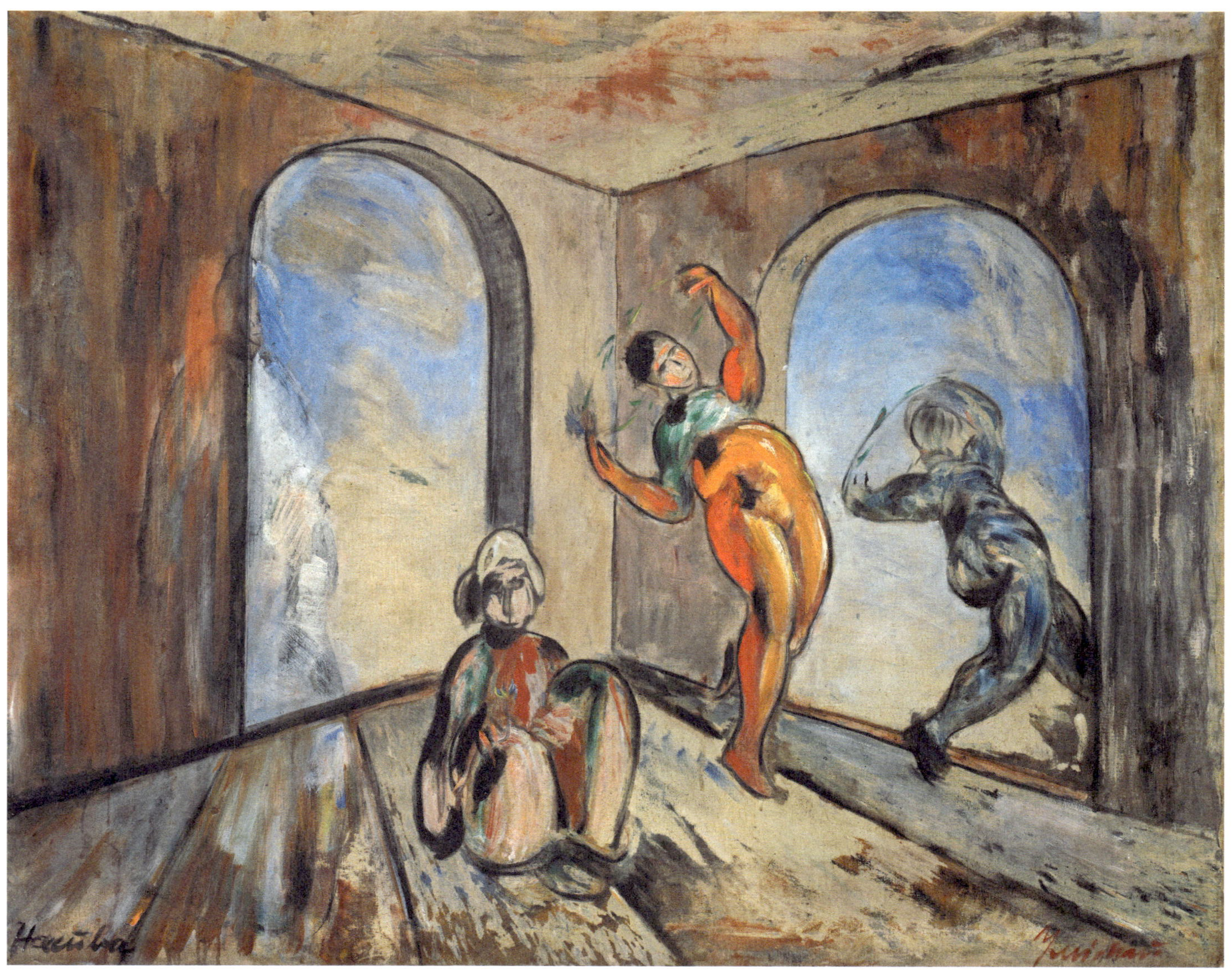

95 *Hecuba*, 1916

93 *Dante*, 1916

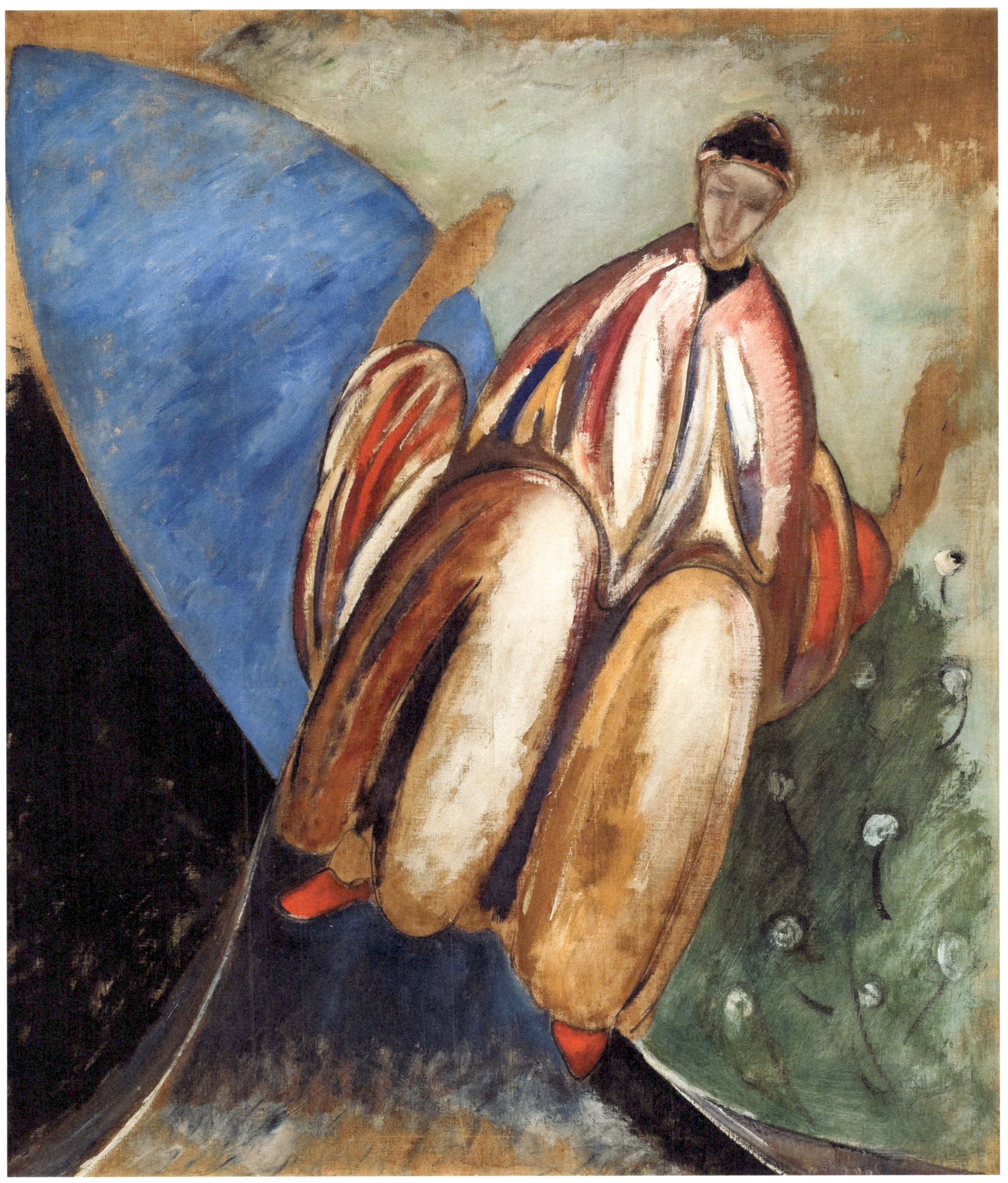

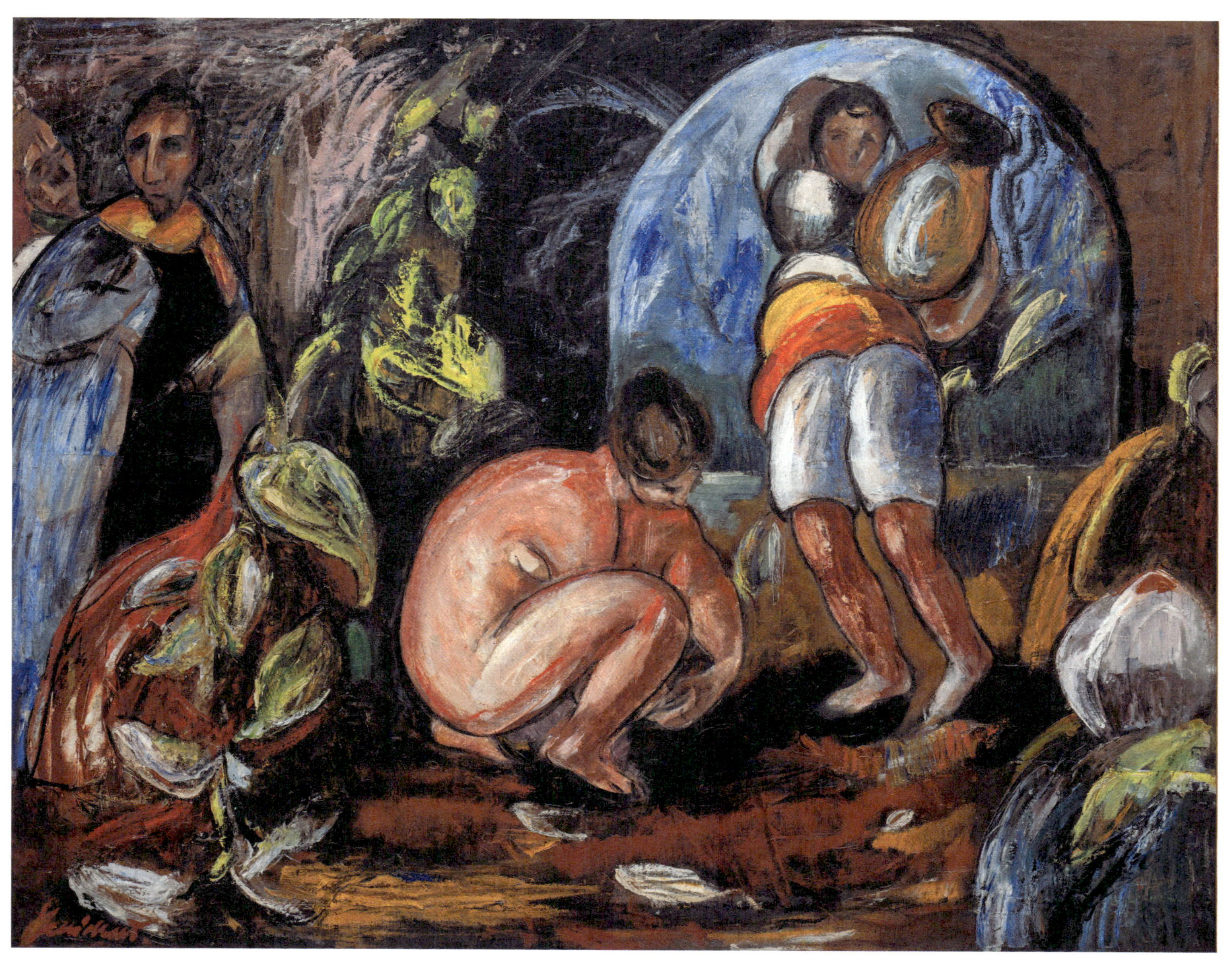

96 *Susanna Bathing*, 1916

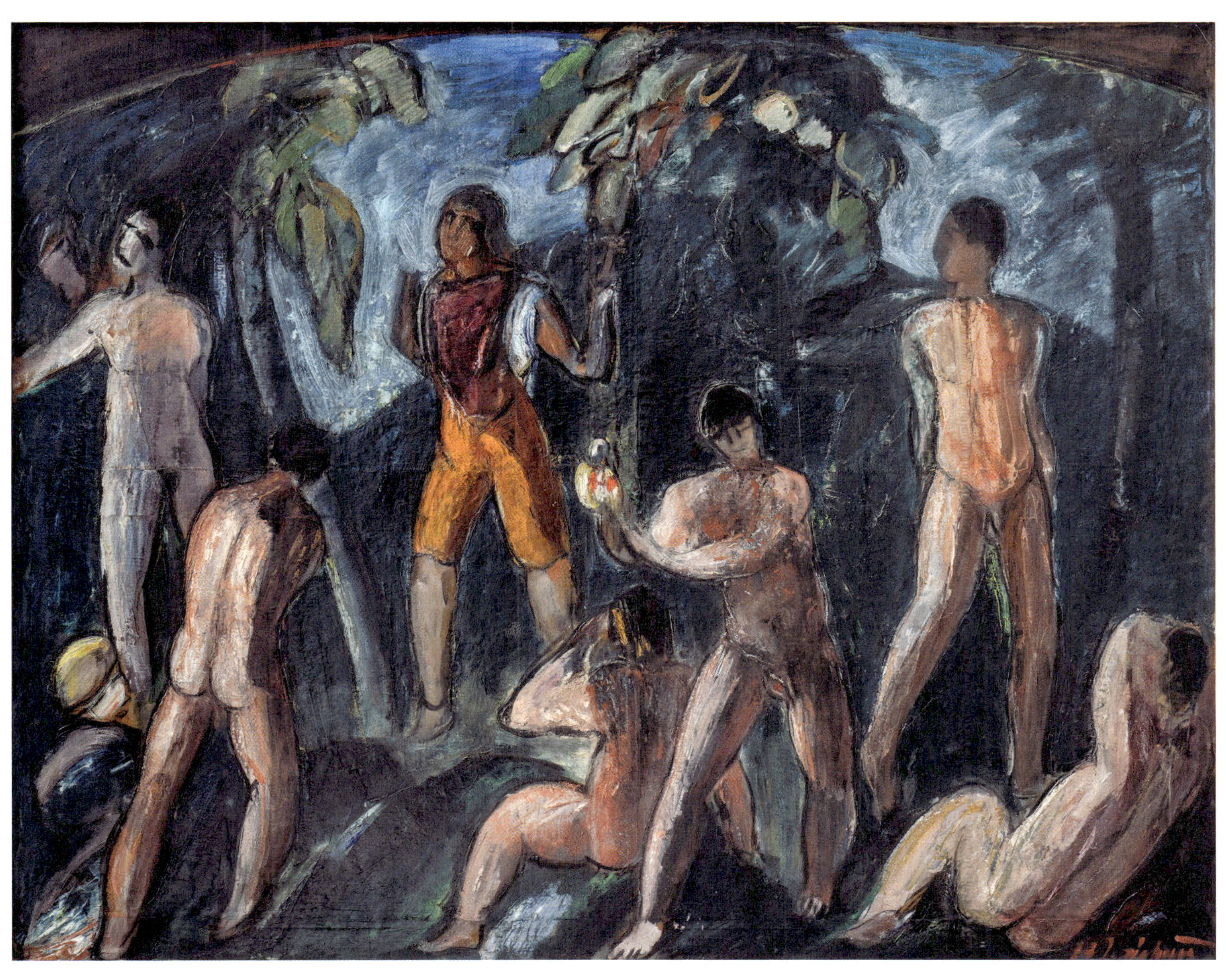

94 *The Golden Bird. From the Glorious Times of Ancient Greece. Opus III*, 1916

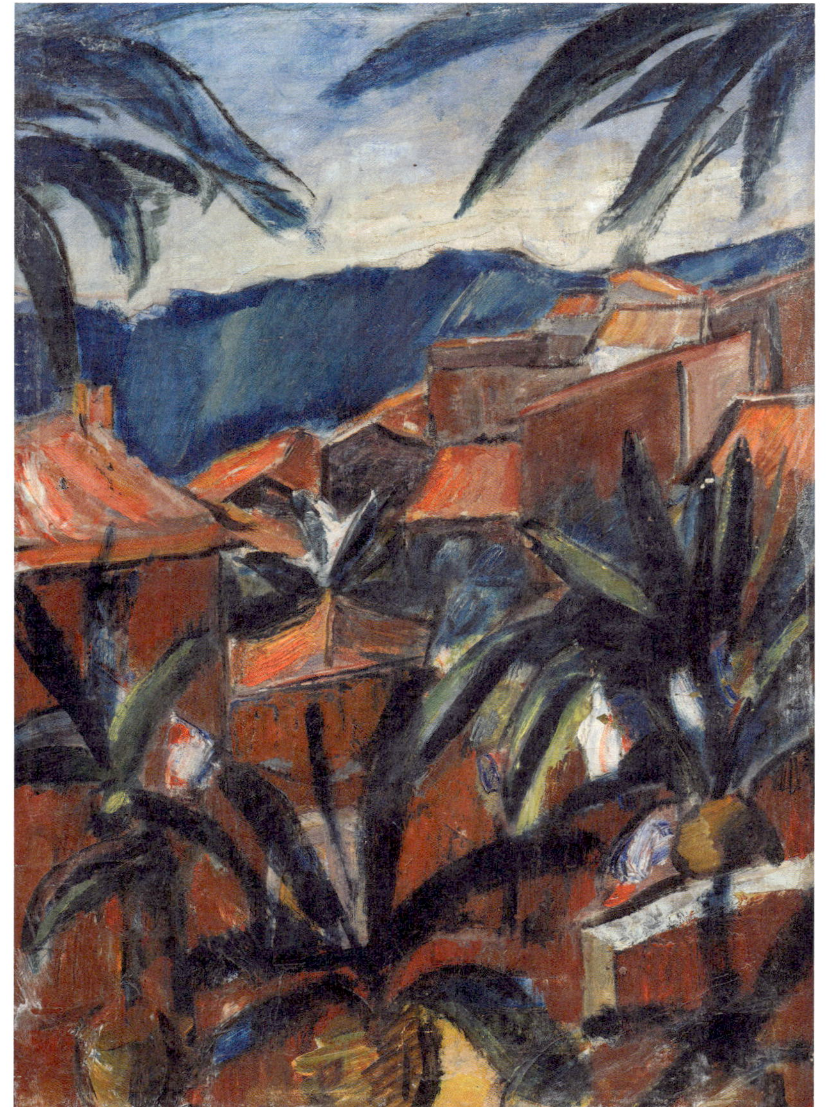

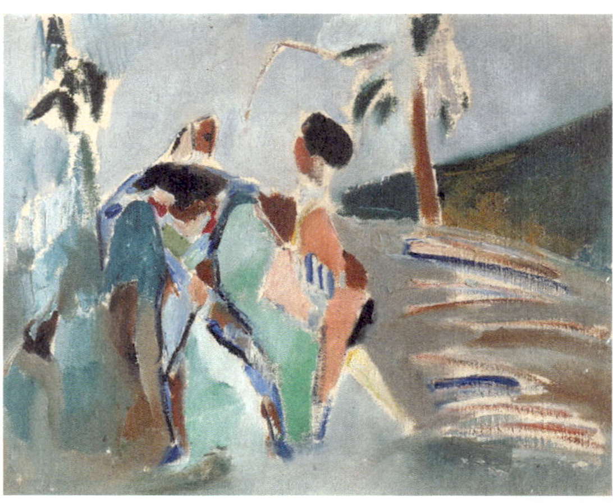

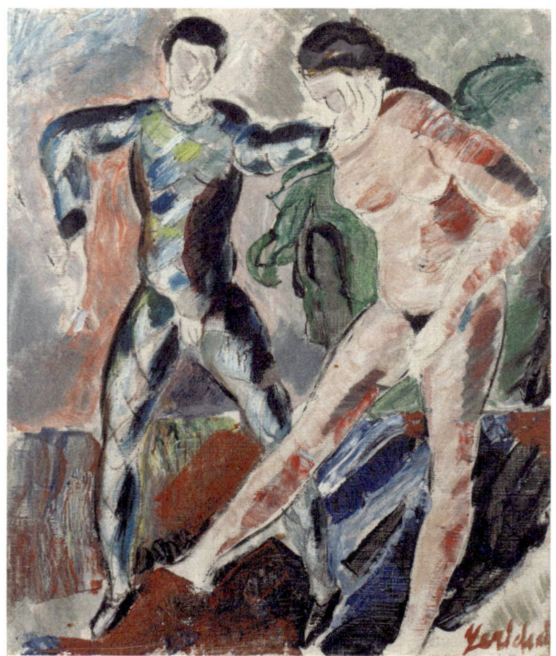

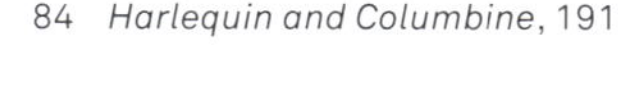

84 *Harlequin and Columbine*, 1916

83 *Harlequin and Columbine,* 1916

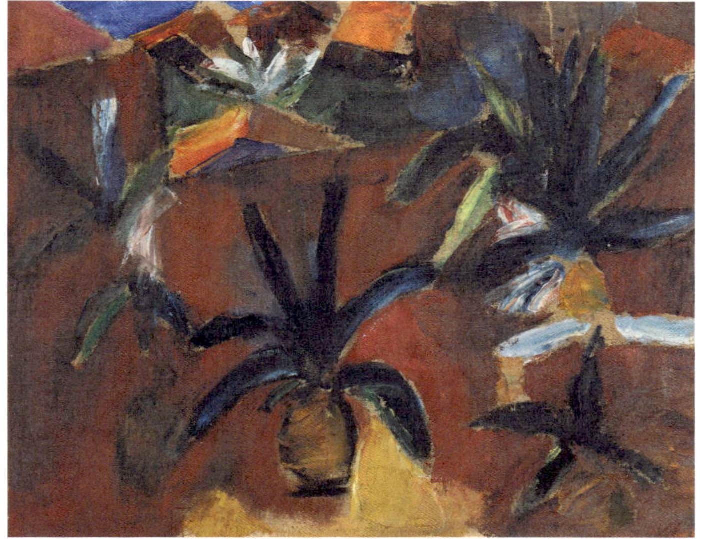

80 *Landscape*, 1916

81 *Landscape*, 1916

85 *Composition with a Centaur*, 1916

78 *Landscape*, 1916

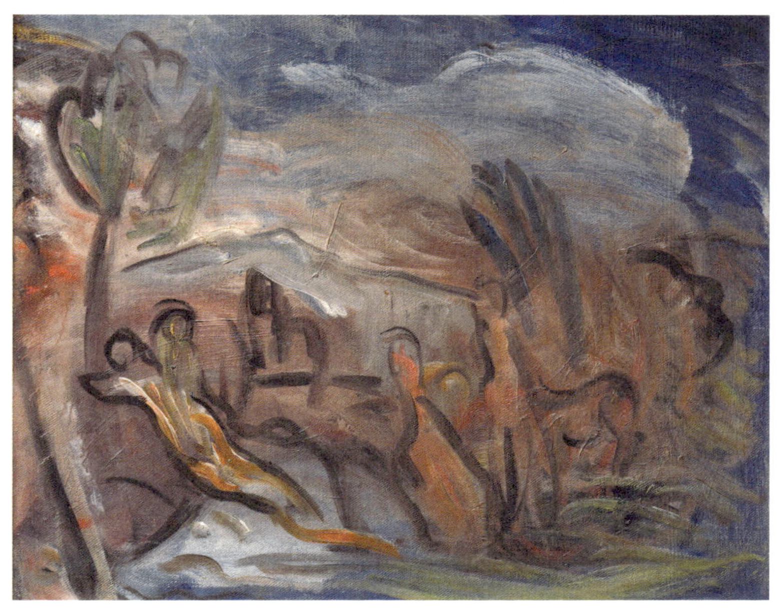

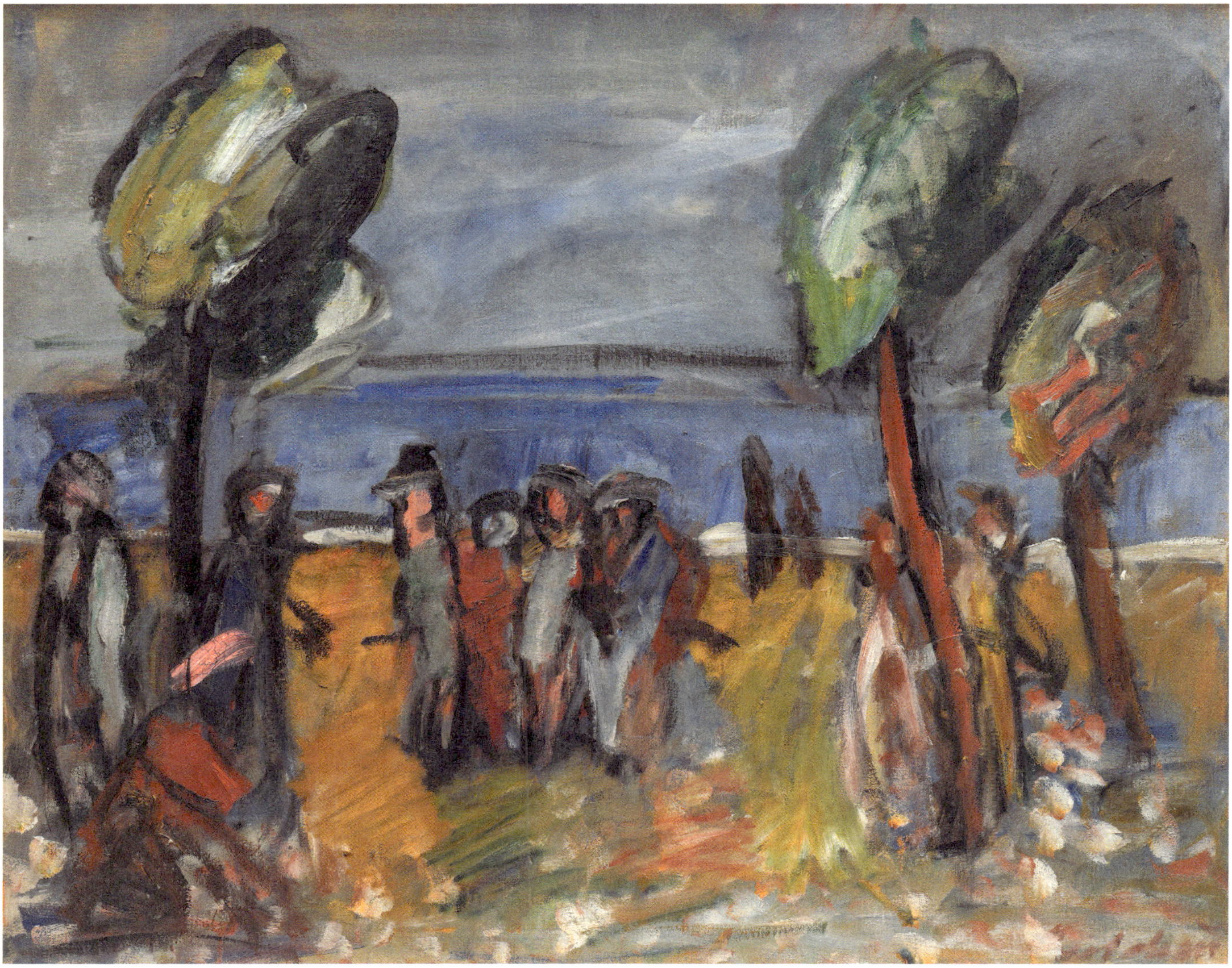

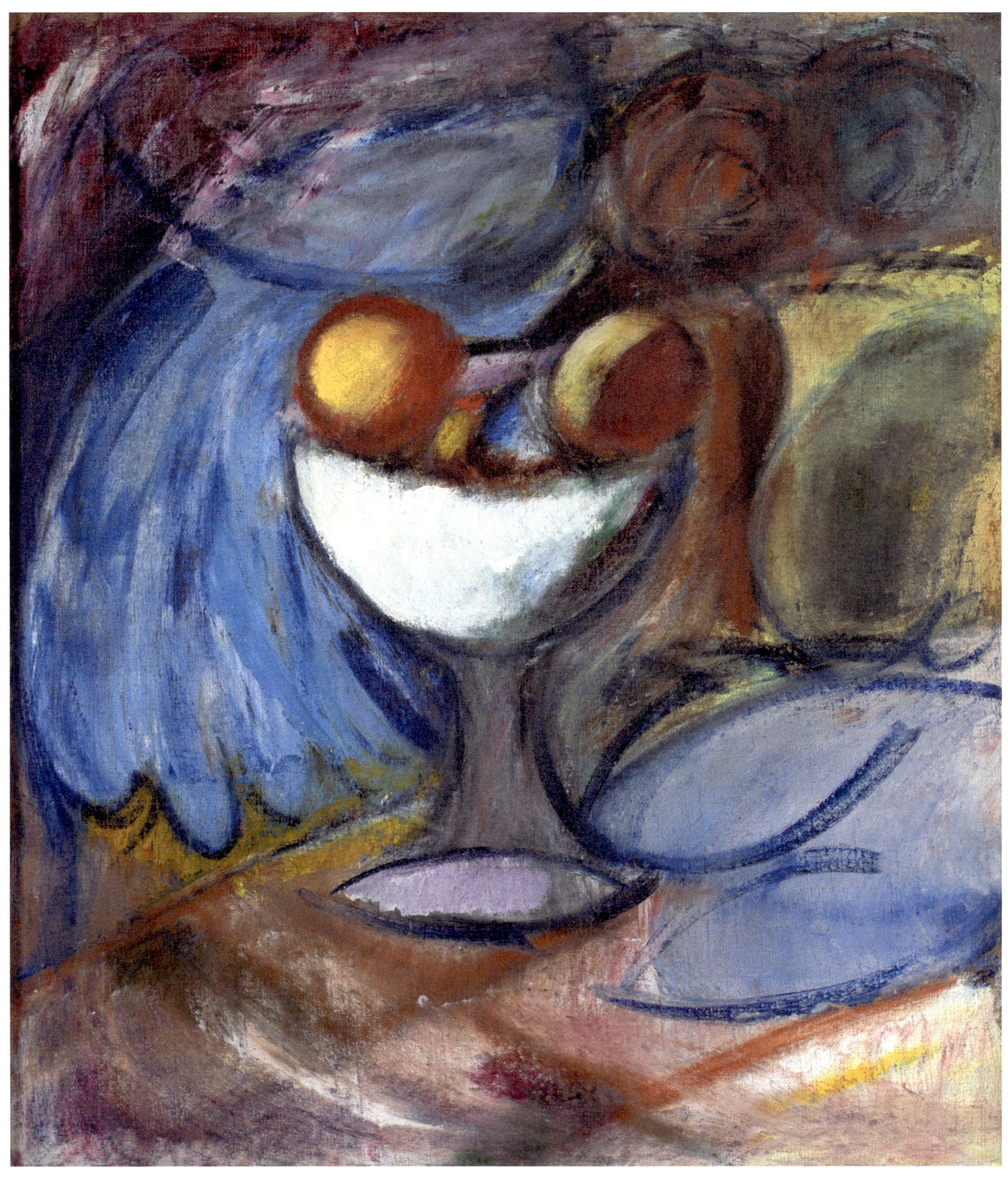

82 *Still Life*, 1916

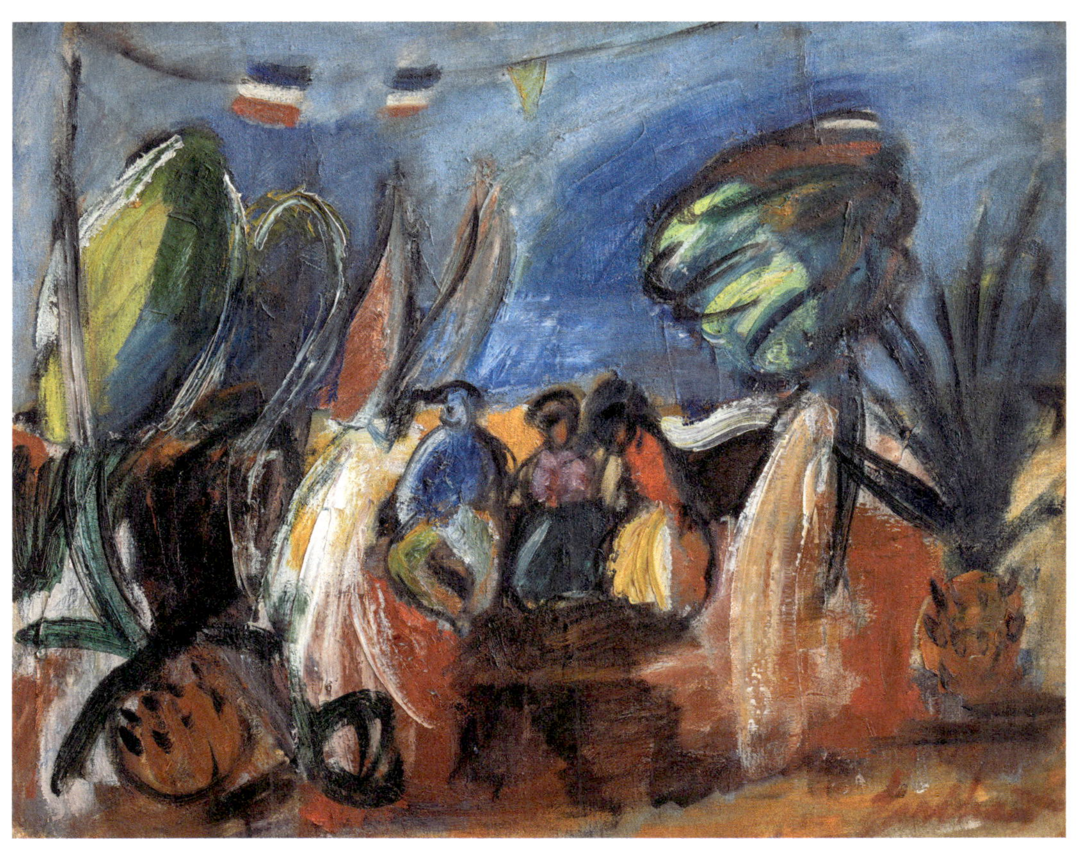

79 *At the Pier*, 1916

90 *The Graves of Fallen Warriors*, 1916

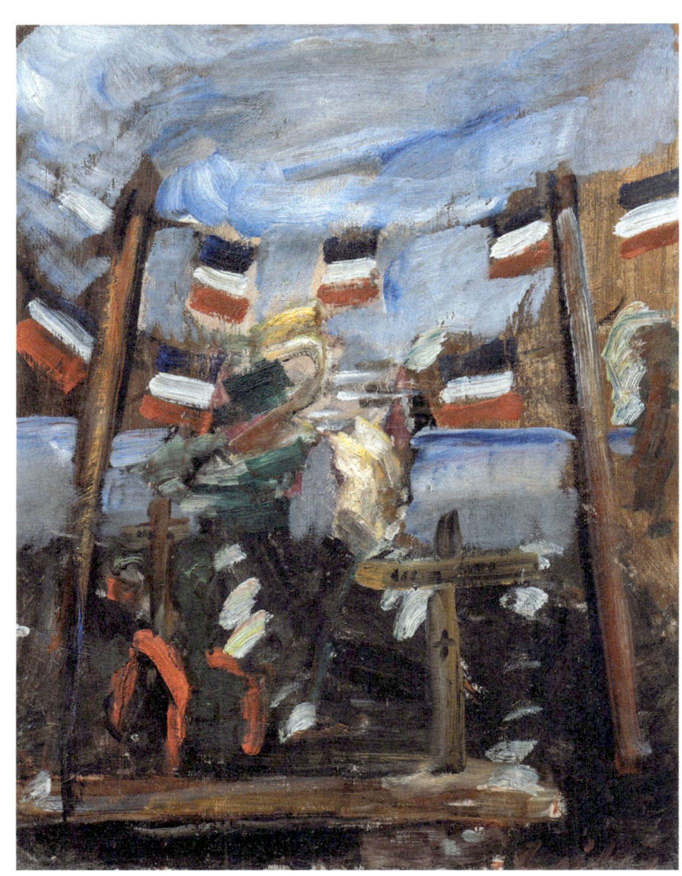

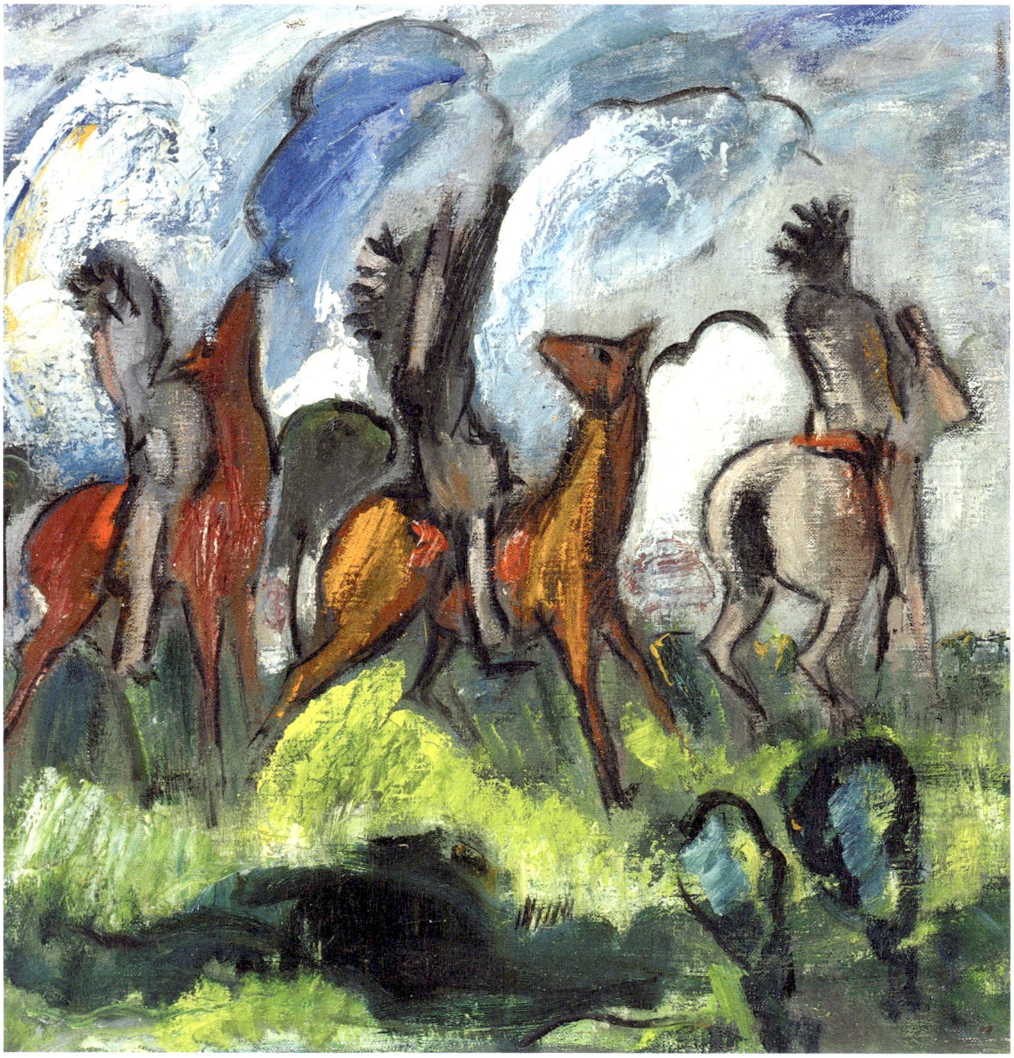

89 *Native Americans on the Prairie*, 1916

88 *The Dragon Lion*, 1916

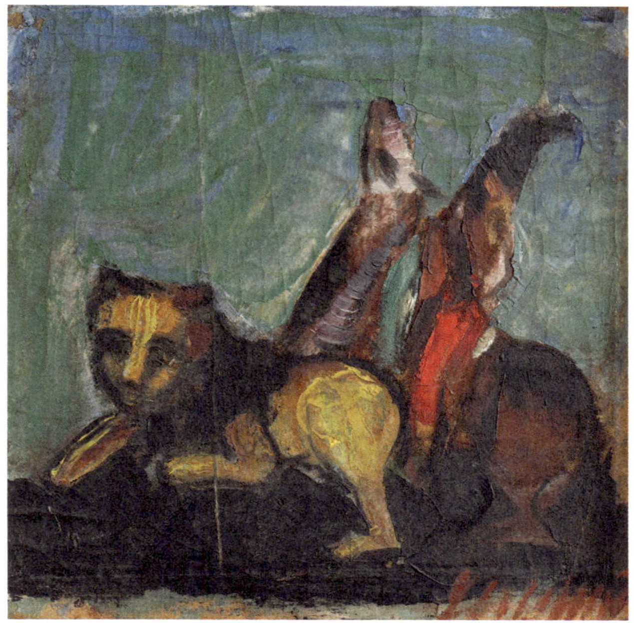

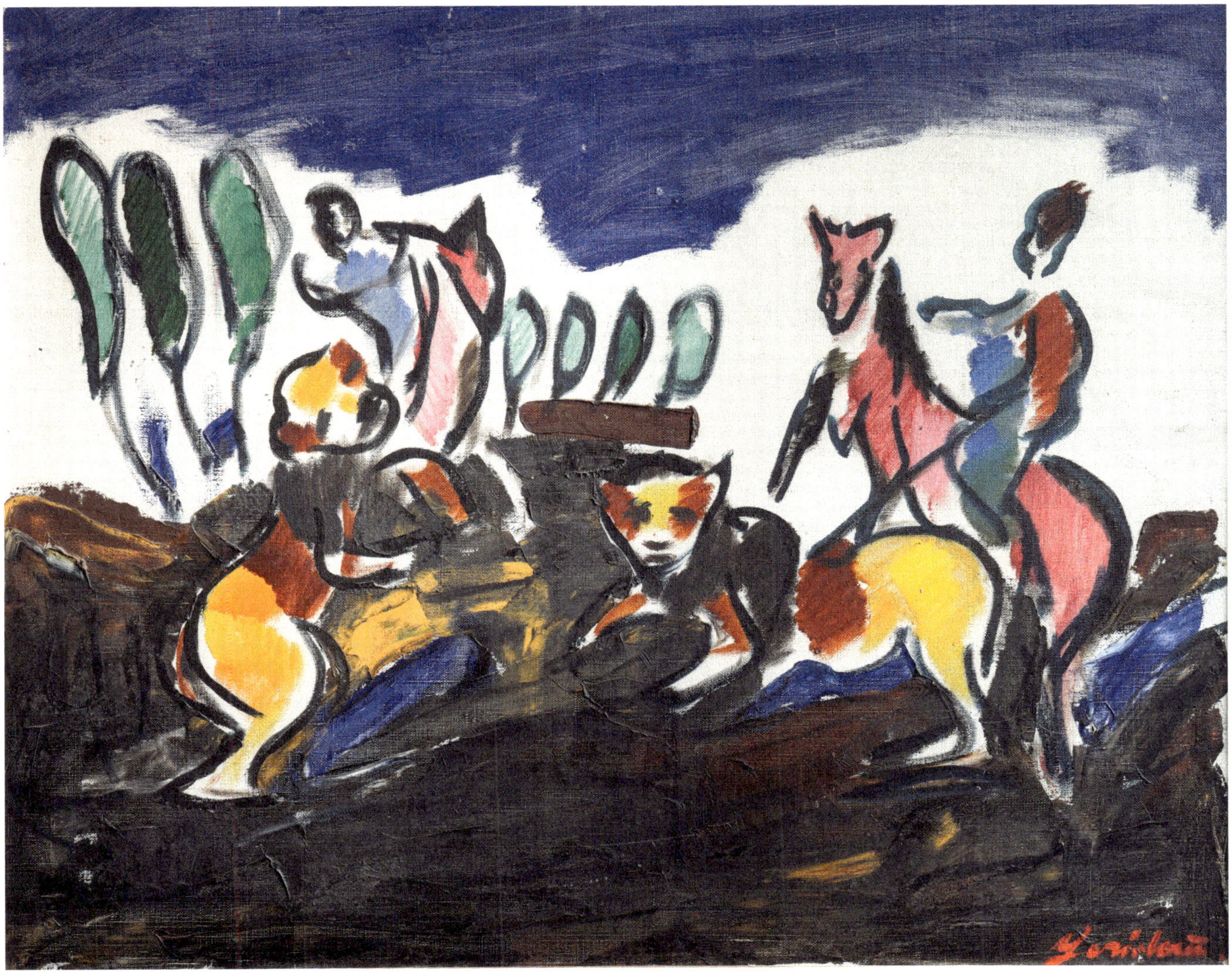

86 *Composition with Riders and Lions*, 1916

87 *The Dragon Lion. Sketch*, 1916

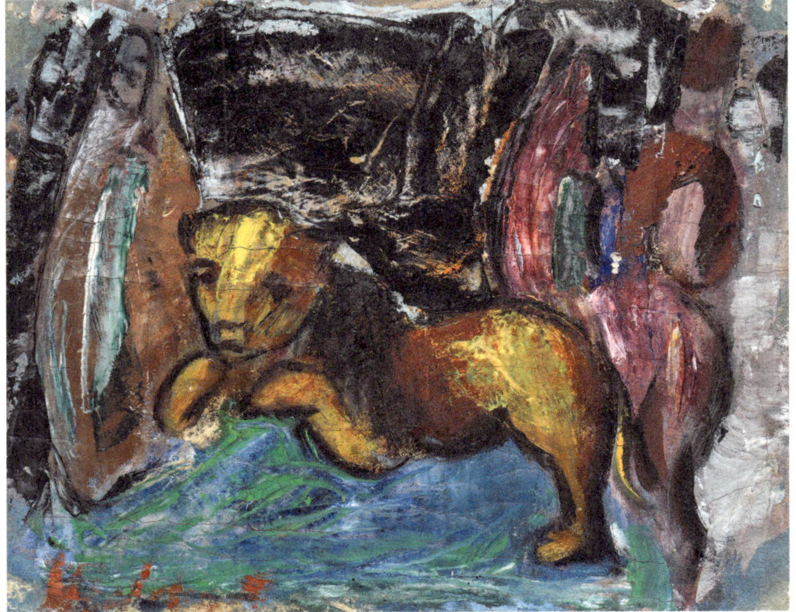

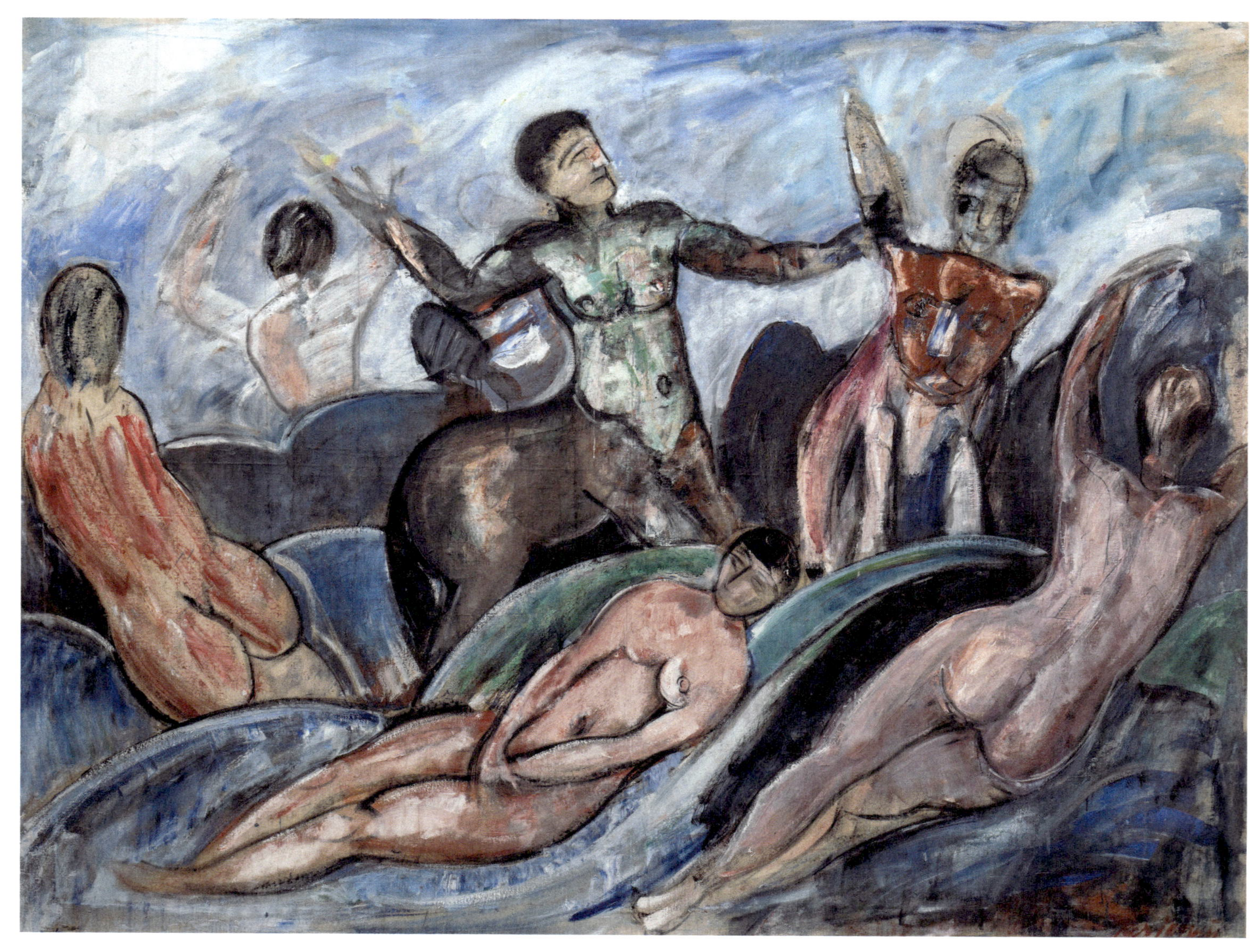

92 *Sea Deities*, 1916

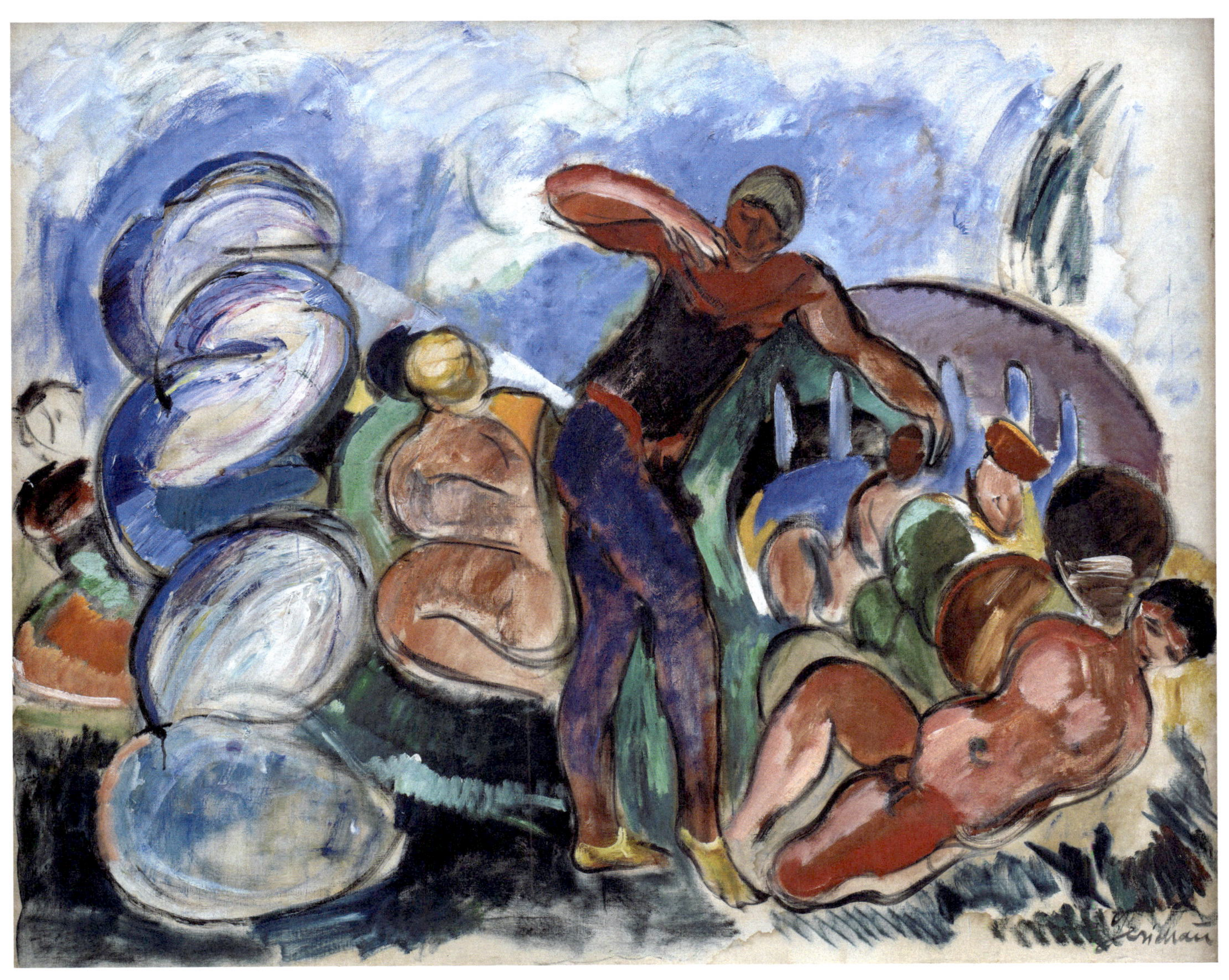

91 *Composition*, 1916

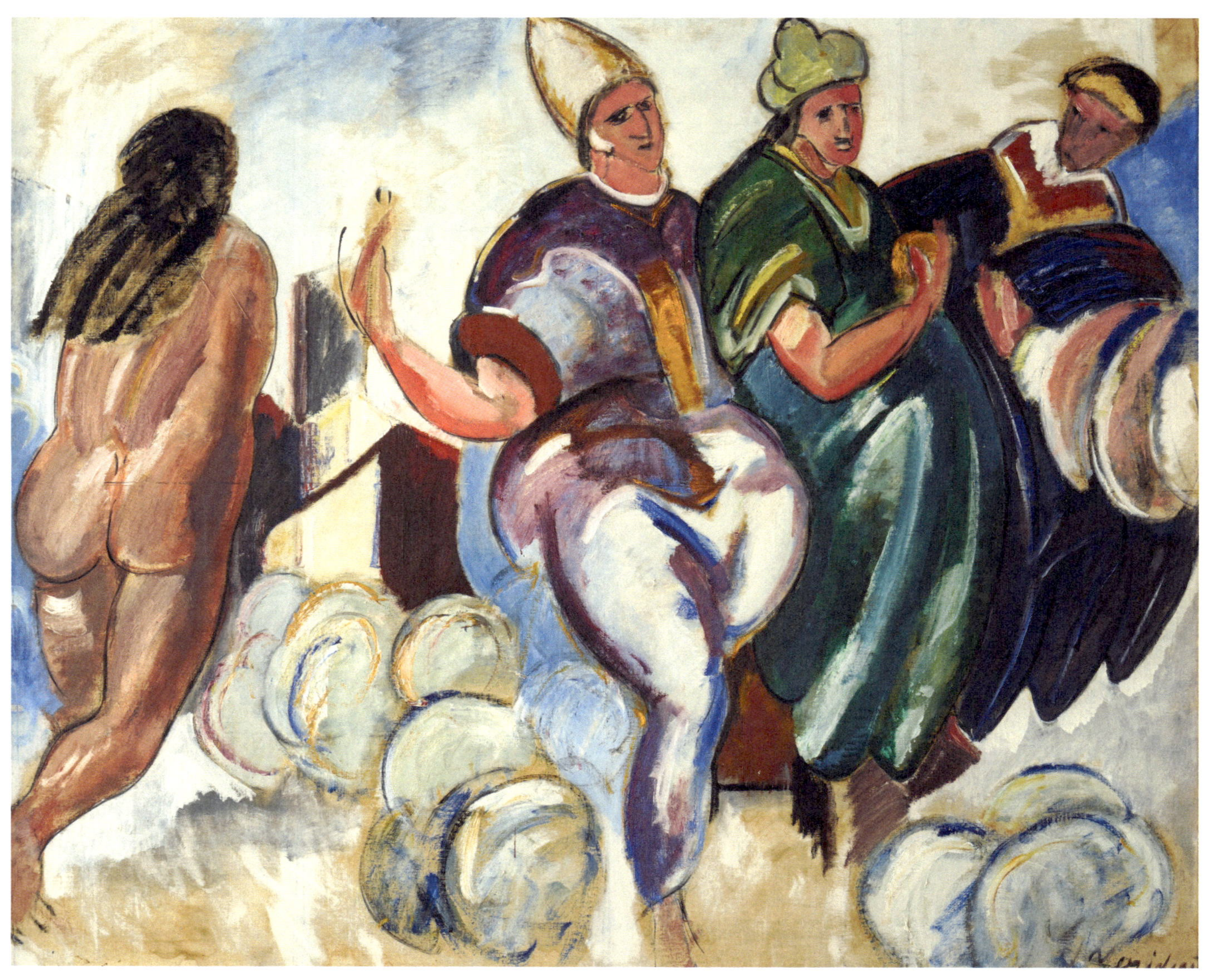

97 *The Magi and the Whore of Babylon*, 1916

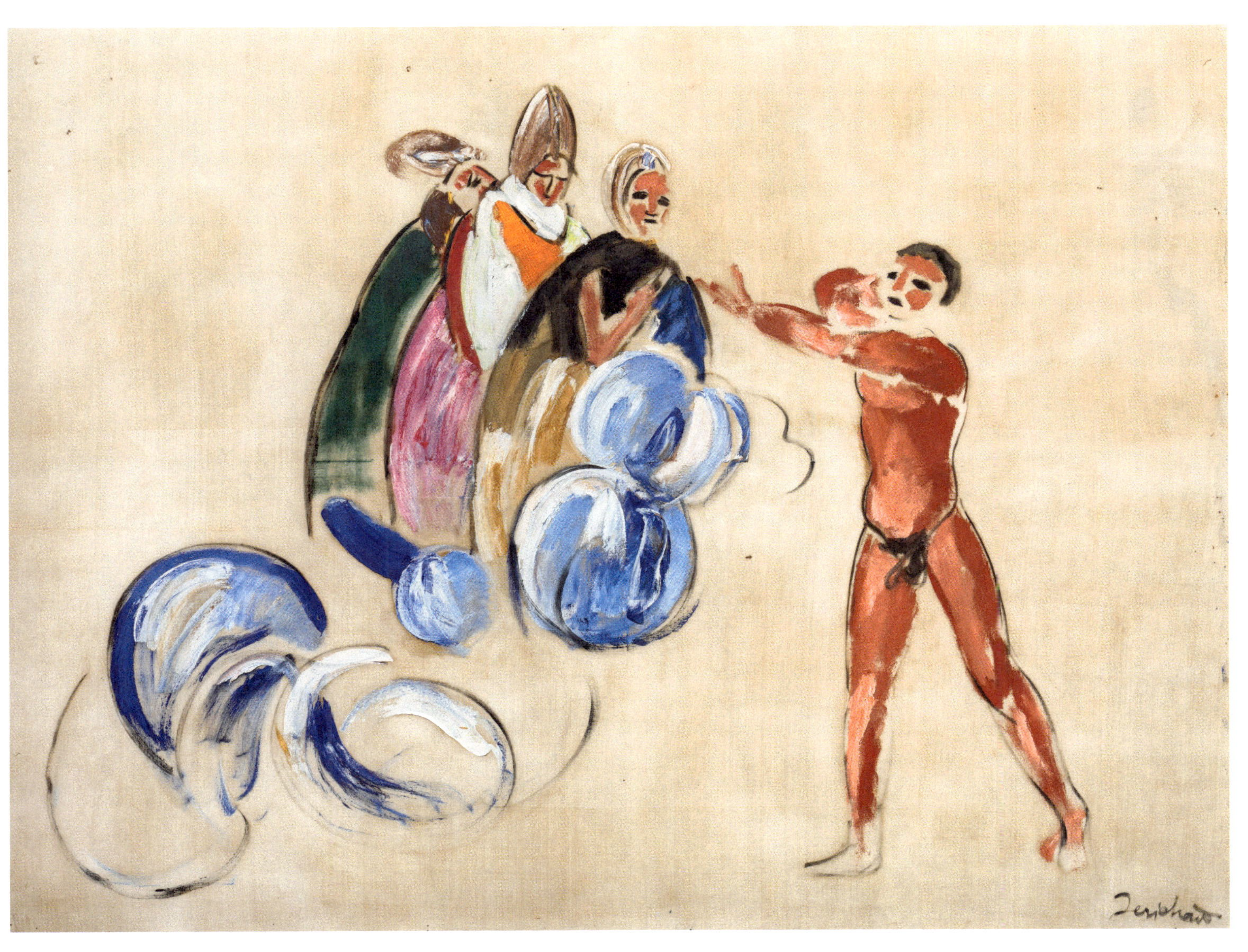

98 *The Ancestors Beckon*, 1916

Jens Adolf Jerichau
1890-1916

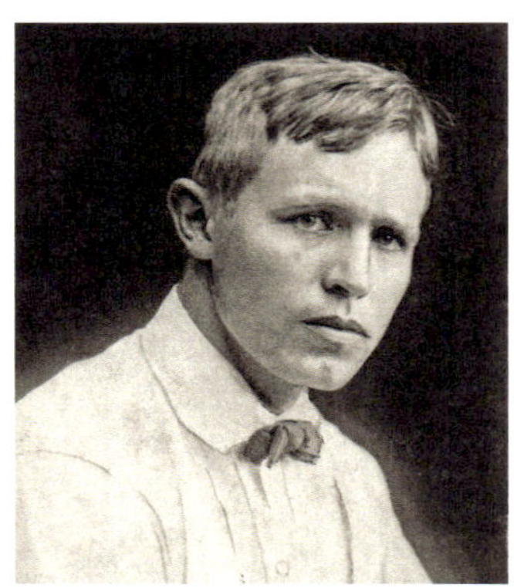

Jens Adolf Jerichau, Odder, 1914

1890:

Jerichau was born on 11 December into a family of artists. His grandfather, the sculptor Jens Adolf Jerichau (1816-1883), who he was named after, and his grandmother, the painter and author Elisabeth Jerichau-Baumann (1819-1881), were among the most prominent artists in Denmark in their time. Throughout Jerichau's life it was important for him to honour his family name. "I have only wanted one thing, one thing always: to uphold my family's legacy," Jerichau wrote. After the early death of his father, Jerichau grew up in Hørsholm with his mother, aunt, grandmother and three sisters. Archived letters attests to close, loving, but also conflicted relationships.

1905-1909:

Jerichau began painting and drawing - mainly subjects from Hørsholm, where his family lived, and from Hjørring, where he was an apprentice stonemason.

1909:

At the age of 18, Jerichau met the charismatic 30-year-old writer Aage Barfoed. "Our eyes met in an exchange of souls, unconscious sympathy, understanding," Jerichau wrote in one of his sketchbooks. Their correspondence testifies to an intimate and spiritual love affair that lasted for over a year. Barfoed introduced Jerichau to the great world literature that became motifs in his work, and encouraged him to change from the study of architecture to the painting programme at the Royal Danish Academy of Fine Arts. Jerichau became part of an ambitious artistic milieu that included Axel Salto, Sigurd and Leo Swane, Ivar Rosenberg and Einar Dyggve. Jerichau's family was greatly against his decision to become an artist, but he himself was in no doubt. "Now or never, I say, now I must become a painter. I feel it more and more as a calling, as what I was born to do," he wrote in a letter to one of his sisters.

1910:

In the summer of 1910, Jerichau developed his style further during an inspiring stay on Funen. Jerichau visited Danish artists including Johannes Larsen and Anna and Fritz Syberg. Later he went to Hesselø, where some of his relatives owned an estate. Jerichau began to study under the art historian Vilhelm Wanscher, who until Jerichau's death was a very important mentor and friend to Jerichau.

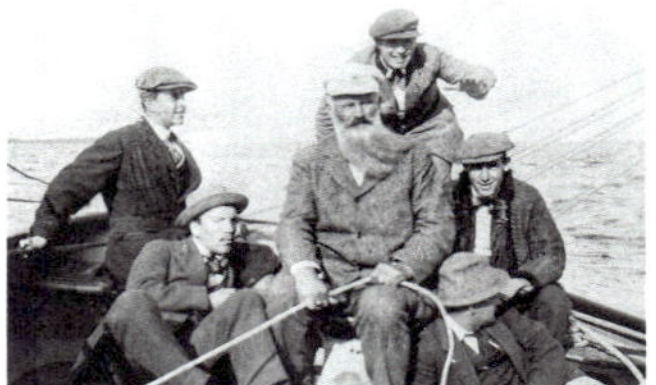

From the left: Jean Hakon Schalburg, Andreas Friis, Emil Holstein Rathlou, Jens Adolf Jerichau, Asger Bremer and Axel Saltoreclining. From a journey to Hesselø, c. 1914

In Copenhagen, Jerichau saw exhibitions with some of the most influential artists on the international art scene, such as Paul Cézanne, Paul Gauguin and Edvard Munch.

1911:

In July 1911, Jerichau travelled around Germany and to Vienna, where he saw works by old masters as well as by contemporary artists: from Titian, Raphael, El Greco, Rubens and Veronese to Vincent van Gogh, Claude Monet and Max Liebermann. On his way home, he described a feeling of profound gratitude and inspiration.

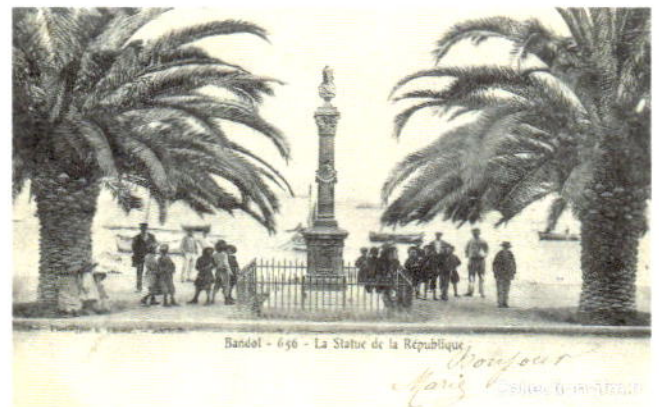

Historical postcard, Bandol

1912:

In April 1912, Jerichau spent a month in Paris, where he visited the most important museums, galleries and art collectors, and saw many works by Cézanne and El Greco. Jerichau also enjoyed

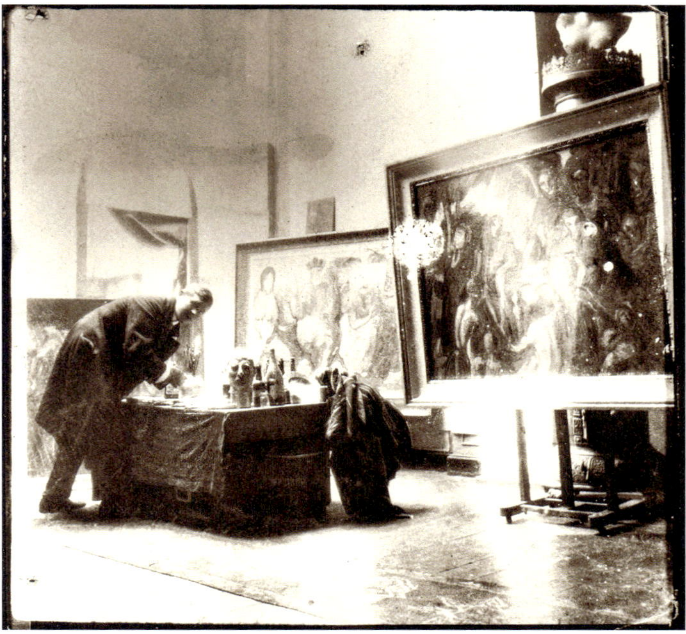

Jens Adolf Jerichau in his studio in Tordenskjoldsgade, c. 1914

the Parisian city life, visiting tailors, cafés and music venues. He saw the world's second colour film in the cinema as well as a staging of Racine's *Phaedra* with Sarah Bernhardt in the title role. Enthused, he wrote home: "France and Paris are the heart from which all the new ideas come or, at least, are promoted." After Paris, Jerichau travelled south, first to Sanary and then to Bormes, "down to the sun and the colours." There he painted with Jean Hakon Schalburg, his friend from the Academy. Jerichau had, however, spent too much money on clothes, good food and Parisian city life, and most of the postcards he sent home therefore included pleas for money.

1913:

After his return to Copenhagen, Jerichau isolated himself and began to paint day and night. He rented a studio in Tordenskjoldsgade in Copenhagen, where he mounted blue arches of cardboard above the doors, black arches above the windows, and painted a circle and a star (or a pentagram) on the floor. He also became more fascinated by the mystical, the occult and astrology, and he experimented in his sketchbooks with grand theories of world history and mankind's connections with the stars. A prophecy found among Jerichau's papers foretold his early death in a country far from Denmark. In Copenhagen he experimented with other artistic mediums, including sculptures and the splendid illustrated *The Book of Wisdom*. In those years, international art was well represented at exhibitions in Copenhagen with, among others, exhibitions of Gabriele Münter and a large collection of icons whose stylized faces may have inspired Jerichau's simplified human figures and faces.

1914:

Jerichau exhibited his paintings for the first time in the Autumn Exhibition at Charlottenborg. Around the same time he began a relationship with Sigrun Schalburg, a divorcée and the mother of four children. Jerichau was frustrated at again meeting resistance, especially from his mother: "Why won't Mother and those closest to me ever take me as I am ... All that I want or do is grief to them back home and has been so since I was small," he wrote to one of his sisters.

1915:

After a productive period in Copenhagen, Jerichau was frustrated at the reception of his paintings in Denmark, and wrote about his critics: "They are stupid and ignorant, as people always are in the face of something new or original". He took out a large loan and travelled south, first to Venice, from where he managed to leave again just before the First World War broke out, and after that to the South of France, Barcelona and Madrid with Schalburg. The Museo Prado in Madrid was a special high point for Jerichau, who was given permission to make copies of the pictures. He also visited the Danish painter J.F. Willumsen in Toledo, where he lived and worked, and together they painted the landscape and saw works by El Greco in nearby churches. During the whole journey Jerichau had great financial problems, and this also strained his relationship with Sigrun Schalburg.

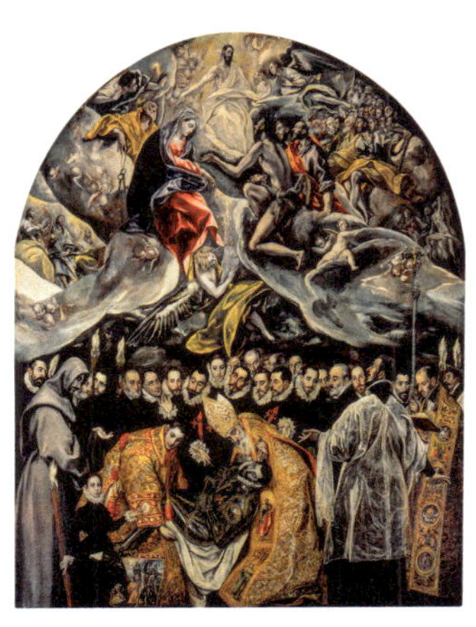

El Greco: *The Burial of the Count of Orgaz*, 1586. Iglesia de Santo Tomé, Toledo

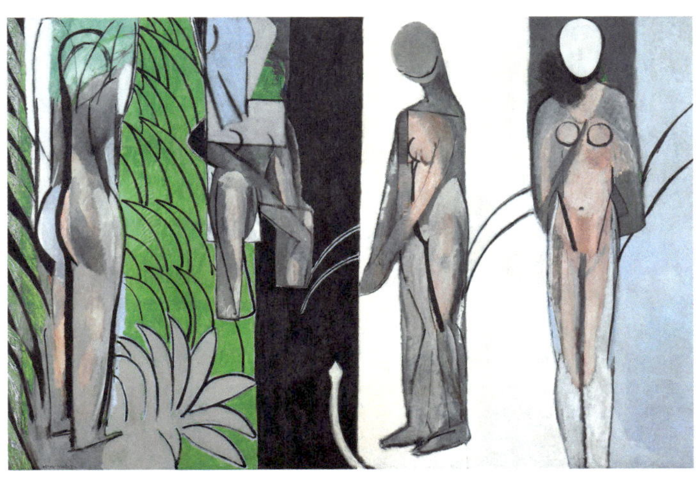

Henri Matisse: *Women Bathing by a River*, 1909-1917. The Chicago Art Institute

1916:

In spring, Jerichau held his biggest exhibition and an auction, where he sold nearly all works. Ecstatic, Jerichau wrote to Sigrun Schalburg in Madrid that they could now get married. However, she had already sent him a letter in which she ended their relationship. Despite the war, Jerichau travelled back to Paris. He rented a studio in a back yard in the artists' neighbourhood Montparnasse upstairs from his friends from the Royal Academy, Axel and Kamma Salto. Together they enjoyed the Parisian city life. Picasso gave them a private tour of the exhibition where he showed *Les demoiselles d'Avignon* for the first time. They also visited Henri Matisse in his lush garden on the outskirts of Paris and saw some very experimental paintings he was working on, among others *Women Bathing by a River*. On Bastille Day, 14th July, Jerichau wrote his will, and at the end of July he wrote on a loose sheet: "I think only of death, this beautiful death that will fill me and swallow me up."
On 16th August, Jerichau took his own life in his studio.
The last thing Jerichau wrote was characteristically grandiloquent and yearning: "Great times are upon us – and a glorious art awaits."

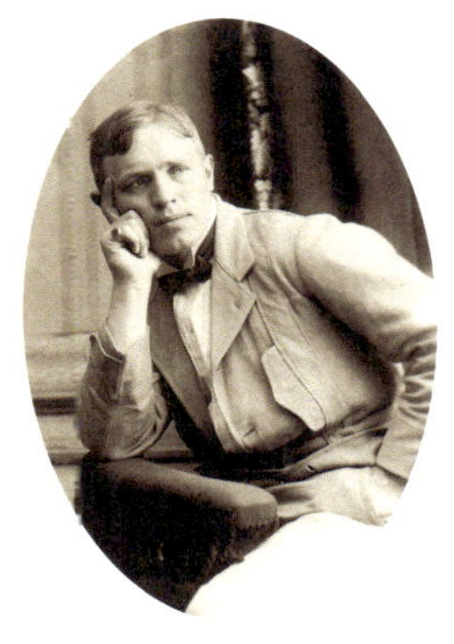

Jens Adolf Jerichau, Paris, 1916

List of Works

Paintings

1 *Kirkebroen*, 1906
The Bridge to the Church
Oil on canvas, 27 × 36 cm
Museum Nordsjælland

2 *Udsigt mod Børsen*, 1909
View of the Copenhagen Stock Exchange. Oil on canvas, 46 × 28 cm. Private Collection

3 *Landskab*, 1910
Landscape. Oil on wood, 32.5 × 53 cm. Private Collection

4 *Sjællænderbonde*, 1910
A Farmer from Zealand
Oil on canvas, 33 × 35.5 cm
Private Collection

5 *Landskab*, 1910
Landscape. Oil on wood, 32.5 × 53 cm. Private Collection

6 *Landskab*, 1911
Landscape. Oil on canvas, 69 × 81 cm. Museum Jorn, Silkeborg

7 *Hesselø*, 1911
Hesseltop. Oil on canvas, 54 × 81 cm. Private Collection

8 *Tomatplante*, 1911
Tomato Plant. Oil on canvas, 47 × 40 cm. Private Collection

9 *Blomstrende Valmuer*, 1912
Poppies in Bloom. Oil on canvas, 46 × 71.5 cm. Private Collection

10 *Matrosernes dans*, 1912
Dance of the Sailors. Oil on canvas, 67 × 76 cm. Private Collection

11 *Fra Provence*, 1912
From Provence. Oil on canvas, 77 × 98 cm. Private Collection

12 *Mennesker på stranden*, 1912. Beachgoers. Oil on canvas, 50.5 × 68 cm. Private Collection

13 *Place Gambetta*, 1912
Oil on canvas, 48 × 58 cm
Private Collection

14 *Markedsplads*, 1912
A Market Place. Oil on cardboard, 37 × 45 cm
Private Collection

15 *Folkefest, Sydfrankrig*, 1912. Traditional Festival, Southern France. Oil on board, 48 × 66 cm
Private Collection

16 *Susanna for Rådet (Mødet i himlen)*, 1912
Susanna and the Elders (The Meeting in Heaven)
Oil on canvas, 29 × 25 cm
Private Collection

17 *Rytter*, c. 1912
Rider. Oil on panel, 52 × 38 cm
Private Collection

18 *Dante. Profeter, Opus I*, 1912
Dante. Prophets, Opus I
Oil on canvas, 135.5 × 135.7 cm
SMK, National Gallery of Art

19 *Dante. Skitse*, 1912
Dante. Sketch. Oil on canvas, 46 × 39 cm. Private Collection

20 *Dante*, 1912. Oil on canvas, 55 × 46 cm. Private Collection

21 *En biskop*, 1912
A Bishop. Oil on canvas, 74 × 60 cm. Private Collection

22 *Salomons dom*, 1912
The Judgement of Solomon
Copy after painting by Rubens at The National Gallery of Art, Copenhagen, Oil on canvas, 44 × 48 cm. Jesper Christiansen & Anna Grue

23 *Sokrates (Portræt af Vilhelm Wanscher)*, 1912. Socrates (Portrait of Vilhelm Wanscher)
Oil on canvas, 52 × 44 cm
Private Collection

24 *Skolen i Athen. Kopi efter Rafael*, 1913. The School of Athens. Copy after Raphael
Oil on canvas, 55 × 81 cm
The Nivaagaard Collection

25 *Filosoffer*, 1913
Philosophers. Oil on canvas, 46 × 55 cm. Private Collection

26 *Alkibiades*, 1913
Alcibiades. Oil on canvas, 110 × 84 cm. Private Collection

27 *Figurkomposition*, 1913
Figure Composition. Oil on canvas, 139 × 116 cm
Private Collection

28 *Komposition (Susanna for det tænkte Råd)*, c. 1913
Composition (Susanna and the Elders). Oil on canvas, 46 × 55 cm. Finn Blakstad

29 *Slangen der frister Eva*, 1913. The Serpent Tempting Eve
Oil on plywood, 92 × 120 cm
Esbjerg Art Museum

30 *Susanna i badet*, 1916
Susanna Bathing
Oil on canvas, 144 × 175 cm
Randers Kunstmuseum

31 *Korsnedtagelsen*, 1913
The Deposition
Oil on canvas, 122 × 146 cm
Ribe Kunstmuseum

32 *Gangen til Golgatha*, 1913-1914. The Road to Calvary
Oil on canvas, 116 × 141.5 cm
SMK, National Gallery of Art

33 *De hellige tre konger og den babyloniske skøge*, 1913-1914
The Magi and the Whore of Babylon. Oil on cardboard, 116 × 136 cm. The Canica Art Collection, Oslo

34 *Guldfuglen. Fra Grækenlands skønne tid. Opus I*, 1913-1914. The Golden Bird. From the Glorious Times of Ancient Greece. Opus I. Oil on canvas, 127 × 150 cm. Trapholt

35 *Pietà*, 1914
Oil on canvas, 113 × 135 cm
Ribe Kunstmuseum

36 *Englen (Mariæ Bebudelse)*, 1914 . The Angel (The Annunciation). Oil on canvas, 80 × 65 cm. Private Collection

37 *Den sorte profet. Profeter. Opus II*, 1914
The Black Prophet. Prophets. Opus II. Oil on canvas, 137 × 115 cm. SMK, National Gallery of Art

38 *Susanna for Rådet*, 1914
Susanna and the Elders
Oil on cardboard, 22 × 24 cm
Private Collection

39 *Babylonisk stjernetyder*, 1914. A Babylonian Astrologer
Oil on canvas, 55 × 46 cm
Private Collection

40 Adam og Eva, 1914
Adam and Eve. Oil on canvas, 47 × 49 cm . Private Collection

41 *Offerfesten. Menneskene søger varsler. Opus I*, 1914
The Sacrificial Feast. Man Seeking Omens. Opus I.Oil on canvas, 148 × 172.5 cm. Esbjerg Kunstmuseum

42 *Figurkomposition med bakkanter*, 1914-1915
Figure Composition with Bacchants. Pencil and oil on cardboard, 133 × 195 cm
SMK, National Gallery of Art

43 *Figurkomposition (Dante på vej til himlen – Dantesymbol)*, 1914-1915. Figure Composition (Dante Ascending – Dante Symbol). Oil on canvas, 155 × 190 cm. Museum Jorn, Silkeborg

44 *Opstandelsen. Hyldest til renæssancen. Symboler. Opus IV*, 1914-1915. The Resurrection. Tribute to the Renaissance. Symbols. Opus IV. Oil on canvas, 117 × 137 cm. Private Collection

45 *Den hellige Georg og drageløven*, 1916. Saint George and the Dragon Lion. Oil on canvas, 115 × 138 cm. Private Collection

46 *Offerfesten. Menneskene søger varsel. Opus II*, 1915
The Sacrificial Feast. Man Seeking Omens. Opus II
Oil on canvas, 146 × 162 cm
The Canica Art Collection, Oslo

47 *Offerfesten. Menneskene søger varsel. Opus III*, 1915.
The Sacrificial Feast. Man Seeking Omens. Opus III.
Oil on canvas, 143 × 170 cm.
Louisiana Museum of Modern Art

48 *Forårets komme. Fra Grækenlands skønne tid. Opus II*, 1915. The Arrival of Spring. From the Glorious Times of Ancient Greece. Opus II. Oil on canvas, 142 × 180 cm. Private Collection

49 *Elskov. Baccanter. Opus I*, 1915. Love. Bacchants. Opus I
Oil on canvas, 116 × 140 cm
ARoS Aarhus Kunstmuseum

50 *Den tykke palme. Udsigt fra Villefranche*, 1915. The Thick Palm Tree. View from Villefranche. Oil on canvas, 50 × 61.5 cm. SMK, National Gallery of Art

51 *Palmen mod St. Sir*, 1915
The Palm Tree, View of St. Sir
Oil on canvas, 46 × 38 cm
Private Collection

52 *Gorgettes store palme*, 1915. Gorgette's Large Palm Tree.
Oil on canvas, 41 × 61 cm
Mads Jørgensen

53 *Kajen*, 1915. The Quay
Oil on canvas, 33 × 46 cm
SMK, National Gallery of Art

54 *Kajen*, 1915. The Quay
Oil on canvas, 38 × 46 cm
Kunsten Museum of Modern Art Aalborg

55 *Udsigt over Middelhavet*, 1915. View of the Mediterranean
Oil on canvas, 38 × 46 cm
The Canica Art Collection, Oslo

56 *Store crier*, 1915
The Large Crier. Oil on canvas, 46 × 55 cm. Private Collection

57 *Stranden*, 1915
The Beach. Oil on canvas, 45 × 55 cm. Private Collection

58 *Det "lille crier"*, 1915
The "Small Crier". Oil on canvas, 37 × 45 cm. Kunsten Museum of Modern Art Aalborg

59 *Den lille bugt*, 1915
The Small Bay. Oil on canvas, 46 × 55 cm. Private Collection

60 *Strandbred med træ*, 1915
Tree by the Beach. Oil on canvas, 37 × 45 cm. Private Collection

61 *Vej i Bandol*, 1915. Street in Bandol. Oil on cardboard on wood, 53 × 63 cm. Private Collection

62 *Gade i Bandol*, 1915
Street in Bandol. Oil on canvas, 46 × 55 cm. Private Collection

63 *Det blå bjerg*, 1915. The Blue Mountain. Oil on cardboard, 54 × 46 cm. Private Collection

64 *Det blå bjerg*, 1915
The Blue Mountain. Oil on canvas, 55 × 49 cm. Private Collection

65 *Fra Provence*, 1915.
From Provence. Oil on canvas, 45 × 61 cm. Private Collection

66 *Havguder. Skitse*, 1915. Sea Deities. Sketch. Oil on canvas, 39 × 32 cm. Private Collection

67 *Havguder. Skitse*, 1915.
Sea Deities. Sketch
Oil on canvas, 41 × 29 cm.
Private Collection

68 *Havguder. Skitse*, 1915.
Sea Deities. Sketch
Oil on board, 49 × 73 cm.
Private Collection

69 *Drageløver*, 1914-1915.
Dragon Lions
Oil on canvas, 103.5 × 114 cm.
Museum Jorn, Silkeborg

70 *Kirkegårdsvejen i Toledo*, 1915
The Cemetery Road in Toledo.
Oil on canvas, 50.5 × 61.3 cm.
SMK, National Gallery of Art

71 *Udsigt over klosteret Christus de la Vega*, 1915
View of the Monastery of Cristo de la Vega. Oil on canvas, 50 × 61.5 cm. Private Collection, long-term loan to Museum Jorn, Silkeborg

72 *St. Laurentius Kapel*, 1915
The Chapel of St. Lawrence
Oil on canvas, 50 × 61.5 cm
Private Collection

73 *Fra Domus Gotika*, 1915
From Domus Gothika. Oil on canvas, 69 × 65 cm. The Canica Art Collection, Oslo

74 *Påklædt Kristusfigur i træ*, 1915. Dressed Figure of Christ in wood. Oil on canvas, 46 × 33 cm. Private Collection

75 *Evas Skabelse. Komposition. Opus II*, 1915. The Creation of Eve. Composition. Opus II. Oil on canvas, 159 × 196 cm. SMK, National Gallery of Art

76 *Den store kardinal. Opus III*, 1915. The Great Cardinal. Opus III. Oil on canvas, 130 × 112 cm
Museum Jorn, Silkeborg

77 *Spinderskerne. Madrid (Kopi efter maleri af Velázquez Las Hilanderas)*, 1915
The Spinners. Madrid (Copy after painting by Velázquez Las Hilanderas). Oil on canvas, 27 × 35 cm. The Canica Art Collection, Oslo

78 *Landskab*, 1916
Landscape. Oil on canvas, 81 × 99 cm. Private Collection

79 *Fra promenaden*, 1916
At the Pier. Oil on canvas, 65 × 81 cm. LB Forsikring

80 *Landskab*, 1916
Landscape. Oil on canvas, 70 × 48 cm. Private Collection

81 Landskab, 1916
Landscape. Oil on canvas, 50 × 60 cm. Private Collection

82 *Nature morte*, 1916. Still Life. Oil on canvas, 55 × 46 cm. Tangen Collection, AKO. Kunststiftelse

83 *Harlekin og Columbine*, 1916. Harlequin and Columbine Oil on canvas, 45 × 37 cm Private Collection

84 *Harlekin og Columbine*, 1916. Harlequin and Columbine Oil on canvas, 38 × 46 cm Private Collection

85 *Komposition med en kentaur*, 1916. Composition with a Centaur. Oil on canvas, 46 × 55 cm. Private Collection

86 *Komposition med ryttere og løver*, 1916. Composition with Riders and Lions. Oil on canvas, 60 × 73 cm Private Collection

87 *Drageløven. Skitse*, 1915 The Dragon Lion. Sketch. Oil on canvas, 27 × 27.5 cm Private Collection

88 *Drageløven*, 1915 The Dragon Lion. Oil on canvas, 18 × 21 cm. Private Collection

89 *Indianere på prærien*, 1916 Native Americans on the Prairie Oil on canvas, 50 × 47 cm Marion & Jörg Schwandt, Berlin

90 *Faldne krigeres grave*, 1916 The Graves of Fallen Warriors Oil on canvas, 64 × 49.5 cm Museum Jorn, Silkeborg

91 *Komposition*, 1916 Composition. Oil on canvas, 131.5 × 161.5 cm. SMK, National Gallery of Art

92 *Havguder*, 1916 Sea Deities. Oil on canvas, 146 × 180 cm. Museum Jorn, Silkeborg

93 *Dante*, 1916. Oil on canvas, 155 × 132 cm. The Canica Art Collection, Oslo. Long-term loan at KODE Kunstmuseer og komponisthjem

94 *Guldfuglen. Fra Grækenlands skønne tid. Opus III*, 1916 The Golden Bird. From the Glorious Times of Ancient Greece. Opus III. Oil on canvas, 130 × 163 cm. Frederiksberg Gymnasium

95 *Hæcuba*, 1916. Hecuba Oil on canvas, 133 × 164 cm Private Collection

96 *Susanna i badet*, 1916 Susanna Bathing. Oil on canvas, 132 × 163 cm. Randers Kunstmuseum

97 *De hellige tre konger og den babyloniske skøge*, 1916 The Magi and the Whore of Babylon. Oil on canvas, 140 × 170 cm. Kunstmuseum Brandts

98 *Slægten kalder*, 1916 The Ancestors Beckon. Oil on canvas, 153 × 197.5 cm Museum Jorn, Silkeborg

Sculpture

99 *Hoved*, 1913 Head. Unburnt clay, 21.5 × 16 × 19 cm. Museum Jorn, Silkeborg

100 *Mandshoved*, 1913 Head of a Man. Unburnt clay, 23 × 22 × 20 cm. Museum Jorn, Silkeborg

101 *Skulpturgruppe*, 1913 Sculptural Group. Unburnt clay, 20 × 24 × 20 cm. Museum Jorn, Silkeborg

Etchings

102 *Antonius*, 1916. Anthony. Etching. Plate mark: 6.5 × 6 cm, Paper size: 18 × 15.5 cm. Museum Jorn, Silkeborg

103 *Uden titel*, 1916 Untitled. Etching. Plate mark: 10.6 × 12 cm, Paper size: 13.6 × 18.6 cm. Museum Jorn, Silkeborg

104 *Figurkomposition*, 1916 Figure Composition Etching Plate mark: 12.8 × 17.5 cm, Paper size: 24 × 32.5 cm SMK, National Gallery of Art

105 *Allegorisk komposition*, 1916. Allegorical Composition Etching. Plate mark: 12.8 × 17.5 cm, Paper size: 24 × 32.5 cm SMK, National Gallery of Art

106 *Komposition*, 1916 Composition. Etching on yellowish paper. Plate mark: 11 × 14.6 cm, Paper size: 16.3 × 23.7 cm. SMK, National Gallery of Art

107 *Kopernikus*, 1916 Copernicus. Etching Plate mark: 6.3 × 5.7 cm Paper size: 14.3 × 9.1 cm SMK, National Gallery of Art

108 *Palme ved havet*, 1916 Palm Tree by the Sea Etching. Plate mark: 10.8 × 9.2 cm, Paper size: 24.4 × 16.1 cm SMK, National Gallery of Art

109 *Komposition (Slægten kalder)*, 1916. Composition (The Ancestors Beckon). Etching. Klingen art portfolio No. 1, 10 original etchings, printed 1918 Plate mark: 11.1 × 14.7 cm, Paper size: 27 × 33 cm Private Collection

110 *Menneskene søger Varsler*, 1916. Man Seeking Omens Etching. Klingen art portfolio No. 1, 10 original etchings, printed 1918. Plate mark: 11.6 × 12.9 cm, Paper size: 27 × 33 cm Private Collection

111 *Dante*, 1916. Etching. Klingen art portfolio No. 1, 10 original etchings, printed 1918 Plate mark: 12.9 × 9.8 cm, Paper size: 27 × 33 cm Private Collection

112 *Komposition*, 1916 Composition. Etching. Klingen art portfolio No. 1, 10 original etchings, printed 1918. Plate mark: 4.9 × 6.1 cm, Paper size: 27 × 33 cm. Private Collection

113 *Kejser Karl den Femte*, 1916. Charles V, Holy Roman Emperor. Etching. Klingen art portfolio No. 1, 10 original etchings, printed 1918. Plate mark: 6 × 5 cm, Paper size: 27 × 33 cm. Private Collection

114 *Loke og Sigyn*, 1916. Loki and Sigyn. Etching. Klingen art portfolio No. 1, 10 original etchings, printed 1918. Plate mark: 11.1 × 14.6, Paper size: 27 × 33 cm. Private Collection

115 *De hellige tre konger og den babyloniske skøge*, 1916. The Magi and the Whore of Babylon Etching. Klingen art portfolio No. 1, 10 original etchings, printed 1918. Plate mark: 9.4 × 10.7 cm, Paper size: 27 × 33 cm Private Collection

116 *Eventyrfuglen*, 1916 The Golden Bird. Etching. Klingen art portfolio No. 1, 10 original etchings, printed 1918 Plate mark: 11.2 × 14.7 cm, Paper size: 27 × 33 cm Private Collection

117 *Gravlæggelsen*, 1916 The Entombment. Etching. Klingen art portfolio No. 1, 10 original etchings, printed 1918 Plate mark: 7.2 × 9 cm Paper size: 37 × 33 cm Private Collection

118 *En biskop*, 1916. A Bishop Etching. Klingen art portfolio No. 1, 10 original etchings, printed 1918. Plate mark: 6.5 × 6.1 cm, Paper size: 27 × 33 cm. Private Collection

Drawings

119 *Selvportræt*, not dated Self-portrait. Charcoal on paper, 40 × 34 cm. Private Collection

120 *Selvportræt*, 1910. Self-portrait. Pencil on paper, 24.5 × 18 cm. Museum Jorn, Silkeborg

121 *Studie efter Dürer: Den hellige Christophorus I*, 1910? Study after Dürer: Saint Christopher I. Version No. 1 of 3. Pencil on brown paper, 36 × 27.3 cm SMK, National Gallery of Art

122 *Studie efter Dürer: Den hellige Christophorus II*, 1910? Study after Dürer: Saint Christopher II. Version No. 2 of 3. Pencil and watercolour on brown paper, 36.3 × 26.5 cm SMK, National Gallery of Art

123 *Studie efter Dürer: Den hellige Christophorus III*, 1910? Study after Dürer: Saint Christopher III. Version No. 3 of 3. Pencil and watercolour on brown paper, 36 × 31 cm SMK, National Gallery of Art

124 *Studie efter Dürer: Den hellige Christophorus*, 1910? Study after Dürer: Saint Christopher. Pencil and watercolour on paper, 36 × 26 cm Private Collection

125 *Fra Ny Guinea til Europa*, 1913-1914. From New Guinea to Europe Page cut from *The Book of Wisdom*. Pen, ink, watercolour on paper, 33.7 × 20.7 cm Private Collection

126 *Mandlig model set fra ryggen*, 1914. Male Nude, Back Pencil, 25.2 × 18.9 cm SMK, National Gallery of Art

127 *Kvindelig model, liggende*, 1915. Female Nude, Reclining Pencil, 25.3 × 18.7 cm SMK, National Gallery of Art

Sketchbooks

128 Self-portrait. Sketchbook, probably Copenhagen and Hørsholm, 1909. Pencil, pen, black ink, 29.7 × 24.2 cm SMK, National Gallery of Art

129 Self-portrait. Sketchbook, probably Copenhagen, Hørsholm and Hesselø, 1909-1910. Pencil, watercolour, 33.9 × 24.6 cm SMK, National Gallery of Art

130 Saint Christopher. Sketchbook, Copenhagen, 1910. Pencil, pen, black and brown ink, 25.4 × 20.4 cm. SMK, National Gallery of Art

131 Self-portrait. Sketchbook, Kerteminde, Fyns Hoved, Ratlousdal [eastern Jutland], and Scania, 1910. Pencil, 25.4 × 20.4 cm SMK, National Gallery of Art

132 Self-portrait. Sketchbook, Svanninge Bakker, Vissenbjerg, Hesselagergaard [near Nyborg], and probably Copenhagen, 1910 Pencil, 23 × 30.4 cm SMK, National Gallery of Art

133 Standing Female. Sketchbook, Hørsholm and Copenhagen, 1910. Pencil, 25.4 × 20.4 cm. SMK, National Gallery of Art

134 Self-portrait. Sketchbook, Hørsholm and possibly Copenhagen, 1911. Pencil, 25.7 × 20.3 cm. SMK, National Gallery of Art

135 Self-portrait. Sketchbook, Hørsholm and possibly Copenhagen, 1911. Pencil, 25.5 × 20.3 cm. SMK, National Gallery of Art

136 Female Nude and Hands. Sketchbook, Marseille, Toulon, Le Lavandou, and probably Bormes, 1912. Pencil, charcoal, 25.3 × 20.3 cm SMK, National Gallery of Art

137 Studies of Female Nude. Sketchbook, southern France, including Le Lavandou, 1912 Pencil, brush, brown ink, black and red oil pastel, 34.1 × 27.2 cm. SMK, National Gallery of Art

138 Self-portrait, Standing Nude. Sketchbook, Paris, Versailles, southern France, and possibly Copenhagen, 1912 Pencil, charcoal, red oil pastel, watercolour, 25.3 × 20.4 cm SMK, National Gallery of Art

139 Model with Raised Arms. Sketchbook, Vincennes, Suresnes, Paris, and Chartreuse, 1912 Pencil, 20.9 × 13.3 cm SMK, National Gallery of Art

140 Model with Raised Arms and Seated Model. Sketchbook, Copenhagen, c. 1913. Pencil, pen, brown ink General: 21.5 × 17.2 cm. SMK, National Gallery of Art

141 The Book of Wisdom. Sketchbook, Probably Copenhagen, 1913-1914. Pencil, pen, brush, brown, black and greyish black ink, watercolour, oil, gold bronze, 33.7 × 20.7 cm. SMK, National Gallery of Art

142 Standing Nude, Male. Sketchbook, Copenhagen, 1914. Pencil, brush, watercolour, 25.5 × 20.3 cm. SMK, National Gallery of Art

143 Female Nude. Sketchbook, Madrid and Copenhagen, 1915-1916. Pencil, brush, watercolour, 25.5 × 20.4 cm. SMK, National Gallery of Art

Notes

Mathias Ussing Seeberg

1 Undated fragment, 1916, Jens Adolf Jerichau Archive, Museum Jorn, Silkeborg.
2 Letter from Jens Adolf Jerichau to Lisbeth Jerichau, Bandol, 18 July 1915, Jens Adolf Jerichau Archive, Museum Jorn.
3 Jerichau, sketchbook, 1909-1910, Royal Collection of Graphic Art, inv. no. 1993-84, National Gallery of Denmark.
4 See, e.g., Emil Nolde's *Palm Trees by the Sea*, which was painted the year before Jerichau's pictures of Bandol, a port city near Marseille. At the time, they were singled out by Jappe Nielsen, a respected Norwegian art critic and close friend of Edvard Munch, in a review in Dagbladet of Jerichau's memorial exhibition in Kristiania (Oslo), 1919. Nielsen wrote that Jerichau here "had achieved results that belong among the most beautiful things in modern, Nordic painting." Jappe Nielsen, "Exlex og Jerichau", *Dagbladet*, Wednesday 26 November, Oslo 1919, No. 291, p. 6.
5 One was his grandfather J.A. Jerichau (1816-1883), whom Mikael Wivel describes as depressive and bipolar. Mikael Wivel, *Penslen og pistolen – Maleren Jens Adolf Jerichau*, Strandberg Publishing, Copenhagen, 2019, p. 395-396.
6 Letter from Jerichau to Lisbeth Jerichau, Bandol, 18 July 1915, Jens Adolf Jerichau Archive, Museum Jorn. Mikael Wivel very generously shared with me transcriptions of Jerichau's correspondence and notes.
7 Letter to Anna Jerichau, Copenhagen, 25 February 1915, Jens Adolf Jerichau Archive, Museum Jorn.
8 See Wivel, op. cit,. p. 359-426.
9 Vilhelm Wanscher, *J.A. Jerichau, Vor tids kunst 2*, Rasmus Naver, Copenhagen 1931, p. 8.
10 Jerichau dedicated this masterpiece from his last days in Paris to Vilhelm Wanscher.
11 In this catalogue, Wivel writes about Wanscher and Jerichau (p. 24), while Lise Villemoes Grønvold describes Jerichau's relationship with Barfoed (p. 50).
12 Mikael Wivel, op. cit., p. 52.
13 Jerichau, draft of a letter, 17 July 1910, sketchbook, Royal Collection of Graphic Art, inv. no. 1993-83, National Gallery of Denmark.
14 Sketchbooks, Royal Collection of Graphic Art, National Gallery of Denmark, 1993-90.
15 Wanscher, op. cit., p. 8.
16 Troels Andersen, *Jens Adolf Jerichau*, Borgen, Copenhagen, 1983, p. 150.
17 Wivel, op. cit., p. 52.
18 There are only three monographic works on Jens Adolf Jerichau: 1. Vilhelm Wanscher, op. cit. Wanscher's monograph provides the foundation for the following ones, because it describes his life and work in parallel. The book is full of personal observations and statements, e.g., Jerichau was "the sweetest, most loving son and brother". Wanscher points out Jerichau's erotic duality and its importance to his figures but does not elaborate further in the book, which mainly deals with Jerichau's compositions and "colourististic beauty." 2. Troels Andersen, op. cit. Andersen's book on Jerichau was the culmination of extensive research into the artist's life and work. Starting in the 1960s, Andersen interviewed key persons from Jerichau's life who were still alive. One was Kamma Salto, who was with Jerichau and her husband, Axel Salto, in Paris during Jerichau's last days. Over the years, Andersen received and archived a great deal of material, which today constitutes the Jens Adolf Jerichau Archive at Museum Jorn, Silkeborg. In Andersen's book, we learn for the first time about Jerichau's relationship with the writer Aage Barfoed, and how, in a draft of a letter, Jerichau denies being homosexual, Andersen also locates the reason why Jerichau was drawn to Barfoed in the "lasting loss" of his father's death when he was 10. Andersen does not pursue Jerichau's possible bisexuality but simply concludes, without further elaboration, that Jerichau was torn "between sexual forces and the death drive". In the beginning of the book, he also labels Jerichau's infatuation with a female cousin as "platonic". Wanscher and Andersen both merely insinuate, likely reflecting their times, that there is something significant about Jerichau's sexuality. It is important to add that Andersen, during a visit to my home on 25 May 2021, said that what he really meant was that this is all there is to it. 3. Mikael Wivel, op. cit. Wivel's book on Jerichau is without compare the most comprehensive work on the artist. Of the three monographers, it is also Wivel who most extensively describes Jerichau's relationship with Barfoed and Jerichau's introduction to Oscar Wilde through Barfoed. He is the first to say straight out that Jerichau was probably bisexual. Moreover, in a note, Wivel mentions Jerichau's acquaintance with the homosexual German painter Rudolf Levy. While Wivel emphasizes Jerichau's bisexuality, his "duality", he does not make an attempt to systematically regard this duality as a generator of pictures.
19 See, e.g., my essay on the work of Marsden Hartley: Mathias Ussing Seeberg, "Introduction to Marsden Hartley's Life and Work", in Lærke Rydal Jørgensen and Mathias Ussing Seeberg (eds.), Marsden Hartley: *The Earth is All I Know of Wonder*, Louisiana, Humlebæk, 2019, p. 6-17.
20 For another local example, a queer reading of Kristian Zahrtmann's work, see Rasmus Kjærboe, *Liv, værk og hjemsteds: Et queer portræt af Kristian Zahrtmann*, 2019, accessed at https://perspective.smk.dk/liv-vaerk-og- hjem-sted-et-queer-portraet-af-kristian- zahrtmann. For an American example of how artists in Jerichau's day used codes to express their gender and sexual identity, see Jonathan D. Katz & David C. Ward, *Hide/Seek: Difference and Desire in American Portraiture*, Smithsonian Books, USA, 2010.
21 Asger Jorn, "Brev om J.A. Jerichau", in Uffe Harder and Richard Winther (eds.): *Hvedekorn* No. 6, December 1962, p. 183-184.
22 See, e.g., the pencil drawing of a female figure with her arms raised above her head, in a sketchbook in the Royal Collection of Graphic Art, inv. no. 1993-90, National Gallery of Denmark. Working from the sketch, Jerichau coloured in the figure on the reverse side of the page.
23 Andersen, "Om Jerichaus figurkompositioner", in Poul Vad (ed.), *Signum – Tidsskrift for moderne kunst*, Vol. 2, No. 1, Gyldendal, Copenhagen, 1962, p. 47.
24 Wivel also touches on this in his analysis of the image on the back of Hecuba, mentioning that the hidden may have given Jerichau a unique satisfaction. Wivel, op. cit., p. 422.
25 Ibid., p. 218.
26 Jerichau, sketchbook, Royal Collection of Graphic Art, inv. no. 1994-3, National Gallery of Denmark.
27 Jerichau, sketchbook, Royal Collection of Graphic Art, inv. no. 1993-21, National Gallery of Denmark.
28 Wivel, op. cit., p. 184.
29 "I see you lying stretched out, Jens Adolf, / on the wide bed and the light in your eye / blown out. Your strong painter's hand so / bitterly unmoving and no dulcet and perilous word amusing your mouth anymore. / O eternal youth's child, you Alcibiades, / who burns star-distant in the dark, / flickering and lonely". Axel Salto, *Fugleskyen – Digte og Raderinger*, Copenhagen, 1935, p. 22.
30 Timothy Hyman, *The World New Made: Figurative Painting in the Twentieth Century*, London: Thames & Hudson, 2016, p. 8.
31 Jerichau, sketchbook, Royal Collection of Graphic Art, inv. no. 1994-3, National Gallery of Denmark.
32 Wivel also mentions this in op. cit., p. 150.
33 Jerichau's interest in antiquity also derives from his grandfather, the sculptor J.A. Jerichau, who had a large collection of antique objects, including reliefs, fragments of statues, and portraits. A relief from this collection was placed on Jerichau's tombstone at Hørsholm Cemetery. Flemming Johansen, "Rosenkrantz og Guildenstern", in *Meddelelser fra Thorvaldsens Museum*, 1989, p. 297-303, accessed at https://arkivet.thorvaldsensmuseum.dk/artikler/udskriv/rosenkrantz-og-guildenstern-i-hoersholm
34 Michael Hatt, *Zahrtmanns symposion: Etik, historie og begær*, 2019, accessed at https://perspective.smk.dk/zahrtmanns-symposion-etik-historie-og-begaer
35 In a notebook, Jerichau wrote a number of short, diary-like entries on his relationship with Aage Barfoed. He does not outright state that their relationship is sexual. He describes how they have taken a bath together and that he spent a night with Barfoed. Jerichau writes, "It ended with me staying there that night with him, and he followed me out in the morning, wonderful morning. I myself was in a daze." Elsewhere, relating a conversation with Barfoed about their relationship, Jerichau writes, "I was fond of him, but did not love him and could not give him my love." Sketchbook, Royal Collection of Graphic Art, inv. no. 1993-82, 16r-18v, National Gallery of Denmark.
36 It is not known whether Jerichau had any other relationships with men. There are, however, insinuations here and there in his notes and letters. In a letter of 8 April 1915, he writes to his mother from Venice, "The day before yesterday, I went on a gondola ride through a number of small canals where one does not usually go. I have made the acquaintance of a gondolier named 'Francesko', a real tar with [?] and completely olive coloured, and he smells of garlic and resembles everything southern by the way." Letter from Jerichau to Anna Jerichau, Venice, 8 April 1915, Jens Adolf Jerichau Archive, Museum Jorn, Silkeborg.
37 Jerichau, draft of a letter, 17 July 1910, sketchbook, Royal Collection of Graphic Art, inv. no. 1993-83, National Gallery of Denmark.
38 "A brief survey and guideline about my acquaintance with A. Barfoed", sketchbook, Royal Collection of Graphic Art, inv. no. 1993-82, National Gallery of Denmark.
39 Stefano Evangelista: "Lovers and Philosophers at Once: Aesthetic Platonism in the Victorian 'Fin de Siècle'", *The Yearbook of English Studies*, Vol. 36, No. 2, Victorian Literature, 2006, p. 235.
40 Ibid.
41 "The appeal to Plato also serves to distance homosexual practice from the connotations of vulgarity prevalent at the time: this process is best captured in Wilde's attempt during the trials to shift the setting of modern homosexuality from the brothels and seedy hotel rooms invoked by the prosecution to the high-cultural and noble rhetoric that Platonism carries with it." Ibid., p. 244.
42 Jerichau's notes also imply that Barfoed and he were discussing gender. They discussed how men are more refined than women and how men have a necessary need for sexual satisfaction, whereas women do not. Jerichau writes, "Talked about human sexual drives. Man's necessary satisfaction and Woman's non-necessary, since she has her monthly menstruation." Sketchbook, Royal Collection of Graphic Art, inv. no. 1993-82, 16r-18v, National Gallery of Denmark.
43 Andersen, 1962, op. cit., p. 46.
44 Wivel notes that the origin of Jerichau's interest in Dante is not known, but mentions Barfoed as a possibility. See op. cit., p. 196.
45 Jerichau, sketchbook, Royal Collection of Graphic Art, inv. no. 1993-21, National Gallery of Denmark.
46 Evangelista, op. cit., and Havelock Ellis: *Studies in the Psychology of Sex, 1:*

Sexual Inversion, University Press, London, 1897, p. 13-14.

47 Gary Cestaro, "Queering Dante", in Gragnolati Manuele, Elena Lombardi, Francesca Southerden (eds.): *The Oxford Handbook of Dante*, Oxford University Press, 2021, p. 694.

48 I thank Lise Villemoes Grønvold for directing my attention to the resemblance between Jerichau's painting and Canto 26 of Dante's *Purgatorio*.

49 Dante Alighieri, *The Divine Comedy*.

50 "Dante prefigures for us the passion and colour and intensity of Italian painting." Oscar Wilde, The English Renaissance of Art, p. 118, accessed at https://celt.ucc.ie//published/E800003002.html

51 Cited in Wivel, op. cit., p. 274.

52 Vilhelm Wanscher, *Rafael og Michelangelo*. Nordisk forlag, Copenhagen, 1908, p. 108.

53 Wivel mentions that the painting could be an image of Jerichau's own "emancipation, artistically as well as erotically". That is why Jerichau gives the two nude figures ideal proportions, while suggesting both the physicality and spirituality of their interaction in the open space between them. Wivel does not consider the erotic references implied by Michelangelo and Dante. Op. cit., p. 274.

54 As Wivel notes, we do not know what avant-garde treatments of primitive cultures Jerichau actually saw. His artworks are the closest we get to an actual testimony. Ibid., p. 146.

55 Ibid., p. 159.

56 Letter from Jerichau to Lisbeth Jerichau, Bandol, 18 July 1915. Jens Adolf Jerichau Archive, Museum Jorn.

57 Sketchbook (Book of Wisdom), ca. 1913-14, Royal Collection of Graphic Art, inv. no. 1994-1, National Gallery of Denmark.

58 Jerichau, sketchbook, Royal Collection of Graphic Art, inv. no. 1994-3, National Gallery of Denmark.

Mikael Wivel

1 As the art historian Erik Fischer (1920-2011) wrote much later, Wanscher was the only one of his Danish colleagues who ever had any great significance for the development of the art of his own time. Erik Fischer, "Den store stil i dansk kunst," article in *Politiken*, 10 March 2004.

2 Vilhelm Wanscher, *Italien og den store Stil*, Copenhagen, 1921, p. 140.

3 Ibid., pp. 64 and 67.

4 Letter from Vilhelm Wanscher to Astrid Birch, dated 31/10. Museum Jorn, Silkeborg.

5 Vilhelm Wanscher, "Efteraarsudstillingen" in *Hovedstaden*, 22 November 1914.

6 Sketchbook ("The Book of Wisdom"). KKS inv. no. 1994-1, p. 5, SMK. The whole process is quoted in Troels Andersen: *CRAS*, 1983, p. 6.

7 The picture is now attributed to Rubens and his workshop – see Olaf Koester, *Flemish Paintings 1600-1800*, Copenhagen: Statens Museum for Kunst, 2000, pp. 198f. In Wanscher's and Jerichau's time, there was no doubt, however, that it was painted by the master himself.

8 Vilhelm Wanscher, *J.A. Jerichau*. Copenhagen, 1931, pp. 16-17.

9 Ibid., p. 18. Troels Andersen, *Jens Adolf Jerichau*. Copenhagen, 1983, p. 82.

Lise Villemoes Grønvold

1 Jerichau, draft of a letter, 17 July 1910, KKS-1993-83, p. 2v-5v, Royal Collection of Graphic Arts.

2 Uffe Andreasen, Chr. Rimestad, "Aage Barfoed", in Dansk Biografisk Leksikon at lex.dk. Accessed 30 August 2021 at https://biografiskleksikon.lex.dk/Aage_Barfoed.

3 Jerichau, notes, late January 1910, KKS-1993-82, p. 16r-18v, Royal Collection of Graphic Arts.

4 Ibid.

5 *The Trial of Oscar Wilde: From the Shorthand Reports*, Paris, private edition, 1906, pp. 58-59, Project Gutenberg. For more on paiderastia and the role of this concept in the homosexual intellectual milieu of the late 19th century, see Linda Dowling, *Hellenism and Homosexuality in Victorian Oxford*, Cornell University Press, 1997.

6 Jerichau, notes, late January 1910, KKS-1993-82, p. 16r-18v, Royal Collection of Graphic Arts.

7 Cecilie Bønnelycke, "'De uappetitligste fyre' – om følelsernes rolle i dækningen af Sædelighedsskandalen 1906-1907", *TEMP*, 2018.

8 Johannes V. Jensen, "Samfundet og Sædelighedsforbryderen", in *Politiken*, Copenhagen, 30 November 1906.

9 Letter to Anna Jerichau, 12 March 1910, Museum Jorn, Silkeborg.

10 Jerichau, notes, late January 1910, KKS-1993-82, p. 16r-18v, Royal Collection of Graphic Arts.

11 Aage Barfoed, letter to Jens Adolf Jerichau, ca. March 1910, Museum Jorn, Silkeborg.

12 Letter to Lilla Jerichau, 14 February 1910, Copenhagen, Museum Jorn.

13 For a queer reading of Dante and the role of love in his work by a writer that Jerichau likely knew, since Wanscher references his writing, see John Addington Symonds, "The Dantesque and Platonic Ideals of Love", 1893.

14 Vilhelm Wanscher, *J. A. Jerichau*, Copenhagen, Naver, 1931, p. 8.

15 Jerichau, notes, late January 1910, KKS-1993-82, p. 16r-18v, Royal Collection of Graphic Arts.

16 Jerichau, draft of a letter, 17 July 1910, KKS-1993-83, p. 2v-5v, Royal Collection of Graphic Arts.

17 Barfoed, letter to Jens Adolf Jerichau, 25 July 1910, Skagen, Museum Jorn.

18 Ibid.

19 Barfoed, letter to Jens Adolf Jerichau, 30 July 1910, Museum Jorn.

20 Visdommens bog, KKS-1994-1, p. 3v, Royal Collection of Graphic Arts.

21 Undated fragment, Museum Jorn.

22 Axel Salto, op. cit., p. 37.

23 Letter to Anna Jerichau, 6 April 1916, Copenhagen, Museum Jorn.

24 Last will and testament, Paris, 14 July 1916, Museum Jorn.

Marilyn McCully

1 Letter from Jerichau from Hôtel de Londres, 3 rue Bonaparte, Paris, to one of his sisters, April 1912; Jens Adolf Jerichau Arkivet, Museum Jorn.

2 Leroy Breunig, *Apollinaire on Art: Essays and Reviews 1902-1918*, trans. Susan Suleiman, New York: Viking, 1972, p. 409.

3 Billy Klüver and Julie Martin, *Kiki's Paris: Artists and Lovers 1900-1930*, New York: Harry N. Abrams, 1989, p. 11.

4 The Russian sculptor Ossip Zadkine, who lived at La Ruche, described the place as "a sinister Brie cheese, where every artist had a piece; a studio which began at a point and ended in a large window." Ibid. p. 59.

5 Jeanine Warnod, *La Ruche & Montparnasse*, Geneva/Paris: Weber, 1978, p. 34.

6 Pierre Sichel, *A Biography of Amedeo Modigliani*, New York: E.P. Dutton, 1967, p. 308.

7 For further discussion of Apollinaire's relationship with the Scandinavian community in Paris, see Peter Read, "L'Attrait du Nord: Apollinaire et les artistes scandinaves," *La Place d'Apollinaire*, ed. d'Anja Ernst and Paul Geyer, Paris: Classiques Garnier, 2014, pp. 221-240.

8 In 1916 Halvorsen decided to organize an exhibition of modern French art in Oslo. With the advice of Matisse and Albert Marquet, he shipped off 94 paintings from Rouen; the exhibition opened at the Kunstnerforbundet on 22 November. The catalogue contained a preface by Apollinaire and texts by Cocteau and André Salmon.

9 Axel Salto, "Jens Adolf Jerichau", *Klingen* no. 1, Oct. 1917.

10 Letter from Jerichau to his mother from 70 bis rue Notre-Dame des Champs, 25 May 1916; Jens Adolf Jerichau Arkivet, Museum Jorn.

11 Salto, *Klingen* no. 1.

12 Ilya Ehrenberg, *People and Life*, trans. Anna Bostock and Yvonne Kapp, New York: Alfred A. Knopf, 1962, pp. 142-143.

13 Gunnar Cederschiöld, *Efter levande modell*, Stockholm, 1949, quoted in Klüver and Martin, p. 71.

14 Walter Pach, *Queer Thing, Painting: Forty Years in the World of Art*, New York: Harper and Brothers, 1938, p. 219.

15 Etienne-Alain Hubert, "Pierre Reverdy et le cubisme en mars 1917", *Circonstances de la poésie: Reverdy, Apollinaire, surréalisme*, Paris: Klincksieck, 2000, p. 68, n. 24.

16 Ibid.

17 Kenneth Silver, *Esprit de Corps: The Art of the Parisian Avant-Garde and the First World War*, 1914-1925, London: Thames & Hudson, 1989, p. 85.

18 Jacques Vernay, "La Triennale, exposition d'art français", *Les arts* no. 154 (April 1916), pp. 25-29.

19 Jean Paul Crespelle, quoted in Sichel, p. 322.

20 The Société Lyre et Palette, which was created in 1916, was financed by Pierre Bertin, Blaise Cendrars and Félix Delgranges. Among the musical events they put on were early performances by members of "Les Six" (Georges Auric, Louis Durey, Arthur Honegger, Darius Milhaud, Francis Poulenc and Germaine Tailleferre).

21 My thanks to Peter Read for pointing out the significance of this exhibition to me.

22 Axel Salto, *Klingen* no.7, April 1918; illustrated with a reproduction of *The Moroccans*.

23 Ibid.

24 Both *The Moroccans* and *Bathers by a River* were worked on over a number of years. For a detailed discussion of the different states of these paintings, and Matisse's work during the summer 1916 on the plaster for *Back III*, see Stephanie d'Alessandro and John Elderfield, *Matisse: Radical Invention 1913-1917*, New Haven and London: Yale University Press, 2010, pp. 294-309.

25 Picasso occupied a studio in the artists' complex known as the Cité Nicolas Poussin.

26 Axel Salto, "Pablo Picasso", *Klingen* no. 2, November 1917; trans. by P.S. Falla, "Axel Salto, Visiting Picasso in Paris", in Marilyn McCully, *A Picasso Anthology*, London: Arts Council of Great Britain/Thames & Hudson, 1981, p. 126. Picasso's painting *Violin and Grapes*, 1912, The Museum of Modern Art, New York, is illustrated with the article.

27 Ibid.

28 Ibid. The construction he describes has not survived.

29 Ibid.

30 Marie Wassilieff later claimed that Jerichau had acquired the puppet directly from her. After Jerichau's suicide, the puppet was sent to his mother, and Wassilieff is said to have asked Picasso if he wanted her to make another for him, to which he responded negatively. He believed that in the circumstances the doll could be considered a "portrait malheur"; see Lennart Gottlieb, *Modernisme og maleri*, Aarhus: Aarhus Universitetsforlag, 2011, pp. 236-237. In fact, Wassilieff did make at least one more Picasso puppet (with Henri Matisse and an African mask) in the following year; see exh. cat. *Matisse Picasso*, London: Tate Modern, 2002, p. 369.

31 Henri-Pierre Roché, diary entry, 12 August 1916, Carlton Lake Collection, Harry Ransom Humanities Research Center, University of Texas at Austin.

32 Wassilieff later claimed that the Picasso puppet Jerichau had acquired was found at the foot of his bed; see Gottlieb, pp. 236-237.

J. A. Jerichau
Great Times Are Upon Us

Edited by Lærke Rydal Jørgensen and Mathias Ussing Seeberg
Graphic Design: Marie Lübecker
Translations: Glen Garner (foreword, Mathias Ussing Seeberg, Lise Villemoes Grønvold), James Manley (Mikael Wivel, Asger Jorn, Biography)
Photo Editors: Sidse Buck and Kim Hansen
Mathias Ussing Seeberg's article has been peer-reviewed

Cover, front: Jens Adolf Jerichau: *Dante*, 1916
Oil on canvas, 155 × 132 cm
Canica Kunstsamling, Oslo. Long-term loan at KODE Kunstmuseer og komponisthjem
Photo: Dag Fosse
Cover, back: Jens Adolf Jerichau: *The Palm Tree, View of St. Sir*, 1915
Oil on canvas, 46 × 38 cm
Private Collection
Photo: Anders Sune Berg
Inside of cover, front: Jens Adolf Jerichau: Self-portrait. Sketchbook. Probably Copenhagen and Hørsholm, 1909
Pencil, pen, black ink, 29.7 × 24.2 cm
SMK, National Gallery of Art
Photo: SMK Foto/Jakob Skou-Hansen
Inside of cover, back Jens Adolf Jerichau: *Male Nude, Back,* 1914
Pencil, 25.2 × 18.9 cm
SMK, National Gallery of Art
Photo: SMK Foto/Jakob Skou-Hansen

Litho/Print: Narayana Press
ISBN: 978-87-93659-46-9
Printed in Denmark 2021
www.louisiana.dk

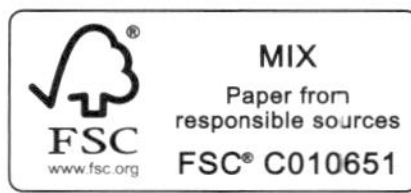

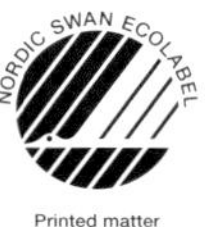

The catalogue is published on the occasion of the exhibition:
J. A. Jerichau
Great Times Are Upon Us
28 October 2021 – 6 March 2022

Curator: Mathias Ussing Seeberg
Co-Curator: Mikael Wivel
Curatorial Assistant: Lise Villemoes Grønvold
Udstillingskoordinator / Registrar: Eva Lund
Exhibition Architect: Jens Kamp
Graphic Design: Marie Lübecker
Conservator / Exhibition Producer: Jesper Lund Madsen

The exhibition is supported by:

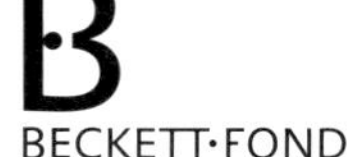

LEKTOR PEER RANDER AMUNDSENS LEGAT

Photos: Album/Ritzau Scanpix: p. 65 top left., 91 top; Akg-Images/Ritzau Scanpix: p. 65 top right; Anders Sune Berg: p. 7-10, 20 right, 20 top left, 21, 22-23, 26 left., 27 top right, 29 left, 30-32, 34-35, 37-40 bottom, 41, 42 bottom, 46, 47 bottom, 48 top, 48 bottom right, 49, 54 top, 55, 57 bottom, 58, 59 top, 60 bottom, 61-63, 67-68, 70, 76, 78-81, 83, 84 bottom, 85 top, 86, 88-89; Bridgeman Art Library/Ritzau Scanpix: p. 72 left, 74 middle; Bruun Rasmussen Kunstauktioner: p. 84 top; Poul Buchard: s.5, 43, 45, 85 bottom; Canica Kunstsamling: p. 29 right, 40 top, 42 top, 59 bottom, 66 bottom; CCØ Paris Musées/Musée Carnavalet – Histoire de Paris: p. 72 middle; Dag Fosse: p. 77; Ole Hein: 44 top, 54 bottom; Kunsten Museum of Modern Art Aalborg: p. 60 top; Museum Jorn: p. 2-3, 24,52, 75 left, 90, 91 bottom right; Museum Nordsjælland/Ole Tage Hartmann: p. 2, 6; Nivaagaards Malerisamling: p. 47 top; RMN-Grand Palais (Musée national Picasso-Paris)/image RMN-GP: s. 73 left, 75 middle; Scala, Florence: p. 73 middle, 74 left, 91 bottom left; SMK Foto/ Jakob Skou-Hansen: p. 17 right,19 right., 25 right, 26 right, 33, 36, 39 top, 44 bottom, 51, 56 top, 57, 66 top, 69, 87; The State Hermitage Museum: p. 17 left.; Øystein Thorvaldsen: p. 48 bottom left, 71.

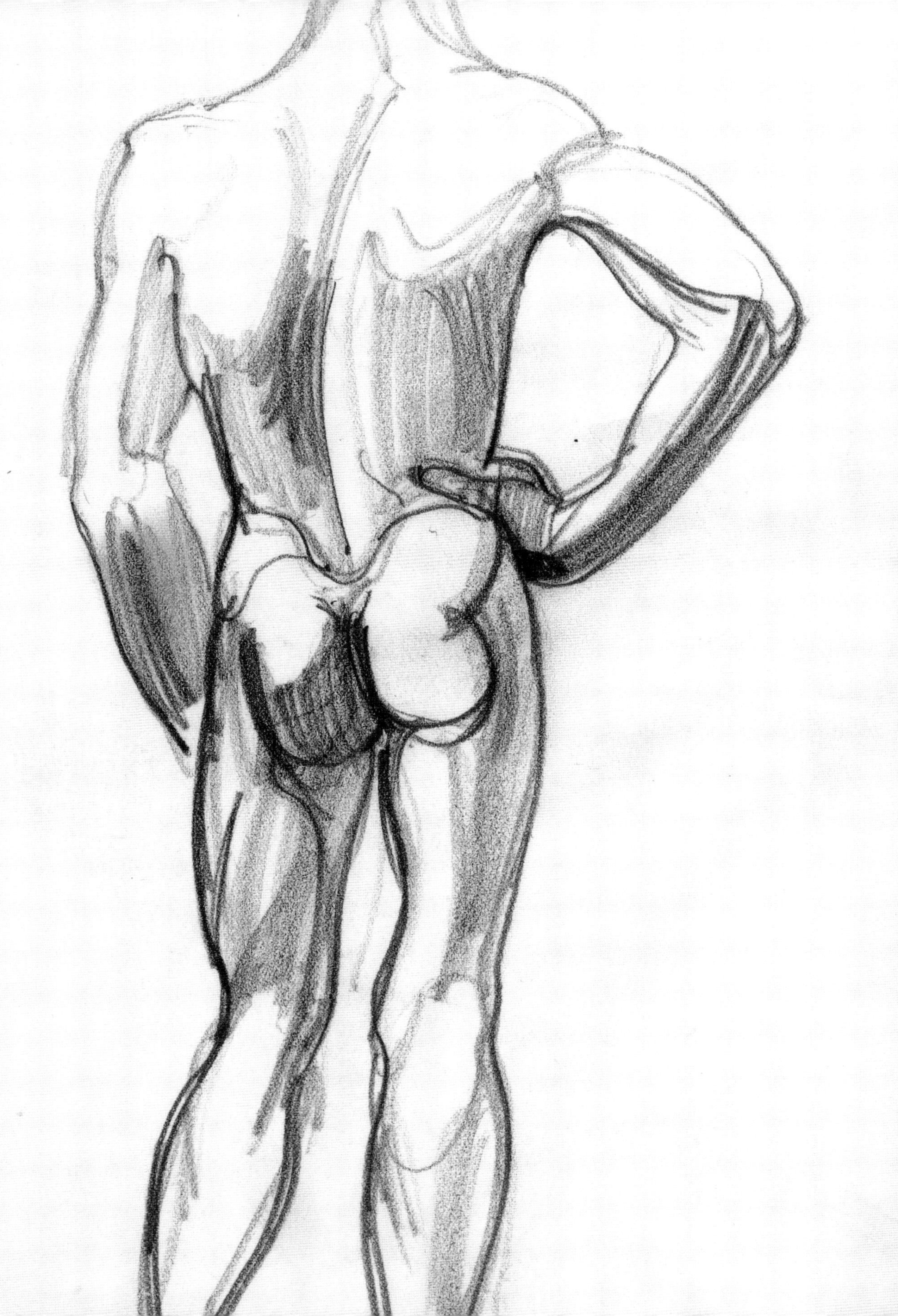